A CONCISE HISTORY OF THE CINEMA
Volume One   £1.25

Above: Laurel and Hardy

in the same
SCREEN SERIES
edited by Peter Cowie
produced by The Tantivy Press

EASTERN EUROPE
by Nina Hibbin

SWEDEN 1 and 2
by Peter Cowie

FRANCE
by Marcel Martin

GERMANY
by Felix Bucher

JAPAN
by Arne Svensson

THE AMERICAN MUSICAL
by Tom Vallance

THE GANGSTER FILM
By John Baxter

Forthcoming

ITALY
by Felix Bucher

THE WESTERN
by Allen Eyles

screen SERIES

A Concise History of
THE CINEMA

Edited by Peter Cowie

A. ZWEMMER LIMITED, LONDON
A. S. BARNES & CO., NEW YORK

Acknowledgements

THE PUBLISHERS would like to thank all the contributors in various countries, who have worked so carefully to make this project possible. They also acknowledge the assistance of the following where stills are concerned: J. S. L. Barnes, Felix Bucher, Cinemabilia (New York), Goswin Doerfler, Leonhard H. Gmür, Jugoslavija Film, Anthony Slide (*The Silent Picture*), and the various companies (some, alas, no longer in existence) who originally issued the pictures.

The two Volumes are divided somewhat arbitrarily at 1940, and readers will note that certain films made after 1940 are mentioned in Volume One and certain films made earlier are mentioned in Volume Two.

The dates after titles in the text usually refer to the date of release in a film's country of origin.

COVER STILLS

Front: GONE WITH THE WIND (courtesy of M-G-M, London)
Back: THE NEW BABYLON, directed by Kozintsev and Trauberg

FIRST PUBLISHED 1971
Copyright © 1971 *by* The Tantivy Press

Library of Congress Catalogue Card No.: 73-118807
SBN 498 07715 2 (U.S.A.)
SBN 302 02063 2 (U.K.)

Printed in the United States of America

Contents

	INTRODUCTION	*page*	7
1	U.S.A.		9
2	BRITAIN		77
3	FRANCE		85
4	ITALY		104
5	GERMANY AND AUSTRIA		106
6	SCANDINAVIA		125
7	EASTERN EUROPE		134
8	JAPAN AND ELSEWHERE		159

Japan 159; *India* 163; *Spain* 164; *Buñuel* 165; *Canada* 167; *Greece* 168; *Australia* 168; *Switzerland* 169

9	DOCUMENTARY AND ANIMATION		170
10	ECONOMIC TRENDS		181
11	TECHNICAL DEVELOPMENTS		191
	SELECT BIBLIOGRAPHY (for both Volumes)		200
	INDEX TO FILM TITLES		205

Introduction

MOST FILM ENTHUSIASTS born before the Second World War have probably come to the cinema via such standard histories as those written by Rotha, Griffith, Knight, and Jacobs. But however knowledgeable one writer may be, certain personal prejudices are bound to lead him to omit this or that director. He may have seen no Danish films but Dreyer's, no underground movies save Warhol's, and no Australian or Bulgarian films whatsoever. And unless, like H. G. Wells in his *Short History of the World*, he is a writer of considerable power and vision himself, he is likely to strike a somewhat shrill and petty note by this summary dismissal of a *genre* or period with which he is ill-acquainted.

So, in this new, two-volume work, we have attempted to improve the situation, and to provide the student and the film follower with a balanced, reasonably priced primary history in English. There are over thirty contributors, each chosen for his expert interest in a particular field. Instead of printing the various articles higgledy-piggledy, we have assembled them into at least a fairly readable and logical sequence, moving from country to country, from director to director, to the major technical and economic developments of the cinema since its inception.

If neither volume offers the reader the comprehensive data of a dictionary or an encyclopaedia, it does give him the basic facts of interest —dates of birth, release dates for most films cited, original-language titles, production statistics and so on. Figures of major importance appear in bold type when first mentioned in the text, and the margin headings should help the casual reader to pick his way through the books.

Of course there are areas of film history where the work of two or three contributors may overlap. Rather than distort the articles in an effort to avoid this, we have often left them as they stand. Thus Hawks, for example, appears in the sections on gangster movies and Westerns as well as in the chapters devoted to the U.S.A. as a whole. The more opinions, the livelier the book; only the facts should be unimpeachable (forgive us if they aren't!)

Howard Suber, writing in *Cinema Journal* about our trio of books on Hollywood, says: "The primary function of the film historian is to help make some sense out of the massive body of works that have been left to us. His job is not merely to tell us that these films exist; it is to tell us which ones we ought to see and why we ought to see them. It is not enough simply to list great numbers of directors, the films they have made, the stars who have appeared in them, and some brief

Opposite: Kathryn McGuire and Buster Keaton in THE NAVIGATOR

descriptions of plots." At the start of a decade that promises an ever more discriminating approach to movies and their past, that advice is excellent. Problems of space in these two volumes have made us guilty of compression in certain chapters. But at other junctures we have tried to select for discussion only those directors, films, and stars that we feel to have significance *now,* in 1971, for the student of the cinema. Contributors have been encouraged to write about the films that appear significant to *them* and not merely to resort to a catalogue of titles. *pdc*

KEY TO CONTRIBUTORS

Each contributor is identified by his initials, which appear at the end of his piece, irrespective of its length.

Roy Armes	*ra*	Peter Harcourt	*ph*
John Baxter	*jb*	Nina Hibbin	*nh*
Suzanne Budgen	*sb*	Dorothea Holloway	*dh*
Ivan Butler	*ib*	Ronald Holloway	*rh*
Russell Campbell	*rc*	Alan Howden	*ah*
Peter Cowie	*pdc*	Claire Johnston	*cj*
Chidananda Das Gupta	*cdg*	Leonard Maltin	*lm*
Langdon Dewey	*ld*	Hanspeter Manz	*hpm*
Goswin Doerfler	*gd*	Paul O'Dell	*po*
William Dyckes	*wd*	Gerald Pratley	*gp*
Allen Eyles	*aje*	David Rider	*dr*
Ken Gay	*kg*	Anthony Slide	*as*
Mirella Georgiadou	*mg*	John M. Smith	*jms*
Ulrich Gregor	*ug*	Ralph Stephenson	*rs*

1. U. S. A.

THE AMERICAN FILM INDUSTRY was born in 1900, when Thomas Edison (for details of Edison's involvement in the cinema see Chapters Ten and Eleven) appointed Edwin S. Porter to be in charge of production at his studios. Porter was responsible for the first important American film production, *The Life of an American Fireman*, released in 1903, and generally considered to be the first American film to tell a story, although, of course, two years earlier Williamson in England had produced a film with a similar story, *Fire*.

The initial success of Edison in the film-making field led to the setting up of other film companies. One of the first was the Vitagraph Company, founded as early as 1896 by J. Stuart Blackton and Albert E. Smith. Vitagraph was responsible for introducing a host of famous names to the cinema; stars such as Valentino, Alice Terry, Betty Blythe and Corinne Griffith, plus, of course, the first internationally renowned film comedian, **John Bunny** (1863–1915), and the cinema's first star, Florence Turner. One of the silent screen's finest dramatic actresses, **Norma Talmadge** (1896–1957), served her screen apprenticeship with Vitagraph, and probably learnt much of her art from the Company's first *matinée* idol, Maurice Costello. Vitagraph was the only one of the early companies to accept that the future of the film industry lay in feature-length production, and it was the only one to survive the break-up of the Motion Picture Patents Group (set up by Edison to protect his supposed copyright interests in cameras and projectors), and remained in existence until 1925 when it was sold to Warner Brothers.

Other early companies were the Lubin Company, founded by Sigmund "Pop" Lubin in Philadelphia, and remaining in existence from 1897 to 1917; the Kalem Company, founded in 1907 by George Kleine, Samuel Long and Frank Marion, and now best remembered for its six-reel feature of 1912, *From the Manger to the Cross* (*dir* Sidney Olcott) and *The Hazards of Helen* series, featuring Helen Holmes and Helen Gibson; and the Essanay Company, also founded in 1907 by George K. Spoor and G. M. Anderson, which produced some of the earliest popular Westerns featuring Anderson, and also a number of Chaplin comedies and the first American films of Max Linder.

American Biograph, because of its association with the juvenile work of D. W. Griffith, is still remembered, and still in existence today are Universal (founded by Carl Laemmle in 1909 as the Imp Company) and Fox (founded in 1913 by William Fox). *as*

D. W. GRIFFITH   David Wark Griffith was born January 22, 1875 in Crestwood, Kentucky, the son of "Roaring Jake" Griffith, a Civil War veteran. It can be imagined that such a nickname was earned on the battlefield and this gives a graphic indication of the character of Griffith's father. This is interesting à *propos* of Griffith's pictures taking as their subject the Civil War, especially *The Birth of a Nation*. It is obvious that Griffith felt very close to his father, and indeed the whole of Griffith's future career may well have been infused with the passionate nature of his parent's character.

Griffith's importance in the development of the cinema is undeniably great, and his contribution to that development started in 1908 when he directed his first film for what was then The American Mutoscope and Biograph Company in New York. The events leading up to this directorial *début* had nothing to do with any ambition of Griffith's to make motion pictures. Griffith's ambition had always been to become a writer; he had worked on a local newspaper, toured with a theatrical company to New York from his native South and had written several plays, poems and stories. In New York, work was scarce, and he found himself with no alternative but to approach one of the film companies for work. The Edison company hired him as an actor when Edwin S. Porter, then head of Edison, refused to buy a script from Griffith. The great Southern pride of David Wark Griffith must have suffered terribly when he was forced to act in movies—then the lowest to which any actor worth his professional title could possibly sink. His first screen

D. W. Griffith

appearance was in *Rescued from an Eagle's Nest* (1907) for Edison. But when, a little later, he approached the Biograph company, his literary efforts met with at least a qualified success and he became permanently employed there first as a writer and actor, and later as a director. The American Mutoscope and Biograph Company—it later dropped the "Mutoscope" productions in favour of straightforward filmed stories—was by no means the most successful of the rash of producing companies which had sprung up in New York during the first decade of this century. It had formidable competition for one thing; the emphasis was on quantity rather than quality, speed rather than care. It was to happen, however, that in just over a year from March 1908 when Griffith joined the staff, he would cause Biograph to eclipse all competition. It is also worth adding, to underline the point, that after he left the company, it again relapsed to anonymity and very slowly came to an ignominious end.

Griffith's output was prodigious and his films ranged from melodrama through romantic stories, adaptations of plays, conventional or historical novels, spy stories and poems. He also took social problems as subjects. Working with him as cameraman was Gottlieb Wilhelm Bitzer, born in Boston of German immigrant parents, who was to Griffith what the Lithuanian Tissé was to Eisenstein. He, like Griffith, was an experimentalist, and it was this element in both of their characters which helped form the foundations for cinematic technique as we know it.

It was in these films—almost five hundred of them between 1908 and 1913—that Griffith felt his way with this new medium and found the most effective way of presenting a narrative in visual terms. Flashbacks, close-ups, intercutting were all techniques he explored and developed in anticipation—perhaps unconsciously—of the great cinematic masterpieces he was to make in the years between 1914 and 1917, *The Birth of a Nation* and *Intolerance.*

Towards the end of Griffith's stay at Biograph he was beginning to explore further and tended to expand his ideas in films which were of a stipulated length, dictated by the Biograph management. When they refused to allow this after he overstepped the mark with *Judith of Bethulia* (four reels as against the maximum two, 1913) he left Biograph. Taking with him many of their stock company, among them Mae Marsh, Lillian and Dorothy Gish, Bobby Harron and Henry B. Walthall, he became head of production with Reliance Majestic. He was eager to begin his epic of the Civil War and postwar chaos based on *The Clansman,* plus material from *The Leopard's Spots,* both novels by the Rev. Thomas Dixon of North Carolina. The first estimate of $50,000 meant forming a new company and filming independently. Shot between July and October 1914, editing took three months. *The Clansman* opened in Los Angeles in February 1915, and as *The Birth of*

Henry B. Walthall and Miriam Cooper in Griffith's THE BIRTH OF A NATION

a Nation in New York in March, to run forty-four weeks. Events snow-balled. A print was shown in the White House to the president and cabinet when Wilson said: "It's like writing history in lightning." The Boston opening brought turmoil and violence after white liberal and Negro factions tried to prevent its showing. Under similar pressures Mayor Mitchell of New York summoned Griffith to hear a critical committee, resulting in the deletion of 170 scenes, though 1,374 remained to run 165 minutes. Newspaper reports and pulpit protests stirred wide interest; litigation followed. Though the cost was $110,000, money poured in and $18,000,000 was grossed in a few years. Lillian Gish created an important prototype of heroine. It was soon considered the most important film yet made, technically comprising panning, contrapuntal editing, natural landscapes, night photography, full-screen close-ups, dream images, lap-dissolves, tinting for mood, irising and hooding.

Since its first appearance *The Birth of a Nation* has continually stirred up controversy and Griffith's reputation has suffered slightly—but only slightly—as a result. He has come to be regarded as anti-Negro, and this despite many scenes in other films which stress the importance of racial equality and what Griffith called "Brotherly Love." Indeed in *The Birth of a Nation* itself there is a title which asks, "Dare we dream of a golden day when the bestial War shall rule no more. But instead—the gentle Prince in the Hall of Brotherly Love in the City of Peace." Griffith also demands the right to show "the dark side of wrong, that we may illuminate the bright side of virtue."

But his next film was to be his most eloquent answer to the critics,

The Babylonian episode in INTOLERANCE, *directed by Griffith*

both those who accused him in 1915 and those who have doubted his integrity since. *Intolerance* does not touch specifically on the subject of race, but it does speak out directly against religious, social and political intolerance. The film was of a magnitude and was conceived in terms as then unknown in the cinema. Italy's epic films *Cabiria* and *Quo Vadis* could not compare with Griffith's masterpiece, to which he applied the whole spectrum of technique as he then understood it, using four separate stories from different periods of history to make his point. A contemporary source described the scene on the *Intolerance* lot: "When the great mob scenes were being photographed, it seemed as though the entire population of Los Angeles had come out to Griffith's place, to take part in the various pageants and mighty rushing armies. Actors from other studios—many of them prominent stars—joined the scenes."

But if his handling of vast crowd scenes was Griffith's major achievement in this picture, he should also be remembered for those intimate scenes in which he was able to convey an emotional intensity worthy of a Goya painting; those quiet, reflective passages where Griffith, Bitzer and the players combined their talents so perfectly to evoke mood and atmosphere. This magnificent work was the peak of Griffith's achievement. So gigantic and complex in its pretentions and yet so simple and basic in its approach, it achieved at times the intensity of a vision.

In 1917, a visit to England with *Intolerance* led to a film for the Allies made in England and on the battlefront in France. *Hearts of the World.* Lillian and Dorothy Gish rose to prominence in this film, and Dorothy showed for the first time her ability to carry a semi-comic role successfully. Footage taken by Bitzer was used in several films Griffith made following *Hearts of the World,* notably *The Girl Who Stayed at Home* and *The Greatest Thing in Life* (1918–19). *True Heart Susie* (1919) was as refreshing as the preceding pictures were intense. A simple story set in rural America, it had great charm and both Lillian Gish and Bobby Harron gave performances which showed the range of their acting ability when compared with their performances in more demanding films. *True Heart Susie* was a "breathe in" for the preparation of *Broken Blossoms* (1919) which achieved in its final moments a dramatic intensity of extraordinary power, with Lillian Gish giving Griffith a performance hardly equalled before or since. Richard Barthelmess played a Chinaman in this adaptation of Thomas Burke's *Limehouse Nights.* It was entirely studio made.

The Greatest Question (1919), *The Idol Dancer* (1920), *The Love Flower* (1920), were followed by *Way Down East* (1920) which was an enormous success despite $175,000 paid for the rights to the melodramatic play. Filmed in a blizzard and on a frozen river for one of the most exciting sequences in any Griffith picture, Lillian Gish's performance was once again as tender and beautiful as only a Griffith movie could produce from her.

Orphans of the Storm (1921) was another triumph for the Gish sisters. A giant spectacle of the French Revolution, it owed a lot to Griffith's greatest films for its elaborate construction and ability to combine both spectacle and intimate scenes—especially between the two sisters—superbly photographed by Hendrik Sartov. *One Exciting Night* (1922) was a murder thriller made when *The Bat* and *The Cat and the Canary* enjoyed huge successes as stage thrillers. *The White Rose* (1923) with Mae Marsh, Carol Dempster, Ivor Novello and Neil Hamilton, was shot in the bayou country of Louisiana and Florida locations which gave it its chief charm. *America* (1924) another historical essay—on the American Revolution—merely earned back its costs. *Isn't Life Wonderful* (1924) photographed by Sartov, was shot on location in Germany to show postwar poverty. Said to be the best of his later pictures, it heralded neo-realism in cinema after the Second World War. *Sally of the Sawdust* (1925) featured W. C. Fields; *The Sorrows of Satan* (1926), planned as an elaborate production, seems to have aborted through conflicting production aims and failed financially. This was followed by a return to Hollywood for *Drums of Love* (1927), *The Battle of the Sexes* and *Lady of the Pavements* (1928), completing Griffith's silent films. *Abraham Lincoln* (1930), with a much altered scenario by Stephen Vincent Benet, Griffith's first talkie, won back considerable acclaim. *The Struggle* (1931) was his last film to all intents and purposes, unless his modest contributions to *San Francisco* and *One Million Years BC* are to be taken as anything more than one technician (Griffith) aiding another. *The Struggle* is an ironic title for Griffith's last picture. It was not well received by critics and this is perhaps understandable. Griffith held fast to pathos as the period became cynical; his last-minute rescues became slapstick to increasingly sophisticated audiences; flappers and vamps were alien to his conviction.

The tragedy of D. W. Griffith was that he made his greatest pictures *Assessment* early in his career, at the time when he was free of producers and people who told him what to do and when to do it. Griffith found himself attacked from all sides and eventually expelled from Hollywood once his particular genius became swamped by the ever-growing influx of these movie-industry tycoons and the big business which came with them. In a sense, Griffith was not interested in money for any other purpose but to make another, and yet another, motion picture. Even today, in retrospect, Griffith is criticised, unjustly, for his "extrovert sentimentality." This very fault caused his retirement from film production. It was claimed, for example, and is still claimed today, that his films sank into absurdity simply because he never held any regard for the rule that true life is not always the same as art, and that straight transposition from life to the screen can often appear very unreal and false indeed. It may well be that Griffith was not entirely innocent of these criticisms; but what ever else, he did what he did genuinely, and straight from the heart. His best films are passionate and tender, terrifying and poignant, works of art certainly, and products too of an imagination far ahead of its time. He died in Hollywood on July 23, 1948. *ld/po*

CHARLES CHAPLIN

The influence and impact of **Charles Chaplin** on the cinema cannot be underestimated, so far-reaching is its effect. Chaplin became a word synonymous with comedy, and at one time he was, without doubt, the most popular and widely known figure in motion pictures. It is to his credit that the incredible publicity which has surrounded both his public and private lives has not greatly impeded his art. His little tramp—known on every continent under a variety of names—has an immediate appeal for all of us, and, it would appear, not least of all for Chaplin himself. He once described comedy as a "benevolent custodian of the mind which prevents one from being overwhelmed by the apparent seriousness of life. It finds compensation in misfortune."

Born in London in 1889, Chaplin came to America in October 1910 with the touring company of Fred Karno. Chaplin had already become an established stage comedian before joining Karno's company at the age of seventeen. His understudy during the American tour was another young man destined to achieve stardom in the movies—Stan Jefferson, later to become Stan Laurel.

Chaplin's talent had not gone unnoticed towards the close of Karno's three-year tour. Kessel and Bauman, who at that time owned several film companies among which were Keystone, Broncho, Domino and Kay Bee, were persuaded by Mack Sennett, the then head of Keystone, to sign Chaplin. Kessel and Bauman offered Chaplin $150 a week, a salary which represented a three hundred percent increase for him. Chaplin left the stage for the movies at the end of 1913.

Mack Sennett is an important figure in cinema history—not only as a result of discovering Chaplin—he can be said to be the father of screen comedy. With Sennett at Keystone at the time of Chaplin's arrival were Ford Sterling, who was the company's leading comic, Mabel Normand, who came with Sennett from Biograph, Roscoe "Fatty" Arbuckle and his wife Minta Durfee, Mack Swain and Chester Conklin.

Chaplin's first film with the company was directed by yet another ex-member of D. W. Griffith's Biograph company of players, Henry "Pathe" Lehrman. The film was *Making a Living,* released February 2, 1914. In it Chaplin played an impoverished Englishman, who begged money from a news photographer, and then stole the hapless man's camera and girl. The film was moderately successful, and the *Moving Picture World* noted Chaplin as "a comedian of the first water."

The first picture in which Chaplin wore his now familiar costume

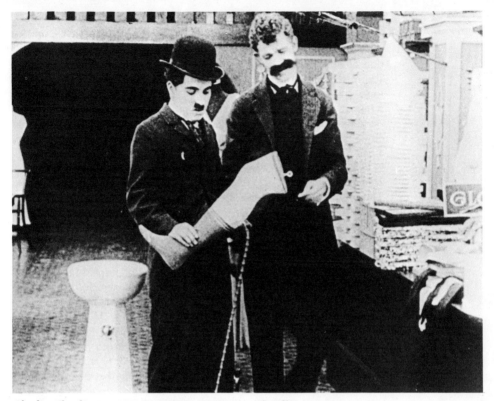

Charlie Chaplin in THE FLOORWALKER, with Albert Austin

was *Kid Auto Races at Venice,* released February 7, 1914. The costume, it is said, was gathered hastily from various dressing rooms about the studio, and included, finally, Arbuckle's trousers, Ford Sterling's shoes (worn on opposite feet in order that they might stay on), and a moustache belonging to Mack Swain. *Kid Auto Races at Venice* was a short "split-reel" comedy, and was released along with an educational film on olives.

When Sterling left Keystone, obviously aware of a greater talent than his own at work, Chaplin very soon became Sennett's biggest attraction. By the end of 1914, his popularity had grown enormously, and Sennett wisely decided to allow Chaplin to write and direct all of his own films.

Of the thirty-five films made by Chaplin while at Keystone, the most important must undoubtedly be *Tillie's Punctured Romance,* released November 14, 1914, although star billing for the film went not to Chaplin but to Marie Dressler. Running to six reels, it has the distinction of not only being the first feature-length comedy, but in all probability the first American full-length feature film, appearing as it did some time before *The Birth of a Nation.* It took Chaplin fourteen weeks to shoot, as opposed to all the other films made during the same period which were completed inside a week. Chaplin plays a villainous city slicker, who attempts to woo simple country girl Marie Dressler, aided and abetted by his partner in crime Mabel Normand.

Other films of importance for Keystone were *Dough and Dynamite, His Trysting Place, Laughing Gas* and *The Face on the Bar-room Floor.* These films all showed that Chaplin was still developing the character of the tramp, and this character was not to flower completely until 1915.

Chaplin used his popularity—which by this time was considerable—to demand a higher salary at the end of Keystone's contract period. Sennett, not unnaturally, was anxious to keep him, but could not give him the $750 a week that Chaplin demanded. Not surprisingly, an offer by the Essanay Company of $1,250 (a figure which, incidentally, Chaplin had himself suggested) drew him away from Keystone. Chaplin left for Essanay in January 1915.

Chaplin at Essanay It is his Essanay period that is widely considered to be Chaplin's most crucial time, inasmuch as it was in the fourteen films made for that company that the real genius of Chaplin began to emerge properly. *The Tramp,* released April 11, 1915, was probably the most significant of all since it included for the first time elements of pathos as well as an unhappy ending. Chaplin also made at this point in his career *Carmen,* released April 22, 1916, a satire on the film versions by Cecil B. DeMille and Theda Bara, although Chaplin had already used elements of satire in some of his earlier films.

It was during his stay at Essanay that Chaplin first met **Edna Purviance** (1894–1963), a blonde with such a sweet, innocent face, who became a perfect partner to Chaplin, and who was to star in no less than thirty-five of his pictures over the next nine years.

At the end of his year with Essanay, Chaplin's popularity had increased to gigantic proportions. Essanay were desperate to keep him, but just could not meet an offer by Mutual of an incredible $670,000 a year. Chaplin was twenty-six.

The Mutual period was one of intense creativity. Many of Chaplin's finest two-reelers were made during this period, among them *The Floorwalker* (1916), *The Pawnshop* (1916) and *One A.M.* (1916). He also made *The Immigrant* (1917) and what has become probably his most well-known picture, *Easy Street* (1917). Chaplin's tramp here reaches near perfection. "That costume," said Chaplin, "helps me to express my conception of the average man . . . the tightly buttoned coat and the stick and his whole manner are a gesture toward gallantry and dash and 'front.' He is trying to meet the world bravely, to put up a bluff, and he knows well that he can laugh at himself and pity himself a little."

In 1917 the Mutual Company offered an unbelievable one million dollars to keep Chaplin, as desperate—perhaps more so—as were Essanay before them to avoid losing him. But once again a rival company went one better. First National offered the same one million dollars, but in addition offered a further fifteen thousand dollars "bonus" for signing with them. This was to cover a total of only eight pictures over an eighteen month period. There was one large difference between this and the other contracts though. Chaplin was to be his own producer and bear the costs of each film, and as he shot an enormous amount of footage for each picture this was likely to take a temporary large amount out of his initial "salary" from First National. An example of Chaplin's shooting ratio would be that for the two-reel *The Immigrant* he shot as much material as Griffith exposed for his twelve-reel *The Birth of a Nation.*

By the end of the first eighteen months of the First National contract only three films had been completed and released, one of which was *Shoulder Arms* (1918), a film which more than any other showed the reaction of the ordinary man in the street to war. It was at this time that Chaplin met and married his first wife, Mildred Harris, an actress from the Thomas Ince studio. But their child died three days after its birth, and the marriage itself broke up soon afterwards. Subsequent divorce proceedings and the production costs of his most ambitious project to date, *The Kid,* reduced Chaplin's once-formidable salary to practically nothing.

The Kid was released early in 1921 and ran to six reels. It starred Jackie Coogan, whom Chaplin had used once previously in the 1919 film *A Day's Pleasure.* Coogan plays "the Kid" adopted by the Tramp, until his rightful mother finds him. *The Kid,* like so many of Chaplin's productions, contains moments of great sentimentality, as well as many scenes of almost bawdy comedy, such as when Chaplin peers under the baby's blanket to discover its sex. The film was a tremendous success and put Chaplin firmly back on the ascendant. Exhausted by coincident divorce proceedings, monetary problems and ill-health, Chaplin interrupted work on his next film, *Pay Day,* in order that he might spend a vacation in Europe.

Pay Day, which was to be his last two-reeler, and *The Idle Class* were followed by *The Pilgrim* in 1922 which completed his contract with First National. Chaplin announced that he was now to be working for United Artists, a company he himself had helped form with Douglas Fairbanks, Mary Pickford and D. W. Griffith in 1919.

A Woman of Paris was his first picture with U.A., starring Adolphe

Menjou and Edna Purviance. It was Chaplin's first film in which he did not star, and although not a financial success has long been acclaimed a masterpiece by critics the world over. It also gave Chaplin the opportunity to give Edna Purviance her first serious acting role.

The Gold Rush   After *A Woman of Paris* in late 1923, Chaplin began filming *The Gold Rush* in the spring of 1924. Production lasted fourteen months and the cost of the film has at one time or another been put as high as a million dollars. This, Chaplin's most widely acclaimed and best-loved film, ended an absence from the screen of two and a half years, and the reception of the film, both critically and in a financial sense, was wildly enthusiastic. *The Gold Rush* contains many scenes and sequences which speak eloquently of Chaplin's genius. The Thanksgiving Day dinner of Chaplin's shoes, the famous dance of the rolls,

Chaplin as the personification of pathos in THE GOLD RUSH

and the cabin see-sawing on the edge of the precipice are some of the most famous moments in movie history. Theodore Huff has remarked that "its laughs, drawn out of tragedy, have a magnified force and meaning. Its principal character symbolises the good, kind and pitiful core of humanity. Moments of the film reach the sublime."

The Gold Rush was followed by *The Circus,* and again Chaplin spared nothing in his insistence on perfection, spending a reputed $900,000 on the film. Work stopped as a direct result of his domestic problems, but the film was eventually completed in January 1928. *The Circus,* like its predecessor, again ended a long absence from the screen for Chaplin, but again earned three times the cost of its production. Chaplin becomes a clown at the circus, and falls in love with the owner's daughter, Merna Kennedy. The film ends with Chaplin leaving the circus, after arranging the daughter's marriage to Rex, the tightrope walker.

The arrival of the talkies early in 1928 put a temporary stop to work on Chaplin's subsequent production; but, after careful considera-tion, he decided that it should be completed—as a silent film. This film was to become *City Lights,* a story of a tramp's love for a blind girl, a theme already used with much success by Harry Langdon in *The Strong Man.* Chaplin built a huge set and exposed thousands of feet of film, spending one-and-a-half million dollars on its production.

Chaplin compromised slightly at the end of two years working on *City Lights* and composed a musical score; the only concession he would make to sound in a film he had conceived as silent. The film was an instant and unqualified success when it appeared in February 1931. Silent films were already a thing of the past when Chaplin brought back to the screen, albeit briefly, the magic of his silent mime. It was, on that *première* evening on Broadway the real swan-song of silent movies.

In 1934 Chaplin began production on his new film, tentatively titled *The Masses,* and described by him as a study of "humanity crusading in the pursuit of happiness." The film, eventually released in 1936 as *Modern Times,* was to be the last appearance of Chaplin as the little tramp. The opening sequence, in which the tramp is discovered working in a factory, mechanically tightening bolts on an endless conveyor belt, conveys the whole meaning of the film: the individual overwhelmed by the advance of mass production systems. *Modern Times* contains some brilliant sequences, such as the scene in which the tramp is chosen as a guinea pig for a feeding machine, but taken as a whole the film is episodic, and the sub-titles tend to hamper the film's flow (only in the final cabaret sequence is Chaplin's voice heard for the first time). The film featured Paulette Goddard (whom Chaplin married in 1936; they were divorced in 1942) and reunited Chaplin with two of his colleagues from Keystone days, Chester Conklin and Hank Mann.

Modern Times was banned in Germany and Italy because of its supposedly anti-Fascist, Communist tendencies, and it is perhaps not surprising that Chaplin's next film should be a bitter attack on Fascism.

Work began on *The Great Dictator* in 1938, but the film was not completed until 1940, and by this time, when Hitler to most of the world was far from a laughing matter, the film had lost some of its impact. The production featured Chaplin in a dual role as a Jewish barber and as Hynkel, dictator of Tomania; in support were Paulette Goddard as a poor girl of the ghetto, Jack Oakie as Napaloni, dictator of Bacteria, Henry Daniell as Garbitsch (Goebbels) and Billy Gilbert as Henning. *The Great Dictator* is a satire on dictatorship and its spirit of ambition-impelled cruelty and greed for power. It contains scenes of inspired, if disturbing, comedy, such as when Chaplin the dictator dances with a globe of the world, but its greatest moment occurs in the final reel, when the barber, mistaken for the dictator, makes an impassioned plea to all soldiers to fight against the enslavement imposed by cruel and power-ridden dictators, to fight to the last for the liberties that they have lost, and to face the future with the hope of a new dawn of peace and freedom. *as*

MACK SENNETT

After a four year apprenticeship at Biograph Company as an actor, writer and director, the famous slapstick comedy film *entrepreneur* Mack Sennett (1880–1960) received financial backing from Adam Kessel and Charles Baumann to form Keystone, a motion picture mill that was to produce over 250 half-, one- and two-reel comedies within two years. From 1908 to 1912 he learned much from director D. W. Griffith, was encouraged by Mary Pickford in his scenario writing for the screen, and was finally allowed to direct his own unit at Biograph.

Al Christie

Sennett became the leading creator of a fast, vigorous type of comedy film but was soon joined by Hal Roach and Al Christie (1886–1951), producers of many effective comic films who have been overlooked by motion picture historians. Sennett lured such talents as Fred Mace, Ford Sterling, and Mabel Normand from other companies—Carl Laemmle's IMP and Biograph. Mace had left for IMP after working with Sennett on many short comedies at Biograph. But it was Ford Sterling (1880–1939) who became the director's leading comedian in the early days of the Keystone Company; Mabel Normand (1894–1930) became his leading comedienne. Miss Normand stayed with Sennett throughout the producer's most creative period of the 1910s. She was featured in many of Keystone's one-and two-reelers, played a lead in the company's first full length comedy, *Tillie's Punctured Romance* (1914), and received tailor-made roles in Mary Pickford type vehicles such as *Mickey* (1918) and *Molly-O* (1921).

Mack Sennett introduced some of the best comedy talent to the screen. Roscoe ("Fatty") Arbuckle, Charlie Murray, Edgar Kennedy, Ben Turpin, Mack Swain, Slim Summerfield, Hank Mann, Al St. John, and Charley Chase were some of the comedians who developed their screen acting skills under the wing of Keystone. Of the silent screen "greats," Charles Chaplin and Harry Langdon served their apprenticeship with Sennett; Harold Lloyd spent a few weeks with the ringmaster of comedy in 1915, but the association was not a success, and the comedian returned to Hal Roach's company. Buster Keaton was a notable exception; he was trained by **Roscoe Arbuckle** (1887–1933) in the arts of screen comedy after the rotund comedian left Keystone and became a director for a minor producing unit called Comique.

Sennett can be credited with the perfecting of the multi-authored comedy scenario technique. He employed a staff of writers with as many as six gagmen being used on one picture. He started this practice because he realised he could cut production costs by more careful planning. Sennett can also be credited with the first feature length comedy. On December 14, 1914 he released his six-reel *Tillie's Punctured Romance* starring Marie Dressler, Charles Chaplin, and Mabel Normand, with a large supporting cast of most of the best Keystone players. And, it may be said, this is his most original contribution to the art of comedy since it was strongly against the grain of production tradition at the time. It was a step that would not have its full effect, however, until the early Twenties.

While Sennett was more of a perfecter than an innovator—he borrowed and adapted plots, gags, comic characterisations, photographic and editing techniques from the early French and Italian comedies— he did create a lusty, fast-paced comedy that was directly tied to the tendencies of the film medium. He departed from the theatrical sketches produced by the genteel comedians of the age such as **John Bunny** (1863–1915) who appeared in such mildly humorous one-reelers as *A Cure for Pokeritis* in 1912. At this time Bunny and Mary Pickford were the big stars, but Sennett was soon to develop and lose one of the greatest stars of all times, Charles Chaplin. After thirty-one films for Keystone, the comedian left for Essanay to achieve a fame that has not been equalled.

When Harold Lloyd went into feature work as his own producer in the mid-Twenties, Roach helped develop **Charley Chase** (*b* Charles Parrot 1893–1940) into an outstanding comedian and, with imagination, paired Stan Laurel and Oliver Hardy in two-reelers in the late Twenties. Al Christie was not as innovative a producer as Roach, nor was the quality of his work as significant. However, in quantity he produced as prolifically as Sennett and helped carry the whole slapstick tradition into the Twenties. He made twenty-three two-reel works for Educational Films Incorporated in 1922, many of which compared to Sennett's best efforts. An actor and director for Nestor in 1912, he organised his own company in 1916 and by the early Twenties was producer of more than 800 comedies.

Ben Turpin   Sennett's best comedian of the Twenties was **Ben Turpin** (1874– 1940), a goose-necked, pear-shaped, cross-eyed man who produced some lively burlesques of the serious adventure feature. After appearing in vaudeville as the tramp-clown character Happy Hooligan at the turn of the century, Turpin appeared in minor roles for Essanay as early as 1909. By 1915 his reputation grew when he appeared in Keystone two-reelers such as *A Night Out* as Chaplin's friend and foil. Like most of the comedians of the silent screen, he was a skilled acrobat; he could execute the most fantastic pratfalls—often promoting laughs from an audience during a chase or fight sequence by somersaulting forward or backwards through the air and landing on his neck and shoulders.

After a year with Vogue Comedies in 1916 and 1917, Turpin returned to Keystone where he finally graduated from the two-reeler to the feature-length film with *Down on the Farm* and *Married Life* in 1920 and *A Small Town Idol* the following year. In this latter film the comedian created some of his strongest comic moments by striking a heroic pose which obviously burlesqued the leading man of serious films. In fact his burlesques of leading men in such films as *The Shriek of Araby* (1923), a spoof of Valentino, and *When a Man's a Prince* (1926), a broad parody on the von Stroheim type of Prussian military officer, he hit his peak as a comedian.

While Turpin seemed to be a comedian with the skills to make features, he could not sustain a long work with such an eccentric comic character—a portrait with a very limited range. With more facile, many faceted characterisations, comedians Chaplin, Lloyd, and Keaton employed a wide variety of comedy scenes in their features because they realised they needed lighter comic sequences to build up to the broader slapstick that came with the chase and the fight. Turpin made only four features and finally stayed with the two-reel work—a length that seemed to fit his limited skills. He made brief appearances in some sound pictures such as *Million Dollar Legs* (1932) but he remained in the background in the sound film as a curious caricature left over from silent days.

Larry Semon   Another minor comedian of merit, **Larry Semon** (1899–1928), was also popular enough to be given some silent feature assignments. In 1924 this sharp-nosed and blank-faced comic appeared in *The Girl in the Limousine* and in 1925, *The Perfect Clown* plus *The Wizard of Oz,* a feature that employed him as the Straw Man. But Semon, like Turpin, was primarily a two-reel comedian. He concentrated on the gag at the expense of the character and he had difficulties in feature works sustaining interest with merely a string of gags. Nevertheless, his fast-paced shorts were popular and he was reported to have earned $100,000 a year for his efforts.

While Hal Roach was making the transition to sound with Our Gang shorts plus Laurel and Hardy films, Mack Sennett's kingdom was collapsing. Hit hard by the depression, he continued as a director, writer and producer in the sound era. By 1933 he filed bankruptcy with debts of nearly a million. Sennett claims to have been worth fifteen million at the peak of his success as a producer. From all indications, his comedy factory had begun to grind out a rather standard product in the Twenties. Also, he was never able to invade the feature film market with any degree of consistency and financial success. Sound seemed even farther from his grasp and most of his shorts were mediocre. Under the banner of Sennett, Incorporated, he produced over eighty pictures between 1929 and 1932. At this time he made only the contribution at which he seemed most apt—the introduction of new talent to the medium. In 1931 he signed up Bing Crosby for a series of shorts under such titles as *I Surrender Dear, Dream House, Blue in the Night,* and *Sing, Bing, Sing.* Under the wing of Paramount in 1932 he obtained a contract with W. C. Fields and allowed him to create his own screenplays for *The Dentist* and in 1933, *The Fatal Glass of Beer, The Pharmacist,* and *The Barber Shop.*

Sennett in Decline

Both Crosby and Field went on to become big stars while Sennett continued his slow fade-out. Both he and Al Christie were producing for Educational by the mid Thirties. The silent screen had been the element of these two producers and they were relegated to the two-reel programme fillers of the age. But they were not alone. Buster Keaton had also seen better days and at this same time was making two-reelers for Educational. Of the important comedy producers of the silent period, only Hal Roach had made a successful transition to the sound motion picture. *dwm*

HAROLD LLOYD

From a humble beginning in small theatrical stock companies and bit roles in films, **Harold Lloyd** (1893–1971), (through a shoe-string production unit formed by Hal Roach) began his steady climb to stardom with a tramp-clown character in such one-reelers as *Just Nuts* (1915). Moving to Keystone for a few pictures and a few weeks in 1915, he found that his humour did not chime with Mack Sennett's. Back with Roach when a contract had been obtained with Pathe, the comedian began to experiment with the character Willie Work and evolved another, similar portrait with more dash called Lonesome Luke. In the years 1916 and 1917 Lloyd made nearly a hundred half-, one-, and two-reel comedies, most of them using some variation on this character.

In this formative period, the comedian grew tired of grinding out films with such titles as *Lonesome Luke's Wild Women,* and *Lonesome Luke's Lively Life* and began to depart from the tramp-clown tradition. He adopted a "straight role" costume of the light comedians and formed his unique trademark badge, horn-rimmed glasses, in *Over the Fence,*

Formative Period

25

Harold Lloyd (at right) with Mildred Davis, in A SAILOR-MADE MAN

a one-reel film copyrighted August 25, 1917. Creating one-reelers at about the rate of one a week between 1918 and 1919, he perfected his breezy, brash young man, who was now simply called Harold, with the assistance of a leading lady, **Bebe Daniels** (1901–1971), providing romantic interest, and walrus-moustached **Snub Pollard** (1886–1962) playing a comic foil. By 1919 he had evolved his comic character well beyond the Sennett tradition even though he retained similar slapstick story material, especially in the climactic scene of his works. While a few of his pantomime bits in this period were Chaplinesque, he strove for originality and innovative gags that were directly related to his character.

Lloyd's distinctiveness caught the fancy of the public, and by the early Twenties his two-reelers brought him a salary of $25,000 each. Under the directing and writing talents of Sam Taylor (1895–1958) and Fred Newmeyer (1888–1968), the comedian moved to three and four-reel works and then into features. His first feature, *Grandma's*

Lloyd dangles from a building in FEET FIRST

Boy (1922), was created only a year after Chaplin embarked on a full-length work, *The Kid.*

Grandma's Boy employed basic story material often associated with the light, genteel humour of Charles Ray, Johnny Hines and Douglas MacLean. But Lloyd did not develop the character and story line with the same soft, often sentimental, touches of the genteel comedians; he employed the best of the slapstick tradition in all of his work, and his uniqueness made him one of the wealthiest men in the film industry.

Safety Last In 1923 Lloyd created one of his best features, *Safety Last,* a film showing a young man who, in striving to succeed, must double as a human fly to keep a promotion scheme that he hatched from falling through. What the comedian labeled "thrill comedy" was developed in this picture by showing his protagonist climbing a twelve storey building—a climb fraught with many obstacles to create comedy. He had used such material in his earlier short works, *Look Out Below* (1918) and *High and Dizzy* (1920), and later he exploited it again in a sound feature *Feet First* (1930).

His popularity rivaled Chaplin's in 1925 when he produced *The Freshman,* a work that revealed the comedian's grasp of the humour of humiliation as his striving, bumbling young man tries to be a college campus hero. He also scored critical and popular successes with *The Kid Brother* in 1927 and *Speedy* in 1928.

After ten silent features, Lloyd made his entrance into sound films with *Welcome Danger* (1929) and produced one of his best pictures, *Movie Crazy,* in 1932. His last film was *Mad Wednesday* (also called *The Sin of Harold Diddlebock*) under Preston Sturges's direction in 1947. In 1962 he released *Harold Lloyd's World of Comedy,* a compilation of many scenes from his silent films, and in 1966 he released *Harold Lloyd's Funny Side of Life,* an anthology of silents that has a complete version of *The Freshman.*

Harold Lloyd can be credited with the development of the silent comic feature to its highest form with films which were carefully structured and which made use of motivated gags in a tightly knit story development. *dwm*

BUSTER KEATON **Buster Keaton** (1895–1966), like Chaplin, was a successful stage comedian before he entered motion pictures. He was to have his name in lights on Shuberts' theatre for a comedy turn of his own invention in *The Passing Show of 1917,* a type of Broadway musical comedy of the period. Roscoe ("Fatty") Arbuckle, who had left Keystone and worked for Joseph M. Schenck in a unit called Comique, talked Keaton into leaving the stage and directed him in his first work, a two-reel comedy called *The Butcher Boy* released in April, 1917. He did fourteen more pictures with Arbuckle—with time off for military service. After learning many of the screen acting and directing techniques from

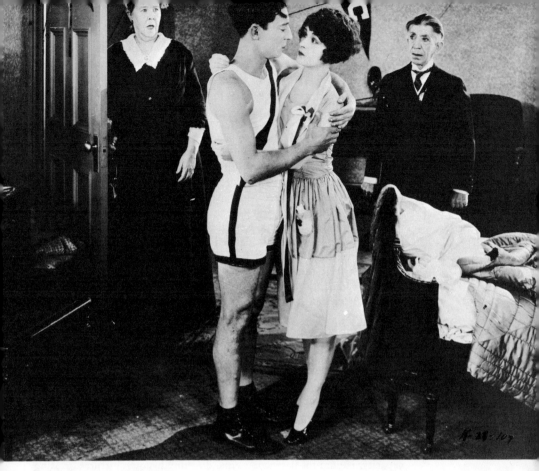

Buster Keaton in COLLEGE

this famous comedian, Metro Pictures Corporation gave him a lead in
The Saphead (1920), an adaptation of the stage hit *The Henrietta*
by Bronson Howard. Before this work was released, the comedian
started writing and directing two-reel works for Metro with the
assistance of Eddie Cline. From 1920 into the year 1923 he created
nineteen two-reel films before he launched into features. His short
works, like Harold Lloyd's, were replete with gags—often developed
by using many variations on one theme. In *Cops* (1922), for example,
he showed his comic character getting into scrapes with the law and
in the climax ending up being chased by the entire city's police force.

After a good reception of the feature, *The Three Ages* in 1923,
Our Hospitality, distributed only two months later, proved even more
successful. The feature in which he did his first job of directing and

starring had three separate stories combined along the same lines (but, naturally, in comic vein) as Griffith's *Intolerance* and used Wallace Beery as a comic heavy. *Our Hospitality* illustrated his ability to sustain his comedy in a clear-cut story line and revealed a character that had greater comic potential. One of his best films followed, *Sherlock, Jr.* (1924) showed Buster, a meek, village dimwit, becoming a super detective in elaborate dream sequences that comprised the bulk of the movie. The same year *The Navigator* employed a rich, bored young man adrift in an ocean liner with his sweetheart.

Keaton's most spectacular feature was *The General* (1926), a picture that incorporated extensive chase material with locomotives during the Civil War. Using black humour in the battle scenes, a Union train plunged into a river after a general declared that the bridge across the water was safe. Press releases claimed the gag cost forty thousand dollars, probably the most expensive gag of the silent period.

Of the twelve features created by Keaton in the Twenties, *Steamboat Bill, Jr.* (1928) also had merit. Buster was revealed struggling with many obstacles in a hurricane. Acrobatic skills in this film, as in his other works, helped create strong, effective gags.

Much in the same fashion as Lloyd, Keaton created excellent comic plots with a wealth of comic twists. Also like his predecessor in films, he varied his character in tone from picture to picture. Both were stars who supervised all aspects of their productions—from story conception to editing.

More than the major comedians Chaplin and Lloyd, Keaton suffered a decline in sound pictures. He claimed in his autobiography *My Wonderful World of Slapstick* that his works suffered from developing assembly line production techniques which cut into his supervisory capacity. He did his best work while directing his own pictures or using a co-operative co-director. His last four features in the Twenties were not under his direction.

The comedian's first sound appearance was a variety film called *The Hollywood Review* (1929) in which he was flanked by many Metro-Goldwyn-Mayer stars such as Norma Shearer, Joan Crawford, and Lionel Barrymore. He was merely a guest star in this extravaganza with other comedians, Jack Benny, Marie Dressler, Stan Laurel and Oliver Hardy. While he was a star in features in the early Thirties, the flare of the Twenties had diminished.

With the revival of interest in Keaton's work today, his rank as a comedian has been elevated by critics who believe the quality and tone of his films increase with time. Relying less on the sentiment of the times, his pictures are sharp gems of comedy that appeal to modern taste. *dwm*

After he was discovered by movie scouts during his vaudeville tour with a skit called "Johnny's New Car," **Harry Langdon** (1884–1944) was introduced by Mack Sennett to the motion picture public in a slight, disjointed comedy short, *Picking Peaches* (1924). The evolution of his distinctive style began to appear when **Frank Capra** (*b* 1897) and Arthur Ripley wrote the script for *Lucky Stars* in 1925. Pitted against a vamp, the innocent, romancing Harry was uniquely comic—such material was to be more elaborately developed in his features. After over twenty two-reel films, he embarked on a three-reel work, *Soldier Man,* that had some of the ear-marks of his features. This 1926 work, again scripted by Capra and Ripley, showed Langdon developing his pantomime skills in a dual role as an American soldier of the First World War and King Strudel XIII of Bomania; the story was obviously a burlesque of the many cloak and dagger serious, romantic works of the Twenties.

When Frank Capra was moved into a directorship of the comedian's pictures, Langdon reached his zenith. He had appeared with Joan Crawford in *Tramp, Tramp, Tramp* (1926) under the direction of Harry Edwards, but his second and third features, *The Strong Man* (1926) and *Long Pants* (1927) under the guidance of Capra, were his best works and firmly established his stardom. Both of these features impressed the New York critics who began comparing his subtle, low-keyed pantomime with that of Chaplin's. His hesitant movements when perplexed or trying to take action intrigued the evaluators. The child-like curiosity also gave his comic portrait distinctiveness.

Unlike the other major comedians of the silent era, Chaplin, Lloyd, and Keaton, he could not effectively supervise his total productions. While his gag ideas contributed greatly to the efforts of his best directors, Capra and Edwards, his attempts to create his own works were disastrous. Misguided in part by the critical recognition of his sad clown pose, he leaned too heavily on Chaplin-like "pathos" in *Three's a Crowd* (1927), although several scenes in this film have a lyrical quality unattained by his rivals. Two more directing-starring efforts, *The Chaser* and *Heart Trouble* in 1928, revealed that the comedian who had captured the attention of the public for so short a time was suffering a decline during the close of the silent screen period.

In several insignificant sound pictures later Langdon nearly achieved a comeback with his role as a whimsical refuse collector in *Hallelujah, I'm a Bum.* But the total film was weak. A 1933 musical with scenario by Ben Hecht, music and lyrics by Richard Rodgers and Lorenz Hart, plus stars such as Al Jolson, Madge Evans, and Frank Morgan did not seem to help sell the movie to the public.

The comedian continued to create two-reel shorts for Paramount and Columbia; he made occasional brief appearances in features. His influence as a writer seemed the greatest in the Laurel and Hardy feature, *Blockheads* (1938), and this work was one of the comedy team's best. Langdon even appeared opposite Hardy in *Zenobia* (1939) during a contract dispute, and it appeared that he might once more become a leading player. But this teaming didn't work and he faded into the background, appearing as comedy relief in many "B" pictures in the Forties. It was a sad fade-out for one of the silent screen's greatest comedians—one who was once considered a serious rival of Chaplin. *dwm*

Mack Sennett once called Hal Roach "my only rival," but by the Thirties, Sennett, once the undisputed "King of Comedy," was facing hard times, while Roach was at the height of his powers. Sennett gave birth to screen comedy, and launched most of movies' great comedians, but it was Hal Roach who added polish to Sennett's frantic style, and produced some of the greatest comedy films of all time.

HAL ROACH   Harold **Eugene Roach** was born in Elmira, New York, in 1892. He left home as a teenager and journeyed to Alaska, travelling along the West Coast of North America, and holding down a variety of jobs. In 1912 he settled in Los Angeles and was attracted to the film industry. He worked as an extra at Universal Pictures, and struck up a friendship with another young actor, Harold Lloyd. In 1914, Roach came into some money and decided to invest it all in film production. With a partner, Dan Linthicum, he founded Rolin Film Corporation, and produced a one-reel comedy starring Harold Lloyd. After several false starts, Rolin established itself, and Roach became a bonafide producer. In addition, Harold Lloyd became a comedy star of the first rank.

By 1920 both Lloyd and Roach were doing well, and the producer decided to expand. He made Lloyd's sidekick, Snub Pollard, the star of his own series. Pollard's director, Charles Parrott, became a star himself several years later as Charley Chase. The Pollard and Chase films produced by Roach during the Twenties were among the most inventive comedies ever made, unsurpassed even by some of the comedy giants. In 1922 Roach inaugurated one of his most durable series: Our Gang. He had always been intrigued with the idea of "kid comedies," and when he originated the Gang in 1922, the idea paid off. He continued to produce these shorts until 1937. In the late Twenties, Roach assembled a contract roster of comedians who appeared in his All-Star Series. James Finlayson, Edgar Kennedy, Anita Garvin, and Max Davidson were all fine comics, but two of the players evolved into a comedy team that had something special. Stan Laurel and Oliver Hardy became Roach's biggest stars, remaining with him through 1940.

While the talkie revolution sent some studios into a state of panic, Roach was quite lucky: Laurel and Hardy, Our Gang, and Charley Chase adapted themselves to sound with ease. To their ranks he added Harry Langdon, who lasted only one year; The Boy Friends, a collegiate series that launched George Stevens as a director; Thelma Todd and Zasu Pitts, the latter replaced by Patsy Kelly in 1934; and The Taxi

Boys, starring Billy Gilbert and Ben Blue. Allied to M-G-M for the distribution of his films, Hal Roach was Hollywood's king of comedy in the Thirties. Then, around 1936, he decided to broaden his horizons by concentrating on feature films instead of short subjects. Only Laurel and Hardy and Patsy Kelly survived the transition to features; Roach sold Our Gang to M-G-M, and his other contractees left for employment elsewhere. Roach didn't worry; his first feature films included such box-office hits as *Topper* (1937), and it looked as if he had a new career ahead of him. He severed his ties with M-G-M and joined United Artists. Among his films for them were *Of Mice and Men* (1939) and *One Million B.C.* (1939), which was partially directed by D. W. Griffith.

Roach entered the Forties with a bright new idea: a compromise between short subjects and feature films called streamliners. Running forty to fifty minutes, Roach produced a score of these films, but they were not successful. During the Second World War, he supervised film production for the U.S. Signal Corps and the U.S. Air Force, and Fort Roach became Hollywood's Army production centre. After the War, however, Roach never regained his civilian prominence as a producer. He and his son produced several successful television series (*My Little Margie, Racket Squad,* etc.) but by the mid-Fifties the firm was bankrupt. Plans to do new Laurel and Hardy television-films collapsed when both men fell ill.

In recent years, Roach has profited by the sale and licensing of his vast backlog of short-subjects and feature films. In 1965 he co-produced *The Crazy World of Laurel and Hardy* for Jay Ward Productions, and of late has been honoured at film festivals. There have been many comeback announcements, but nothing has ever resulted from them.

Hal Roach has been accused of being merely a money-man with no special talent. This is an unfair description of one of the few producers who knew talent when he saw it, and gave his stars, writers, and directors freedom to create great comedy. *lm*

In Hollywood, the film industry, after suffering a temporary setback at the end of the First World War, grew rapidly, becoming the fifth largest industry in the United States and attracting large-scale investments from Wall Street.

The innovations developed by Griffith together with the influence exerted by the Soviet and German Expressionist schools led to a growing interest within the industry in film technique. The mobility of the camera began to be explored by directors, whose role came to be seen as increasingly crucial. At the same time, the use of a written scenario became standard practice in place of improvisation on the set as longer shooting schedules and larger budgets were used, and title writing came to be seen as an art in itself. Editors, cameramen and set designers also assumed far greater importance as the decade progressed. The foremost *genres* during this period were the domestic dramas often depicting the breakdown of established *mores,* costume dramas and spectacles such as DeMille's *The Ten Commandments.* The Western developed significantly during this period and Sternberg directed what were to become the seminal gangster films *Underworld, The Drag Net* and *The Docks of New York.*

Erich von Stroheim   Perhaps the single most outstanding talent which dominated the decade was that of **Erich von Stroheim** (1885–1957). Born in Vienna, Stroheim emigrated to the United States in the early 1900s and began his Hollywood career as an actor, later working as an assistant to Griffith. His first film, made for Universal, *Blind Husbands* (1918) traced

Gibson Gowland and ZaSu Pitts in Stroheim's GREED

GOLDWYN PICTURE

the sexual adventures of an Austrian officer on holiday, a role that Stroheim undertook himself, to great effect. *The Devil's Passkey* (1919) which followed, was a film with a similar theme. Following the success of these films, Stroheim was able to embark on a much more expensive production, *Foolish Wives* (1921), again himself playing a lascivious Austrian officer, one of a group of adventurers on holiday in the South of France. Like Sternberg, Stroheim conjured up a world still very much in its infancy psychologically. It was a grotesque and brutal world, and the bleakness and callousness of his protagonists' lives was revealed with a meticulous realism. *Foolish Wives* was substantially mutilated by its producers, and from this time onwards all his films appeared in truncated versions. *Merry-Go-Round* (1922), the first film in a projected trilogy about the last days of the Hapsburg empire, was in fact completed by someone else, and at this point, Stroheim left Universal for the Goldwyn Company and embarked on what was to be his masterpiece, *Greed* (1924). Based on Frank Norris's novel *McTeague,* this powerful and cruelly realistic story of obsessional behaviour, when completed, ran to twenty-four reels and was released in the drastically reduced form of eight reels. In spite of this, Stroheim made one more film for M-G-M, *The Merry Widow* (1925) an adaptation of the Lehar operetta starring Mae Murray, which he suceeded in turning into a characteristically black comedy. Moving to Paramount, he continued the theme he had begun with *Merry-Go-Round,* the exploration of life in Imperial Vienna, with *The Wedding March* (1927) and its sequel *The Honeymoon* (1927), intended by Stroheim to make one complete film, but released separately by Paramount. His last film *Queen Kelly* (1928) with Gloria Swanson playing the leading role, was interrupted by the arrival of sound and abandoned by the producer Joseph Kennedy. A version was assembled some time later by Gloria Swanson which Stroheim has repudiated. Regarded by producers as hopelessly extravagant, Stroheim was forced to abandon his directorial career after beginning work in 1932 on *Walking down Broadway* (Stroheim was taken off the project, and the film was re-shot as *Hello Sister* by Alfred Werker). Stroheim continued to act in both Europe and America, but he remains a director who must necessarily be seen as one of the cinema's greatest enigmas.

If Stroheim was one of the major casualties of the Hollywood of this period, **Cecil B. DeMille** (1881–1959) was certainly one of Hollywood's most flamboyant successes. His directorial gifts coupled with his entrepreneurial skills had a significant part to play in the growth of Hollywood. Steeped in the literary traditions of Fenimore Cooper and the dramatic conventions of David Belasco, DeMille began his career as a playwright before going into partnership with Jesse Lasky and Sam Goldfish and moving into motion pictures. DeMille's approach to the cinema was essentially didactic; he saw himself as the upholder

Cecil B. DeMille

of the Christian moral code that was constantly in danger of being undermined by an increasingly permissive society. His films in the early Twenties largely consisted of marital comedies and were concerned with the rapidly changing role of women and the consequent breakdown of the family. The *milieu* DeMille depicted was essentially that of the leisured middle-class, where luxury and moral freedom constituted a life style. Among such films were *Old Wives for New* (1918), *Why Change Your Wife?* (1920), *Forbidden Fruit* (1921), *Manslaughter* (1922) and *Adam's Rib* (1922). However, DeMille's directorial reputation rests with his ability to direct action and his narrative power, these qualities being foremost in his spectacles. He made his first epic in 1923, *The Ten Commandments,* which juxtaposed the Biblical story with a modern one, and was notable for its fine action sequences and its moral fervour, combined with a somewhat incongruous predilection for the erotic. After forming his own production company in 1925 and making several less ambitious films such as *The Golden Bed* (1925) and *The Road to Yesterday* (1925), DeMille embarked on a further epic of even more ambitious proportions, *King of Kings* (1927), another Biblical story, taking some extraordinary liberties with the New Testament and employing thousands of extras, that still remains as one of the outstanding films of the *genre.*

Rex Ingram   The achievements of the director **Rex Ingram** (1892–1950) have largely been forgotten today, and yet at the time he achieved a reputation as a director of great distinction and his success with *The Four Horsemen of the Apocalypse* did much to save Metro from bankruptcy. An Irishman born in Dublin, Ingram emigrated to America in 1911 after studying painting, entered the industry as a designer, and later wrote a number of scripts. Ingram made his first film in 1916, *The Great Problem,* and went on to make a number of films for Universal before moving to Metro in 1919. After making two films, *Shore Acres* (1920) and *Hearts Are Trumps* (1920), he was assigned to shoot *The Four Horsemen of the Apocalypse* (1921), based on the Ibañez novel about the First World War. The film proved to be extremely successful and launched Rudolph Valentino in his career. As a painter, Ingram possessed a rare pictorial sense combined with an interest in the exotic and strange. His subsequent films for Metro were *The Conquering Power* (1921), *Scaramouche* (1923) and *Where the Pavement Ends* (1923). Forming his own studio at Nice, Ingram made *Mare Nostrum* (1926), *The Magician* (1926), *The Garden of Allah* (1927), which were followed by *The Three Passions* (1929) and *Baroud* (co-directed by his wife Alice Terry and starring Ingram himself) made in North Africa in 1931, at which time Ingram retired from film-making.

The Frenchman **Maurice Tourneur** (1878–1961) was another director who made a significant contribution to the American cinema of this period. Beginning life as a painter, Tourneur began working in

Brilliant use of light and location in THE FOUR HORSEMEN OF THE APOCALYPSE

the film industry in France with the Eclair Company, and moved to Hollywood to run the studios the company established there in 1914, staying until 1926. During his years in Hollywood Tourneur was a prolific director, and his first film *Mother* (1914) established him as a director with a highly original pictorial sense, and one of the first directors to exploit fully the possibilities of camera technique and the use of light and shade. Tourneur's innovations can best be seen in one of his most celebrated films which he made with **Clarence Brown** (*b* 1890), *The Last of the Mohicans* (1920). Brown came to the film industry after training as an engineer, working as an assistant to Tourneur. His first film, *The Great Redeemer,* was made in 1920. A romantic, considerably influenced by German Expressionism, Brown is best known for his ability to direct actors such as Valentino in *The*

Eagle (1925) and Greta Garbo in *Flesh and the Devil* (1927) and *A Woman of Affairs* (1928).

Vidor and King   Social realism, which was to play such an important part in the American cinema of the Thirties, was not entirely absent in the Twenties. Undoubtedly the major director to emerge during this period with a strong social conscience that pervaded his work was **King Vidor** (*b* 1896). Vidor went to Hollywood in 1915 after making several amateur films, and his first feature *The Turn of the Road* (1918), made for the Christian Science Movement, was indicative of the humanism and idealism that were his guiding principles as a director. He soon succeeded in establishing his own studio, Vidor Village, where he made a number of films independently, including *The Jack-Knife Man* (1919), *Conquering the Women* (1920), and *Alice Adams* (1922). Vidor then decided to join M-G-M, where he made his two most important films of the silent period, *The Big Parade* (1925), a vehement indictment of the horrors of the First World War, and *The Crowd* (1928), a sensitive and moving story of unemployment and hardship. **Henry King** (*b* 1888) was another director to make a significant contribution to the American cinema of this period with two films in particular, *Tol'able David* (1921) and *Stella Dallas* (1926). Beginning his career in the cinema as an actor, King gradually moved into directing short features for such companies as Lubin and Pathe between 1912 and 1917. King was quick to assimilate his craft, and *Tol'able David,* which was made remarkably early in his career, remains a masterpiece of expressive editing. King then made *Sonny* (1922) and *Fury* (1923) before going to Italy to make two films with Lillian Gish, *The White Sister* (1923) and *Romola* (1924). Returning to Hollywood, his most notable films before the coming of sound were *Stella Dallas* with Belle Bennett and Lois Moran and *The Winning of Barbara Worth* (1926), both of which were remarkable for their psychological observation.

Allan Dwan (*b* 1885) was another director who made an important contribution to the cinema of this period. One of Hollywood's most prolific film-makers, Dwan generally directed either domestic comedies such as *Manhandled* (1924), which starred Gloria Swanson, or costume dramas like *Robin Hood* (1922) and *The Iron Mask* (1929), both of which featured Douglas Fairbanks in his characteristically swashbuckling roles. **Fred Niblo** (1874–1948) became well-known as a director of costume dramas, and his *Mark of Zorro* (1920), *The Three Musketeers* (1921) and *Ben-Hur* (1926) are particularly memorable. **W. S. Van Dyke**'s (1899–1943) most outstanding film of the silent period was *White Shadows of the South Seas* (1928), an interesting combination of documentary and fictional techniques. **Mal St. Clair** (1897–1952) was one of the most skilful directors of domestic comedy, with such films as *Are Parents People?* (1925), *The*

Grand Duchess and the Waiter (1926) and *A Woman of the World* (1926). **Frank Borzage** (1893–1961), one of the great Romantics of the cinema, directed *Seventh Heaven* (1927) and *Street Angel* (1928). **William Wellman** (*b* 1896) began making films in 1923; his most outstanding achievements of this period were *Wings* (1927), an extraordinarily ambitious aviation film, and *Beggars of Life* (1928).

With the tremendous expansion that took place within the industry in the Twenties, a policy of importing foreign talent got under way. One of the most brilliant European directors to be tempted by the glitter of Hollywood was **Ernst Lubitsch** (1892–1947). As an established figure in the German cinema, Lubitsch arrived in America in 1923. Mary Pickford invited him to direct her in *Rosita* (1923), a film that was largely unsuccessful, and demonstrated Lubitsch's as yet inadequate understanding of the nuances of American life and manners. However, he soon became accustomed to America and was responsible for some of the finest comedies ever produced. *The Marriage Circle* (1924), his next picture, was enormously acceptable, and traced a typical Lubitsch situation, the relationship between two couples. The underlying melancholy of his satire, and his tremendously effective use of gesture and facial expression in his actors came to be called "the Lubitsch touch." There followed *Three Women* (1924), a satire on female psychology, *Forbidden Paradise* (1924), a costume drama with Pola Negri, *Kiss Me Again* (1925), a sexual comedy, *Lady Windermere's Fan* (1925), *So This Is Paris* (1926), and three costume dramas, *The Student Prince* (1928), *The Patriot* (1928) and *Eternal Love* (1929).

Of the other foreign directors who went to Hollywood, the German F. W. Murnau, Victor Sjöström and Mauritz Stiller from Sweden and Benjamin Christensen from Denmark were the most important. Murnau's *Sunrise* (1927) was one of the greatest Expressionist films, Sjöström's *The Wind* (1927) was a remarkable study of mental disintegration brought about by alien surroundings, and Christensen's horror films, *The House of Horror* (1929) and *Seven Footprints to Satan* (1929) are particularly memorable.

Ultimately the Hollywood of the Twenties belonged to the stars, and such names as Fairbanks, Valentino and Garbo became household words. **Mary Pickford** (*b* 1893) consolidated her popularity, which had been brought about by the *ingénue* roles she had played up to this time, and extended her range with such films as *Daddy-Long-Legs* (1919) and *Rosita* (1923). Her husband **Douglas Fairbanks** (1883–1939) became known largely for his athletic prowess in such films as *The Three Musketeers* (1921), *Robin Hood* (1922), *The Thief of Bagdad* (1924), the colour film *The Black Pirate* (1926) and *The Iron Mask* (1929). **Rudolph Valentino** (1895–1926) is best known for his roles in *The Four Horsemen of the Apocalypse* (1921), *The*

Sheik (1921) and *The Eagle* (1924); his reputation rests on his portrayal of the archetypal romantic hero. From this time onwards, the content, production and publicity of the cinema was focused on the star, and several archetypes emerged particularly for female stars. The fragile innocent developed by such stars as Lillian Gish was counterpointed by the *Femme Fatale,* while another archetype, *la divine,* best embodied by Greta Garbo, who combined mystery with purity, also emerged blending elements of both archetypes. Of the other female stars, **Louise Brooks** (*b* 1906), **Clara Bow** (1905–1965), **Gloria Swanson** (*b* 1898) and **Pola Negri** (*b* 1897) were the most unforgettable. *cj*

The death of Thomas Ince on November 19, 1924 at the relatively young age of forty-two was to rob the silent cinema of its most creative producer. Ince had begun as a director in 1910 with Carl Laemmle's Imp Company, where he had directed Mary Pickford in several one-reelers. The following year he was hired by Kessel and Bauman as director and production head for their New York Motion Picture Company. Ince continued to direct all of his productions until the summer of 1912, after which time he allowed others to direct from a detailed scenario which he provided. During this period Ince was building up the Inceville studios, covering some 20,000 acres of land and comprising five

Mary Pickford riding with Chaplin and Fairbanks while shooting POLLYANNA in 1919

stages. Among the multitude of players that Ince discovered and groomed for stardom were William S. Hart, Charles Ray, Sessue Hayakawa, Billie Burke, Dorothy Dalton and Enid Markey. In 1916 he produced his most famous film *Civilization* (*dir* Raymond B. West), an allegory against war and a plea for brotherhood, with obvious roots in Griffith's *Intolerance*. Ince's finest production was probably the 1923 *Anna Christie* (*dir* John Griffith Wray), the first time that O'Neill had been brought to the screen, and with a magnificent dramatic performance from Blanche Sweet in the title role. *as*

THE WESTERN

The Western can be dated back to the earliest days of story-telling in the American cinema. *The Great Train Robbery* (1903) was probably the first effectively organised piece of dramatic fiction, telling in one reel a complete story of a robbery, the chase, and the triumph of justice. It had been preceded by a few vignettes of Western life, basically moving photographs of the real thing like *Cripple Creek Bar-room* (1898, *dir* W. K. L. Dickson) and *The Life of an American Cowboy* (1902, *dir* Edwin S. Porter), the latter including in embryo a chase sequence that its director was to develop for his *The Great Train Robbery*. In fact, **Edwin S. Porter** (1869–1941), who also scripted, *Edwin S. Porter* photographed and edited *The Great Train Robbery* was the most important American film-maker prior to D. W. Griffith (who began his film career as an actor in a later Porter Western drama, *Rescued from an Eagle's Nest,* 1907). A member of the outlaw band in *The Great Train Robbery* was Max Aaronson (1883–1971) who as **"Bronco Billy" Anderson,** became the first star of Westerns by creating a cowboy hero whose adventures formed the subject of a long series of one-and two-reelers, beginning with *Bronco Billy and the Baby* (1910), a sentimental adaptation of a Peter B. Kyne story with a resemblance to another oft-filmed Kyne work best known in screen form as *Three Godfathers.*

Porter had established the dramatic basis of conflict between good and evil in his story of a train hold-up and his photography in a still wild New Jersey gave some hints of the pictorial splendour the *genre* was to achieve; Anderson evolved the image of the Western hero. The subsequent history of the Western largely lies in an increasing subtlety in the use of characterisation, conflict and landscape. Bronco Billy's exploits (which continued until 1917) also produced the kind of simple moral identification with virtue and integrity on which the *genre* has flourished.

D. W. Griffith, filming in California, brought the epic side of the Old West to the screen, depicting many of the great events in its history like Custer's Last Stand (in *The Massacre,* 1912), the Gold Rush of '49 as part of *Crossing the American Prairies in the Early Fifties* (c 1910), and the story of a historic battle in *Martyrs of the*

Alamo (1915, directed by Christy Cabanne under his supervision). Besides showing the settlers' troubles with the Indians in *Fighting Blood* (1911), Griffith also dealt more directly, and often in a sympathetic manner common to the period, with the aboriginal inhabitants of the West in such films as *The Redman's View, The Heart of a Savage* (both c 1910) and *A Pueblo Legend* (1912). His films sometimes aspired to big action scenes, skilfully made with panoramic views and tense editing techniques, but Griffith's poetic insight maintained the importance of his characters and it is only because of Griffith's more celebrated achievements being in other fields that his major contribution to the development of the Western tends to be overlooked.

Thomas H. Ince

Another important figure of the time was **Thomas H. Ince** (1882–1924) who directed several interesting Westerns and produced the earlier films of the Western star William S. Hart. Ince's two reeler *War on the Plains* (1911) used the members of a Wild West show to create a convincing impression of life in the Old West, and others of his films had sombre endings that sometimes jarred but did something

Bronco Billy (G. M. Anderson) directed and starred in BRONCO BILLY AND THE RED-SKIN. Opposite: William S. Hart as Wild Bill Hickok.

to reflect the hardship, prejudices and basic uncertainties of the period.

The second great star of Westerns was **William S. Hart** (1870–1946) who was raised in the West and had acted in stage Westerns. His frequently austere work (which he sometimes part wrote, directed, and always supervised) breathed dedication to the West as a subject suited for all the artistic possibilities of cinema; he rarely made films outside the *genre,* and in his Westerns a recurring portrayal was of the outlaw who reforms and finds happiness, often from offering his protection to the heroine as in the classic *Hell's Hinges* (1916) when his first gaze on the preacher's sister is enough to cause him to switch sides from the bad element to the good element in the town. But Hart's inflexibility, his refusal to adjust to increasingly sophisticated public taste, plus his advancing age, reduced his popularity in the Twenties when he was supplanted as the top box-office favourite by **Tom Mix** (1881–1940). Mix emerged from a background that was genuinely adventurous (he had fought in wars and worked for the Texas Rangers) and otherwise appropriate (his mother had Cherokee blood). Mix actually began his screen career a little before Hart but the modest, frequently humorous shorts he made between 1913 and 1917 were a far cry from the polished, amiable entertainments he made later—films that were a shrewd blend of action, stunts and comic relief with Mix as a virtuous, incorruptible hero more attached to his horse Tony than any girl. Little of Mix's work survives but he too was a man of the cinema (he had often written and directed as well as starred in his shorts), and he chose his collaborators well, but it is doubtful that his work was as artistically striking as that of Hart. An important star of the later Twenties was **Tim McCoy** (*b* 1891) who appeared in some lavish, well directed Westerns like *War Paint* (1926, *dir* W. S. Van Dyke), *The Overland Telegraph* and *Sioux Blood* (both 1929, *dir* John Waters). **Buck Jones** (1891–1942), **Ken Maynard** (*b* 1895), Douglas Fairbanks, **Hoot Gibson** (*b* 1892) and **Harry Carey** (1880–1947) were other notable stars of the Twenties' Westerns.

The director of two Tom Mix Westerns was John Ford, who also worked extensively earlier in his career with Harry Carey as well as with Hoot Gibson and Buck Jones. But Ford really made his mark with one of the two outstanding and influential major Westerns of the Twenties, *The Iron Horse* (1924), telling on an epic scale of the construction of a railroad to bridge the continent (Cecil B. DeMille's *Union Pacific* in 1939 told the same story and had many similarities of style). Filmed on location in Nevada under arduous conditions that matched those experienced by the original builders, *The Iron Horse* grew to epic proportions as it went along and is still impressive for its overall control, the occasional touches of genius in its style, and Ford's sympathetic identification with the story.

Tom Mix, one of the great cowboy stars of the Twenties

The other key Western was *The Covered Wagon,* made in 1923 by James Cruze and telling the story of a great wagon trek westwards in 1848–9. This, in fact, was the pioneering example of a vast film unit on location and it was staged on a most impressive scale, with fine compositions in depth (photographed by Karl Brown) that were part of its success in relating the more intimate story with the vastness of the setting. The three leading characters enact a triangle drama that would stand up in a modern Western, while the basic conflict is well stated from the start in two shots of a plough showing it first as the key to the future for the settlers, then as the threat to the Indians whose way of life it will destroy. A funeral, simply and eloquently filmed, is followed by a birth, demonstrating a natural balance of human affairs to contrast with the more destructive basic conflict (the main Indian attack is vividly and imaginatively staged). **Cruze** (1884–1942), one of the most successful figures of the period, also made a further silent Western, *The Pony Express* (1925), though it had few of the merits of *The Covered Wagon.*

Sound Period   Surprisingly, the Western—with its strong accent on exteriors—was not inhibited by the restrictions of early sound, and in fact led the way in liberating the medium from static, talkative situations. In the process, some fine pictures were made, two of them by **Raoul Walsh** (*b* 1892): *In Old Arizona* (1929), featuring Warner Baxter as the Cisco Kid, and *The Big Trail* (1930), a wagon train epic starring a young John Wayne who, however, lapsed into B pictures (mostly Westerns) until at the end of the decade his appearance in *Stagecoach* shot him to permanent stardom. Other important films were Victor Fleming's version of *The Virginian* (1930), starring a young Gary Cooper and based on the novel by Owen Wister which had first established the Old West as a challenging subject worthy of literature; King Vidor's *Billy the Kid* (1930), a harshly realistic and violent study of the outlaw (portrayed by Johnny Mack Brown, who eventually took up a long career as a star of superior B Westerns); and Wesley Ruggles's *Cimarron* (1931), the story of a historic land-rush which starred Richard Dix, another Western star of note.

These were the celebrated films of the period, and at least one other film, neglected until recently unearthed by film historian William K. Everson, deserves to be noted, namely *Law and Order* (1932), an austere account of the taming of a "wide-open" town based on the Hickok legend, with agile direction by Edward L. Cahn and good dialogue by John Huston whose father, actor Walter Huston, contributed a thoughtful study of the principal lawman.

In the years following, the Western retained considerable box-office importance but largely through low-budget, unpretentious pictures with **George O'Brien** (*b* 1900), Buck Jones, Ken Maynard, Tim McCoy, **William Boyd** (*b* 1898) (who portrayed "Hopalong" Cassidy), and the singing stars, of whom **John Wayne** was actually the first although **Gene Autry** (*b* 1907) and **Roy Rogers** (*b* 1912) fully exploited the idea (Autry's pictures, in particular, were more musicals than Westerns very often). **Randolph Scott** (*b* 1903) began his lengthy (and relatively undistinguished until the Fifties) career in Westerns in the early Thirties in a series of Zane Grey adaptations mostly directed by Henry Hathaway.

More ambitious Westerns were few and far between, and these were largely undistinguished by the standards set before and to be achieved after. Among them was King Vidor's *The Texas Rangers* (in which the director was handicapped by a routine script) and Cecil B. DeMille's *The Plainsman,* a lavish but lifeless film dealing with the adventures of Wild Bill Hickok (Gary Cooper) that at least rendered the tragic ending to the man's life in contrast to the flamboyant heroics earlier on.

At the end of the decade, DeMille made a railroading epic, *Union Pacific* (1939), with a similarly talkative and ponderous script, but it gained dramatic power from its basic subject (the same as Ford used for *The Iron Horse*) and the big budget DeMille treatment, seen at its best in the Indian attack on the train with some imaginative dramatic effects (like the Indians unwhirling bolts of cloth). But 1939 was more important for *Stagecoach,* John Ford's first Western in more than a decade and a film which opened up new dramatic possibilities for the *genre.* Although marred by dramatic contrivance in the Dudley Nichols script (the contrived variations among the passengers on the stage), it made striking visual use of the Monument Valley location that Ford returned to frequently for later Westerns, and the direction

Monument Valley at its most impressive in John Ford's STAGECOACH

of the key action sequence—the flight of the stagecoach from attacking Indians across the salt flats—was a brilliant exercise in construction and stunt work. The film ended with one of the best gunfights ever staged—against the imaginatively evoked atmosphere of a frontier town after dark. The same year also produced one of the best comedy treatments of the genre, *Destry Rides Again* (earlier a "straight" vehicle for Tom Mix), in which James Stewart sought to stamp out lawlessness without gunplay (the script accommodated some touching moments from the interplay of characters under George Marshall's skilful direction). Michael Curtiz began a trio of lavish Westerns filmed with his typically breezy pace, all starring Errol Flynn and written by Robert Buckner: *Dodge City* (1939, the best), and *Virginia City* and *Santa Fe Trail* (both 1940). *aje*

INTO THE THIRTIES

The two events that had the greatest influence on the Thirties in Hollywood both occurred at the end of the preceding decade. The first, and most fundamental, was the commercial advent of sound, the second the Wall Street crash of 1929 and resulting depression. The staggering success of *The Jazz Singer* compelled all other studios to follow suit, and by the time the Thirties opened the silent film was, with the exception of Chaplin, a thing of the past. Despite the violent upheaval of the first years—the disappearance of a number of famous stars because of their foreign origin (Jannings, Vilma Banky) or their supposedly inadequate voice reproduction (John Gilbert, May McAvoy, Corinne Griffith, Norma Talmadge), and the compensating arrival of stage personalities (Ruth Chatterton, Fredric March, Ann Harding, Paul Muni)—the industry rose to the challenge with commendable speed and vigour. The problems of the static camera imprisoned in its padded booth, and the rudimentary inadequacy of the sound recording devices were relatively quickly overcome, and most directors welcomed the added possibilities of the new dimension. By 1931, 85 per cent of the theatres in the U.S.A. were wired for sound, and 75 per cent in Britain. The majority of the great stars—notably Greta Garbo—successfully made the transition, and at the end of the decade films such as *Gone with the Wind, The Wizard of Oz, Stage Coach, Ninotchka, Mr. Smith Goes to Washington,* and Walt Disney's first feature-length cartoon *Snow White and the Seven Dwarfs* showed Hollywood at the height of its powers.

The second great influence, the depression, was surprisingly delayed in making itself felt in the film industry. Driven by the need for escape from the pervading gloom, and still excited by hearing its favourite stars speak, the public flocked to the picture palaces, and it was not until 1933 that the pinch began to be felt. By midsummer of that year, however, some 5,000 of 16,000 cinemas in the United States had closed, and it was not until the end of the decade, apart from a marked temporary improvement in 1937, that the industry as a whole could be said to have attained a sound financial footing.

A major result of both the arrival of sound (with its enormous installation cost) and the slump (with its consequent lack of funds) was the disappearance of independent companies or their merging into eight major studios: M-G-M, Paramount, 20th Century-Fox, Warner Brothers, RKO, Universal, Columbia and (a distributing organisation only) United Artists. Films of the Thirties were thus more likely to be typed according to the studios from which they came than to a single name such as Griffith or Stroheim: the glitter and gloss of M-G-M, the smart cosmopolitanism of Paramount, the horror cycles of Universal, the swift, hard-hitting social indictments or contrasting lavish musicals of Warner Brothers. Directors worked more closely under the eye of the studios that employed them, but this is not to imply either that such assembly-line productions did not often achieve a high standard of cohesion and individuality, or that most gifted directors found much difficulty in stamping their products with the imprint of their own personalities.

One of the swiftest and most successful transitions from silence to sound was made by a foreigner—Ernst Lubitsch, who carried into the new medium all the wit and point of both his comedies and his serious films. His first three talkies were musicals, *The Love Parade* (1929), *Monte Carlo* (1931), and *The Smiling Lieutenant* (1932), and from the beginning he managed to restore the camera's mobility even while it was still locked in its booth. *The Man I Killed* (1932), a fierce indictment of war, was, most undeservedly, a box-office failure, thus unhappily discouraging him from further dramatic films. There followed *One Hour with You* (1932), a musical re-make of his *The Marriage Circle, Trouble in Paradise* (1932), *Design for Living* (1933), adapted by Ben Hecht from Noël Coward's play with only one line of the original dialogue retained, and other musical and straight comedies (including a brilliant five-minute episode with Charles Laughton in *If I had a Million,* 1932), climaxing at the end of the decade in his only film with Greta Garbo, the brilliantly amusing *Ninotchka* (1939) in which, M-G-M proudly announced, "Garbo Laughs."

Another director to meet the challenge of sound with enthusiasm was King Vidor, whose first talkie was the all-Negro *Hallelujah* (1929)— a melodramatic story, but with highly impressive individual scenes, particularly those concerned with the singing of spirituals. The rest of his output during the Thirties varied in quality but included three worth noting: *Street Scene* (1932), a straightforward but gripping transference from the theatre of Elmer Rice's play, in which he worked ingeniously within the limits of a single elaborate set; *The Citadel* (1939), a smoothly made family film from A. J. Cronin's highly coloured medical novel; and *Our Daily Bread.* The latter, made in 1934, was Vidor's best picture of the period. In it he harked back to the problems of the depression and the unemployed, with a plea for communal work on the farm. The full potential of the film was never quite realised—punches were pulled, possibly on orders from above—but more than one powerful sequence showed Vidor at his best.

Michael Curtiz   One of the most prolific directors of the decade was **Michael Curtiz** (1888–1962) and during it he handled the majority of the famous stars in the Warner Brothers studios, from Richard Barthelmess in *Cabin in the Cotton* (1932) to Bette Davis and Errol Flynn together in *The Private Lives of Elizabeth and Essex* in 1939. His range extended from the classic "lost" horror film *The Mystery of the Wax Museum* (1932) to the Errol Flynn adventure series, *Captain Blood* (1932), *Charge of the Light Brigade* (1936), *The Adventures of Robin Hood* (1938) and *Dodge City* (1939). He also made a number of tough thrillers such as the uncompromising *Twenty Thousand Years in Sing Sing* (1933). With so large an output, much of his work was obviously of ephemeral interest, but at his ruthless best he was one of the most important Warner directors during their most energetic period.

Clarence Brown, having made Greta Garbo's most successful silent film *Flesh and the Devil,* brought her with equal success into sound with his version of Eugene O'Neill's play *Anna Christie* (1930). Thereafter through the Thirties he directed a number of expensively mounted, star vehicle pictures, romantic in style but handled with a cool sensitivity, such as *A Free Soul* (1931) with Norma Shearer, and *Letty Lynton* (1932). Though best known for his Garbo movies *Anna Karenina* (1935) and *Marie Walewska* (*Conquest,* 1937), his most successful film of the period was another O'Neill adaptation, *Ah Wilderness* (1935), in which he successfully captured the essence of a bygone, nostalgic America.

In the early Thirties the work of **Mervyn LeRoy** (*b* 1900) exemplified the film of hard-hitting social criticism: *Little Caesar* (1931), the first realistic gangster film, *Five Star Final* (1932), an exposé of the corrupt methods of unscrupulous reporters after a story, and, most successful of all, *I Am a Fugitive from a Chain Gang* (1932). Later, except for *They Won't Forget* (1937), an excoriating picture of mob fury in the deep South, his films became more diffuse and less typical, including musicals such as the exhilaratingly fast paced *Gold Diggers of 1933,* spectacles (*Anthony Adverse,* 1936) and light comedy. At its best, his work is notable for speed, economy and forceful cutting. In 1939 he produced *The Wizard of Oz.*

Lewis Milestone (*b* 1895) opened the decade with his best-known film, *All Quiet on the Western Front* (1930). Its impact may have lost some of its original power, but it still remains a remarkable achievement and one of the most compelling and relentless anti-war pictures,

Paul Muni (right) in Mervyn LeRoy's I AM A FUGITIVE FROM A CHAIN GANG

using grim and moving irony rather than the bitter ridicule of later films on this theme. *The Front Page,* a fast-moving satire on the ethics of the sensational press, followed in 1931, and a version of Somerset Maugham's *Rain,* only partially successful, in 1932. *The General Died at Dawn* (1936) and the sepia-tinted *Of Mice and Men* (1939) stand out among the routine productions of his following years.

Henry King continued to produce smooth, competent pictures throughout the period, at his best sympathetic and warm, but always at risk of descending to banality and the easy *cliché.* Most notable were *State Fair* (1933) and *Jesse James* (1939). *Stanley and Livingstone* (1939), though condensed for dramatic effect, commendably avoided the sentimental distortions of so many historical re-creations.

Frank Capra (*b* 1897) was chiefly known in silent days for his direction of the brilliant Harry Langdon comedies. In the early Thirties he made for Columbia a number of successful early sound films of surprisingly wide variety, such as *Dirigible* (1931), *Platinum Blonde* (1932), *American Madness* (1932), *The Bitter Tea of General Yen*

Frank Capra

51

(1932) and *Lady for a Day* (1933). In 1934 the enormous and un-expected triumph of *It Happened One Night*—a comedy making use of the current novelty of long-distance coach travel—paved the way for a series of warm-hearted, technically brilliant social comedies extolling the individual against the tyranny of the many: *Mr. Deeds Goes to Town* (1936), *You Can't Take It with You* (1938), *Mr. Smith Goes to Washington* (1939) and *Meet John Doe* (1941). The visually beautiful *Lost Horizon* (1937), based on John Hilton's fantasy about a Tibetan Utopia, had the same underlying theme linked with those of the escape to happiness, and the ivory tower.

Fritz Lang (see also Chapter Five) was brought to Hollywood by M-G-M in 1934, after leaving Germany when Hitler came to power and making one film, *Liliom,* in France. He directed only three Amer-ican films during the Thirties, all on themes of social significance, and two of them among his all-time masterpieces. *Fury* (1936) is still, despite a softened ending, one of the most terrifying and powerful denunciations of mob hysteria and lynch law in the cinema, beautifully constructed in a steady progression from quiet opening to violent climax. *You Only Live Once* (1937) concerned the hopeless attempts of a young ex-convict to go straight and is a harrowing indictment of social values, avoiding both melodrama and sentimentality in its treat-ment. *You and Me* (1938), somewhat similar in subject, was less successful.

Although he did not direct his first feature film until 1941 (*The Maltese Falcon*), **John Huston** (*b* 1906) worked in collaboration on the scripts of several successful films of the Thirties, notably the early adaptation of Poe's *Murders in the Rue Morgue* (1932, directed by Robert Florey), the Bette Davis costume melodrama *Jezebel* (1938, directed by William Wyler) from a play by Owen Davis, and *Juarez* (1939, directed by William Dieterle) in which Paul Muni appeared as the Indian-born Mexican leader.

JOSEF VON STERNBERG   Josef von Sternberg (Josef Stern, 1894–1969) was born in Vienna, spent three years at school in the United States when he was seven, returned to Vienna, and settled in America again when he was fourteen. After a period of considerable financial hardship, he started work as a film patcher in the World Film Company. After a further period of travel he returned to the United States and there, in 1925, made his first film, *The Salvation Hunters,* in conjunction with an un-known young British actor, George K. Arthur. It told a sordid story of a feckless young coward and his wife who find an abandoned child and leave their hovel on the waterfront when a procurer, hoping to make money out of the wife, offers them lodgings. Eventually the young man is aroused by the procurer's ill-treatment of the woman and child, attacks him, and determines to make something more of his future. In its relentless realism, the film was undoubtedly influenced by Stroheim's *Greed*. Symbolic throughout is the lowering presence of a huge dredge working in the mud of the river. Uncompromising in its lack of physical action and its deliberate pace, it nevertheless brought its young director considerable critical acclaim. Chaplin in particular was enthusiastic, and the film was bought by United Artists.

After several false starts, von Sternberg scored his first popular success for Paramount with *Underworld* (1927), scripted by himself from a story by Ben Hecht. *Underworld* set the pattern for countless American gangster films to follow. In it he combined already the realism of setting and *milieu* with poetry of light and composition which was for some time to mark his work. A melodramatic, fundamentally sentimental story was made stringent and believable by the discipline, economy of means and sense of timing which he brought to it. In the following year, 1928, he directed two more stories of the seamier side of life: *The Dragnet,* a tough, hard-hitting crime thriller, and *The Docks of New York.* This visually remarkable film was made, except for one or two stock shots, entirely in the studio, von Sternberg and his art director, Hans Dreier, constructing a wholly convincing section of the waterfront with its bars, its rickety exterior staircases, sleazy rooms, and even a moored tramp steamer. The film was also memorable for Betty Compson's beautiful and moving performance in a part which could so easily have become *cliché*-ridden—the prostitute with a heart of gold. Sternberg's handling of the actress foreshadowed his work with Marlene Dietrich.

The same year also saw the *première* of *The Last Command*. Sternberg had written the script for an earlier Emil Jannings film, *The Street of Sin* (1928), directed by Mauritz Stiller, and this led to his working on the actor's next picture as both writer and director. *The Last Command* was incontestably Sternberg's greatest achievement in the silent period—indeed, one of its finest masterpieces. Together with *Der blaue Engel* (1930), it stands at the head of the director's work. Based on a true story which was told to Sternberg by Ernst Lubitsch, it tells, in a long flashback, of a proud and powerful Russian general who is thrown down by the Communist revolution and is forced to flee the country and seek work in America, penniless, as a humble film extra. There, by a combination of cruelly ironic circumstances, he is made to portray a role similar to his own past position, under the direction of an embittered man whom he had once confronted in a company of touring players in Russia.

The Case of Lena Smith (1929) his last silent film, revealed the rottenness beneath the gaiety of Old Vienna in the story of a peasant girl, an army officer and an illegitimate child. The picture is a rarity today, which is a pity because, in spite of loose construction and conventional characterisation, it is noteworthy for the wonderful fluidity of

Evelyn Brent and Emil Jannings in von Sternberg's THE LAST COMMAND

Sternberg's camerawork (with Harold Rosson), and for the performance he obtains from yet another actress, Esther Ralston.

For his first talking picture he returned to the gangster setting of *Underworld* and *The Dragnet. Thunderbolt* (1929) was made in a mood of uncompromising realism with harsh, flat photography and—unusual in those days—a complete absence of background music. (For comment on *Der blaue Engel* see Chapter Five.)

Aided, in the first three films, by photographer Lee Garmes, Josef von Sternberg made a series of pictures during the Thirties in which he created in the person of Marlene Dietrich a beautiful, totally unreal figure—a modern mythological love goddess: *Morocco* (1930), *Dishonoured* (1931), *Shanghai Express* (1932), *The Blonde Venus* (1932), *The Scarlet Empress* (1934), *The Devil Is a Woman* (1935). The stories were mostly puerile, and even the baroque beauty of lighting and composition eventually began to pall. *Shanghai Express,* with its cunning creation of China in the confines of the studio, and *The Scarlet Empress* (1934) were the most interesting. Other films of this

American period included adaptations of *An American Tragedy* (1931) and *Crime and Punishment* (1935) and a trivial musical with music arranged from Kreisler, *The King Steps Out* (1936). He then went to England to make the ill-fated *I, Claudius* (1937). This project, bedevilled from the start by difficulties between the director and his star, Charles Laughton, and by other troubles climaxed by a car crash suffered by his leading lady Merle Oberon, was abandoned with only some twenty minutes of completed film. The footage, edited and incorporated into a documentary account of the production, is all that can be seen of what might have been Sternberg's masterpiece.

Thereafter he did little of interest. *The Shanghai Gesture* (1941) was a sensational story set in a high-class Chinese brothel, in which his penchant for the baroque and ornamental could have full play. His last completed picture was *The Saga of Anatahan,* made, by invitation, in Japan.

Sternberg brought to the screen new horizons in the art of lighting, particularly of shadowed and broken rays. Scenes from his films that stand out in the memory seem almost always to be seen through streamers and feathers, through loose gauze, through slatted shutters or intricate lattice-work. He also brought the combination of poetry and realism which was so regrettably lost in later years and only rarely recovered. *ib*

John Ford (*b* 1895) is the American director most respected in the world and most honoured in his own country (with six Academy Awards). His work is emotional and popular: he has never resorted to private symbolism, and his films contain no obscurity. Knockabout comedy and tragedy co-exist with perfect ease in his work, which throughout a long career shows a clear development and progression. He has always paid great attention to the photography and pictorial aspects of his films: in all his best films the quality of the images matches the sensitivity of his direction of actors. His career is marked by a remarkable continuity in themes and by his long association with particular scenarists, actors and technicians.

The youngest of thirteen children of Irish immigrants, he was prop man, assistant director and stuntman on the films of his brother Francis, before directing his first film in 1917. His silent period was very prolific, including many short films, and dominated by Westerns (see separate section). Between 1917 and 1921 he worked at Universal studios; between 1921 and 1931, at Fox; his silent work includes the earliest appearances of many of the actors who were to become closely identified with his work (including John Wayne, Victor McLaglen and Ward Bond) and also the remarkable collaboration with photographer George Schneiderman, which lasted well into the Thirties. The distinctive "look" of Ford's films was already established in this period.

JOHN FORD

His earliest non-Westerns came at the end of the period at Universal and at the beginning of the period at Fox: *The Prince of Avenue A* (1920) was a romantic story with a background of civic politics; *The Girl in No. 29* (1920) dealt with the revival of a playwright's inspiration by his friends; in *Jackie* (1921), an American in London helped a Russian girl to realise her ambition of becoming a great dancer. Themes which were to become characteristic already appeared: Ford's concern with the family and poverty emerged in *Little Miss Smiles* (1922); the themes of atonement and sacrifice appeared in *Hoodman Blind* (1923) and *Hearts of Oak* (1924). Stories of horse-racing and prize-fighting recurred, notably in *Kentucky Pride* (1925), *The Fighting Heart* (1925) and *The Shamrock Handicap* (1926). In the last years before the advent of sound Ford gradually ceased to make Westerns: from 1927 to 1938, he made none.

In *Thank You* (1925), an intrigue against a priest was foiled by a man whom the priest had helped; in *The Blue Eagle* (1926) a long-standing feud between two men was continued through civilian and naval life with an occasional truce to fight common enemies. *Upstream* (1927) was a comedy drama about actors in London. Ford's work continued to include assignments, but themes which may be seen as central to his work began to occur with greater frequency: exile and the disintegration of a family were of particular importance. *Mother Machree* (1928) dealt with an Irish mother's sacrifices for her son, with whom she is eventually reunited. *Four Sons* (1928), which was commercially highly successful, concerned a Bavarian mother and her four sons, three of whom were killed in the First World War: the only survivor is the one who went to America, where she joins him after the war. *Hangman's House* (1928) was a drama set in Ireland: a girl is forced by her father into a marriage she dislikes, which is ended when an exiled Irishman returns from America to kill her husband, who has wronged him in the past: her rescuer is an outlaw in his own country and, regretfully, must return into exile.

Ford's entry into the sound period was gradual: the short comedy, *Napoleon's Barber* (1928) in which Napoleon was a customer in a barber shop, was his first talkie; *Riley the Cop* (1928), a comedy set in New York during Prohibition, and in Munich, was released, like *Strong Boy* (1929), with a music score and synchronised effects. *The Black Watch* (1929), a military story, set in British India during the First World War, was Ford's first feature-length sound film, but the dialogue scenes were not directed by him. Happily, he ended the Twenties with *Salute* (1929), a story which particularly attracted him —fraternal rivalry with a service and sporting background.

From 1930 onwards, Ford's work became increasingly substantial and more even in quality; throughout the Thirties he made two or three films each year. The collaboration with photographer Joseph H. August is mainly concentrated in the years 1929–36. The collaboration with Dudley Nichols, which lasted intermittently from 1929 to 1947, is thought by some to have produced Ford's best work; others find many of their films together to be vitiated by pretension and self-consciousness; the deeper continuity of Ford's career was not, however, disturbed. It was in some of the films of this period that Ford's fatalism and expressionism were most pronounced: particularly in some of the work with Nichols, Ford's humour was less in evidence than usual, and these films tended to share a constricted physical situation, a very high proportion of studio work and a heavy atmosphere, though Ford's clarity and directness were never compromised. Nichols and Ford turned to literary sources with great frequency; Nunnally Johnson is notable among other scenarists who worked with Ford in this period.

Men Without Women (1930), the first product of the collaboration with Nichols, was a submarine drama, in which one man was sacrificed to save the rest of the crew. *Born Reckless* (1930) was a comedy-drama dealing with politics and gangsterism. A more important film was *Up the River* (1930), a prison comedy, marked by early appearances of both Spencer Tracy and Humphrey Bogart. *Seas Beneath* (1931) was a First World War naval story; in *The Brat* (1931), a novelist used a waif as inspiration. Doctors have often been of great importance in Ford's work, and the outstanding *Arrowsmith* (1931), based on Sinclair Lewis's novel about the struggles of an idealistic doctor, is a notable example. *Air Mail* (1932) dealt with the early days of air-mail flying (*cf* Hawks's *Only Angels Have Wings*). In *Flesh* (1932), a German wrestler was treated unscrupulously in America. Ford returned to his theme of motherhood in *Pilgrimage* (1933), in which a mother visited the grave of her son killed in the First World War and realised that her treatment of him was tragically wrong. The important Will Rogers trilogy was inaugurated by *Dr. Bull* (1933): the others were *Judge Priest* (1934) and *Steamboat round the Bend* (1935), the last two both scripted by Nichols and Lamar Trotti. They dealt, in a humorous and relaxed way, with small-town life in Connecticut and Kentucky, and with life on and by the Mississippi.

A key film in the relationship with Nichols was *The Lost Patrol* (1934), which daringly mixed acting styles in a story of British soldiers lost in the Mesopotamian Desert during the First World War: all but one were killed by the unseen enemy. The performance of Boris Karloff as a religious fanatic was outstanding. *The World Moves On* (1934) was an ambitious film telling the story of a hundred years in the history of a powerful American business family and its ramifications in Europe, taking in the First World War and ending in the Twenties. A comedy with a deep underlying seriousness was *The Whole Town's Talking* (1935) in which a timid, conscientious clerk was mistaken for a vicious and notorious gangster, whom he physically resembled (both roles being played by Edward G. Robinson). The pattern of the clerk's life is reversed, and he is frightened into complicity with the gangster, until he is instrumental in having him killed. The public is portrayed as sensation-hungry and the police as remarkably stupid. It was *The Informer* (1935), set in Dublin in 1922, which decisively drew critical attention to Ford. It was made cheaply and quickly, but with great care by all concerned. A stupid giant of a man, played by Victor McLaglen, sells his friend to the British troops, hoping to go to America with the money, but his generosity allows him to be cheated of it. He is tried and killed by his former revolutionary comrades, but while lying mortally wounded is able to ask, and be granted, the forgiveness of his friend's mother. The film is heavy in atmosphere and full of powerful compositions. It received four Academy Awards.

Henry Fonda, John Carradine, and John Qualen in John Ford's THE GRAPES OF WRATH

The Prisoner of Shark Island (1936), scripted by Nunnally Johnson, was the true story of the doctor who tended Lincoln's assassin and was wrongly imprisoned as an accomplice; after distinguishing himself in a yellow-fever epidemic, he is able to convince the authorities of his innocence. *Mary of Scotland* (1936), adapted by Nichols from Maxwell Anderson's play, told with dignity of Mary, Queen of Scots, and her eventual martyrdom. Katharine Hepburn's performance is to be noted. Ford and Nichols returned to the Irish "Troubles" with *The Plough and the Stars* (1936), based on O'Casey's play (*cf* Hitchcock's *Juno and the Paycock*), set in Easter week, 1916. A group of minor films followed: *Wee Willie Winkie* (1937), a military story set in British India; *The Hurricane* (1937), a South Seas story in which brutal authorities repeatedly imprisoned a native who repeatedly escaped—a great natural catastrophe concluded the cycle; *Four Men and a Prayer* (1938), and *Submarine Patrol* (1938).

A period of concentrated excellence was inaugurated by Ford's long-delayed return to the Western in 1939 and then to earlier American frontier history. He continued this fine succession of films with *The Grapes of Wrath* (1940), scripted by Nunnally Johnson, an adaptation of Steinbeck's novel of the Depression and the travels of a dispossessed "Okie" family. Ford resisted the final pessimism of Steinbeck, so that his film is an affirmative view of the precariousness and continuity of life. Ma Joad, struggling to hold the family together, and Tom, striding off idealistically into the night, are central to the whole of Ford's work. The many excellent performances include those of Jane Darwell (who received an Academy Award for the film, as did Ford) as Ma and Henry Fonda as Tom. It was photographed by Gregg Toland, like *The Long Voyage Home* (1940), an adaptation by Nichols of short plays by Eugene O'Neill. Ford seemed ill at ease in this sombre and constricted tale of merchant seamen and their dreams of escape from the sea. The result was cold, though by no means a failure. *jms*

John Ford returned to the theme of American poverty and the disintegration of a family in *Tobacco Road* (1941), set in Georgia. His last feature before America entered the Second World War was *How Green Was My Valley* (1941), a nostalgic and moving view of a Welsh childhood in a mining valley: the family gradually breaks up, there is poverty and a pit disaster, and behind it all, the background of the accumulating impact of industrialism on a small community. The film received five Academy Awards. Ford joined the Navy and made a number of wartime documentaries, including *The Battle of Midway* (1942), which he also daringly photographed, *December 7th* (1943) and *We Sail at Midnight* (1943). His first postwar feature was *They Were Expendable* (1945), a warm, elegiac and graceful film, superbly photographed by Joseph H. August, which drew on fact to tell of a group of sailors who proved the worth of the P.T. Boat in defiant actions and rescue operations during the American defeat in the Philippines in the early stages of the war. Apart from *Pinky* (1949) which Ford prepared and began, but which was completed by Elia Kazan, the final product of the Ford-Nichols collaboration was *The Fugitive* (1947), one of the director's favourites and adapted from Grahame Greene's novel, *The Power and the Glory*. It was set in an imaginary police state and concerned the pursuit of a priest; it recalled *The Informer* and contained the theme, dear to Ford, of sacrifice for the community. It was an ambitious work, composed and photographed with extraordinary, perhaps excessive care. This was Ford's last non-Western of the Forties; since 1945, half of his output has consisted of Westerns. *jms*

HOWARD HAWKS

Howard Hawks (*b* 1896) came to the cinema via a varied career that included flying during the First World War and racing car driving —both experiences are to be found in his films. Between 1922 and 1924 he was an independent producer; he then worked as a scriptwriter until he became a contract director for William Fox in 1925. But from 1929 onwards Hawks elected to work without a binding contract over his head. He has been his own producer in most instances, and has worked on virtually all the scripts of his films, often without being credited. His career is divided between comedy and drama. In the Twenties and Thirties Hawks's dramas were at times overtly tragic, dominated by ideas of fatality and necessity. (In his later work, tragedy is usually only implicit; the stress there is on self-control and individual responsibility.) Unlike Ford, he shows little interest in national tradition.

Hawks's first film was *The Road to Glory* (1926), a drama concerning a young girl's reactions to going blind after an automobile accident. The film had a cyclical construction, ending as it had begun. *Fig Leaves* (1926) was a comedy, drawing a parallel between Adam and Eve in the Garden of Eden and a modern story, of Adam and Eve Smith. The art direction was by the distinguished designer William Cameron Menzies.

The extraordinary speed of many of Hawks's later films was foreshadowed in *The Cradle Snatchers* (1927), a farcical comedy. *Paid to Love* (1927) was a tragi-comic love story, set in a mythical country and focusing on a Parisian night club performer and the Prince who falls in love with her. The impact of Murnau's work on Hollywood was indicated by the large amount of trick camerawork in this film. Subsequently, however, Hawks adopted a less complex technical approach. *A Girl in Every Port,* made in the next year, anticipated the director's later work more clearly than any of his silent films. It dealt with the tension between male friendship and an intrusive female; in this case the aggressive companionship of the two sailors triumphed. Louise

Paul Muni (with gun) threatens Vince Barnett in SCARFACE

Brooks played the girl and the film marked the high point of her American career (though she never excelled in her own country as she did in Germany under the direction of Pabst). *Fazil,* also completed in 1928, took place in Paris, Venice, and Morocco, relating the love of a sheik for an emancipated French girl. It was released with synchronised sound effects. *The Air Circus,* shot immediately afterwards, was made by Hawks as a silent picture; dialogue scenes, which he did not direct, were added later. This film concentrated on the instruction of a pilot in a flying school, in almost documentary fashion.

Trent's Last Case (1929), a detective story which was made as a silent film only because of copyright difficulties, signalled the end of Hawks's silent phase and the end, also, of his first and only period under contract. His apprenticeship was now effectively over, and once he had fully adjusted to the sound cinema, his work began to assume the character that it has since retained—its primary attribute being the illustration of human personality in harness and the development of the Hawksian ethic of professionalism and self-respect.

His first sound movie was *The Dawn Patrol* (1930), a sombre Air Force story set in the First World War, in which the inexorable death-rate ends friendships and defeats those who try to reduce it. The flying sequences were outstanding. *The Criminal Code* (1931) was a prison drama, notably acted by Walter Huston and Boris Karloff. This film, violent and humorous, entirely sympathised with the convicts and with the futility of their lives. Hawks, like LeRoy in *I Am a Fugitive from a Chain Gang,* went to considerable lengths to achieve authenticity.

The Crowd Roars (1932) was a motor racing drama, rapid and concise, of professionals in the face of constant danger, a theme Hawks was to return to in *Red Line 7000* in the Sixties. *Scarface,* released the same year, was the best of the cycle of gangster films that came from Hollywood during the Thirties. It created the harsh and rapacious Tony Camonte (inspired by Al Capone), and brought out both his addiction to violence and his incestuous love for his sister. The careers of George Raft and Paul Muni (who played Camonte) were decisively affected by their success in this fast and brilliant film. Significantly, *Scarface* was the first of the five Hawks film scripted by Ben Hecht, one of Hollywood's most controversial and talented scenarists.

The friendship of two men, and a woman who moves between them, was the subject of *Tiger Shark* (1932), in which Hawks used the Pacific as an effective setting. *Today We Live* (1933) was of special interest in that it inaugurated the collaboration of Hawks with novelist William Faulkner. The story on which the film was based was by Faulkner, who also wrote the dialogue. It concerns the relationship of two Englishmen, an English girl and the American who wants to buy their ancestral home, and the crucial result of their participation in the First World War. Ben Hecht shared a credit for the script of *Twentieth Century* (1934), one of Hawks's speedy comedies with over-lapping dialogue, which described the marriage of a director and his actress, and their crumbling relationship in the face of failure and success. John Barrymore and Carole Lombard played the leads here.

Hawks's first film to touch on air mail flying was *Ceiling Zero* (1936); he was to take up the subject again, with happier results, several years later. *The Road to Glory* (1936) was reminiscent of *The Dawn Patrol* in its cyclical and tragic view of the Great War, this time dealing with the trenches. The main players were Fredric March and Warner Baxter, the photography was by Gregg Toland, and the script by Faulkner; a remarkable combination of talents.

Though completed by William Wyler, most of *Come and Get It* (1936) was handled by Hawks. In any event, Wyler's work seemed faithful to Hawks's conception. It was adapted from a novel by Edna Ferber and scripted by Jules Furthman. It followed the life of a logging contractor as he became wealthy. The roles of two women, mother and daughter, were of extreme importance in illustrating the hero's somewhat delayed arrival at self-knowledge. The first part of the film, dealing warmly with his early love, was a fine comic achievement.

Bringing Up Baby (1938) was a classic comedy in which the dry world of a scientist, played by Cary Grant, collapses, as chaos irrupts in the form of Katharine Hepburn. Order and dignity, as so often in Hawks's comedies, are the prime casualties, and in *Bringing Up Baby* they are never given a chance. The pace is extraordinarily fast; the direction as deft as any in the Thirties. In *Only Angels Have Wings* (1939), with a script by Furthman, from Hawks's original story, there was a return to the subject of early air mail flying. The setting: a fog-bound airfield, almost entirely cut off from the outside world; a girl learns to understand the fliers' calm acceptance of death, the ethic by which they live, and the warmth of their comradeship; she earns their respect and the love of one of them. *jms*

The director **Rouben Mamoulian** (*b* 1898) occupies a unique place in the history of the cinema, his career beginning in 1929 and coinciding with the coming of sound. Of Russian origin, born in Tiflis, Georgia, Mamoulian trained at the Vakhtangov Studio of the Moscow Art Theatre where he was a follower of Stanislavsky's teachings. After leaving Russia, he worked as a stage producer first in London, and later in New York on Broadway, producing a wide variety of plays, operas and operettas between 1923 and 1928, when he was put under contract by Paramount. At first the coming of sound led to an over-emphasis in the use of naturalistic noise and a marked inflexibility of camerawork in general. Mamoulian was one of the few directors to use sound expressively from the outset. His experience in the field of musical entertainment combined with his earlier commitment to naturalism contributed to the almost experimental style of his first film *Applause* (1929). This story of an ageing burlesque queen, poignantly played by Helen Morgan, succeeded in capturing the atmosphere of back-stage life with a remarkable use of the mobile camera. Mamoulian next turned to the gangster *genre,* making *City Streets* (1931), with Gary Cooper playing the part of a fairground artist who turns to a life of highjacking. The film was remarkable in that it presented a highly stylised view of the gangster milieu and contained almost no violence whatsoever. *Dr. Jekyll and Mr. Hyde* also made in 1931 proved to be a significant contribution to the horror film, a *genre* more in keeping with Mamoulian's preoccupations. This adaptation of Robert Louis Stevenson's novel was distinctly Freudian in tone, and Mamoulian once more confirmed his growing reputation as an innovator by experimenting with the use of synthetic sound and the use of filters in the transformation scene. *Love Me Tonight* (1932) was his first real musical; based on a stage play by Leopold Marchand and Paul Armont with musical numbers by Rodgers and Hart. In it,

Rouben Mamoulian

John Gilbert and Greta Garbo in the famous inn scene in QUEEN CHRISTINA

Mamoulian established himself as one of the major musical directors. His next film *Song of Songs* (1933) starred Marlene Dietrich in the uncharacteristic role of a peasant girl who goes to Berlin and becomes the inspiration of a sculptor. At this point in his career, Mamoulian left Paramount and was signed by M-G-M to direct Greta Garbo, at her own request. Like *Song of Songs, Queen Christina* (1933) was a romantic melodrama, this time set in Sweden, in which Garbo played the young Queen of Sweden with an uncharacteristic authoritarianism and lack of femininity which were to characterise many of the women Mamoulian was later to depict. In *We Live Again* (1934) Mamoulian chose another historical subject and used the Ukranian actress Anna Sten for the main part. Having now established himself as one of the principal directors in Hollywood, Mamoulian was entrusted with making the first colour film using the new three-colour Technicolor process for Pioneer Pictures, with *Becky Sharp* (1935), a film version of Thackeray's *Vanity Fair*. Mamoulian made full use of this opportunity to use colour dramatically for the first time. *The Gay Desperado* (1936), a comic operetta set in Mexico, and *High,*

Wide and Handsome (1937) a musical Western about the Pennsylvania oil-fields, were both marred by a cloying sentimentality that was not redeemed by Mamoulian's customary inventiveness. After an unsuccessful attempt to get Columbia interested in making a film of *Porgy and Bess,* Mamoulian made *Golden Boy* (1939), an adaptation of the Clifford Odets play about a young violinist, played by William Holden, who becomes drawn into the world of boxing, with tragic consequences. *cj*

Although **Busby Berkeley** (*b* 1895) was active in the cinema for over thirty years, his real impact on the cinema was exerted between 1930 and 1940, when his development of a highly abstract musical spectacular form was in some senses as experimental as the work of the *avant-garde* film-makers in Europe. As a child, Berkeley worked on Broadway as an actor, and later turned to direction. In 1930 he was imported from Broadway to Hollywood by Warner Brothers, and his first film as dance director was the Eddie Cantor musical *Whoopee* (1930). Attracted by the greater freedom the film medium offered when compared to the stage, Berkeley began to experiment with mass choreography, aerial photography, camera movement and the use of

Busby Berkeley

Joan Blondell leads one of Busby Berkeley's remarkable formations in Lloyd Bacon's GOLD DIGGERS OF 1937

close-up, which quickly led to the formation of a highly distinctive style in such films as *Palmy Days* (1931), *Kiki* (1931), *The Kid from Spain* (1932) and *Roman Scandals* (1933). His first directorial assignment came in 1933 with *She Had to Say Yes,* and *Forty-second Street,* made in the same year and directed by Lloyd Bacon, was such a success that a whole series of such films followed: *Gold Diggers of 1933,* the first of a celebrated series, *Footlight Parade* (1933) featuring an extraordinary aquaballet, *Dames* (1934), *Fashions of 1934* and *Wonder Bar* (1934), among others, all of which Berkeley worked on as dance director. In 1935, he directed his second film, *Gold Diggers of 1935,* and from then on most of his energies were engaged in direction, although he continued to work simply as a choreographer on a number of films. He made two more films in 1935, *Bright Lights* and *I Live for Love;* then followed *Stagestruck* (1936), *The Go-Getter* (1937), and *Hollywood Hotel* (1937). With *Men Are Such Fools* (1938), Berkeley tried his hand at straight comedy, followed in the same year by *Garden of the Moon* and *Comet over Broadway. cj.*

HOLLYWOOD COMEDY   The arrival of sound had drastic effects in the field of comedy. The inevitable emphasis on dialogue placed a premium on the services of new comics and writers with Broadway and radio experience in handling the spoken word. The silent comedians were largely displaced by producers unwilling to give them a chance. However, Stan Laurel and Oliver Hardy, who had developed relatively late, bridged the eras without a flurry. They developed dialogue routines that added a new dimension to their established characters and staple situations and both *Men of War* (1929) and *The Perfect Day* (also 1929) show them at peak form. The delightfully protracted tit-for-tat descents into chaos remain part of their work, and Stan adapts to dialogue with the obtuseness of a two year-old, taking phrases at their surface meaning like Harpo Marx only with a puzzled earnestness, while Ollie uses words as an additional expression of his would-be dignified approach to the ladies and life in general. Laurel and Hardy were rather less successful with features, although these were imbedded with sequences as memorable as those in their shorts (*Sons of the Desert/Fraternally Yours,* 1933, and their inevitable excursion to the wide open spaces, *Way Out West,* 1937, are the most fondly regarded of their full-length works).

The Marx Brothers were initially recruited to film two of their Broadway hits at Paramount's East Coast studio. In *The Cocoanuts* (1929), they were somewhat hemmed in by a now hilariously-dated line in supplementary romantic interest, but in their own scenes established the brand of abrasive, vulgar humour for which they are noted. **Groucho** (*b* 1895) contributed his agile wit, deftly coping with any challenge to his absolute authority on any subject under the sun; **Chico**

*The Marx
Brothers cheerfully
menace Esther
Muir in A DAY
AT THE RACES*

(1891–1961) survived ably on a denseness that outfoxed all attempts to deal logically with him (as well as exploiting the confusion potential of a fake Italian accent); **Harpo** (1893–1964) carried on the silent tradition of mute clowning with a zest that defied taming; and **Zeppo** (*b* 1901) stood awkwardly on the side lines, being a creature of a different century, dropping out after the first five films, and leaving the amply-proportioned Margaret Dumont, the butt of many a physical and verbal onslaught, as the fourth figure indelibly associated with the team. This was the pattern that went through their later work; only the targets changed. In *Animal Crackers* (1930), the second stage hit filmed, they were loose in high society; in their first screen original, *Monkey Business* (1931) which introduced humorist S. J. Perelman's malicious and juvenile flavour to their work, they were stowaways on a transatlantic liner involved with gangsters; in *Horse Feathers* (1932) they ran amok on the campus and sent up the Depression; while *Duck Soup* (1933), where they had the guidance of a great comedy director, Leo McCarey, gained more polish and pace than its predecessors, being a deft political satire. Later in the Thirties, they moved to another studio and reached new heights of popularity at some sacrifice to their previous image by allowing in more plot, subsidiary romance, and letting their command of the situation lapse to induce moments of sympathetic identification when they had their backs to the wall. In *A Night at the Opera* (1935), the loss scarcely showed, for the screenplay (by George S. Kaufman and Morrie Ryskind) was so well tailored for their

*The Marx
Brothers*

abilities—its climax, when the suitably aggrieved Marxes reduce an opera performance to havoc, is one of the great scenes of comedy. *A Day at the Races* (1937) was somewhat overpadded with plot and musical interludes, but a new team of writers otherwise ably provided material for the team. Their subsequent work was disappointing—the studio projects were turned out on the cheap and became quite conventional despite a slight rallying with *The Big Store* (1941); while their independent work showed an insufficient awareness of the qualities that had so distinguished them as screen comedians.

W. C. Fields   **W. C. Fields** (1879-1946) was an established comedian of the silent period who reached peak form in the Thirties, even gaining the freedom to write his own pictures (under improbable aliases, from the sketchiest of outlines). Fields mined his coarseness of manner, his awkwardness, his everlasting conflicts with fate and authority to great effect, for beneath it all he had a skill of timing learned on the vaudeville circuits and as a superb conjuror (this latter ability displayed on the screen in his masterful bits of business with objects of every description, particularly golf clubs, straw hats, and billiard cues). Forever harassed (especially by nagging, socially-conscious wives and irritating small children), forever battling on (letting off steam with mumbled imprecations, disguised for censorship reasons as "Godfrey Daniel!" and the like), Fields appealed to audiences as the downtrodden part of themselves (in contrast to the Marx Brothers who displayed a spirit of liberation that audiences could only envy). After such memorable pictures as *Tillie and Gus* (1933, partnering Alison Skipworth as a pair of crooked gamblers), *The Old-Fashioned Way* (1934, recalling the small-time vaudeville era), *It's a Gift* (1934, one of several comical misalliances with child star Baby LeRoy), and *The Man on the Flying Trapeze* (1935, with no sign of a flying trapeze), Fields made such defiantly scrappy, utterly idiosyncratic pictures as *The Bank Dick/The Bank Detective* (1940) and *Never Give a Sucker an Even Break/What a Man* (1941) as enduring memorials to his irreplaceable talent.

Mae West   **Mae West** (*b* 1893) was another vital figure in Thirties comedy: plump in appearance, Rabelaisian in manner, she made fun of sex and slipped as many innuendos as she could across the screen while generally turning out to be a good girl at heart, looking for a simple, honest mate. She was credited with singlehandedly rescuing her studio from economic failure and bringing the Hays Office into existence to tone her down and otherwise handicap the cause of free expression. She wrote many of her own scripts and after such hits as *She Done Him Wrong* (1933, with its suggestively titled song, "A Guy What Takes His Time") and *I'm No Angel* (also 1933), she ultimately went on to team up with W. C. Fields in *My Little Chickadee* (1940), which they jointly scripted and which gave her something of the upper hand.

Mae West and W. C. Fields in MY LITTLE CHICKADEE

Many other comedians thrived in the Thirties in a series of vehicles built around their personalities. **Eddie Cantor** (1893–1964), mooneyed, far from innocent, propped up the comedy side of Goldwyn musicals like *Roman Scandals* (1933); **Joe E. Brown** (*b* 1892), though best remembered these days for his role in *Some Like It Hot,* starred in such well-received comedies as *Local Boy Makes Good* (1931) as a shy botanist and *You Said a Mouthful* (1932) as the inventor of an unsinkable bathing costume; Wheeler and Woolsey dispensed an inferior brand of Marx Brothers' illogic in such films as *Kentucky Kernels* (1934) and *Nitwits* (1935); and Leon Errol was one of the many stars of comedy shorts made during the period as well as an occasional supporting actor in features.

Many of the most successful comedies of the Thirties were based on hit plays, or screen originals, cast not essentially with comedians nor directed by exclusively comedy figures, although the success of players like Cary Grant and Irene Dunne, or directors like Frank Capra and Leo McCarey, leads us to associate them first and foremost with the humorous film.

Gems of the early Thirties included *Three Cornered Moon* (1933,

Elliott Nugent) which depicted the straits of the lovable Rimplegar family when it falls on hard times during the Depression and feather-brained Mary Boland's first reaction to disaster is to think of hiring a taxi and go off to have her hair fixed; *Once in a Lifetime* (1932, Russell Mack) satirising the state of panic in a Hollywood adjusting to sound with Jack Oakie as the inveterate nut-chewer and dumbhead who ascends to the post of production chief at a studio; and *The Thin Man* (1934, W. S. Van Dyke), first and best of a series that described the zany adventures of a husband-and-wife team (played by William Powell and Myrna Loy) in investigating cases of crime. This last film is one of those that came to be designated "screwball comedy" for its carefree delight in the eccentric behaviour of its characters. The same kind of spirit animated Gregory La Cava's *My Man Godfrey* (1936) in which that captivating actress Carole Lombard was a member of a high society family who adopted a "forgotten man" of the Depression and introduced him to a crazy household in which the mother (Alice Brady) allowed her *protégé* (Mischa Auer) to do an unforgettable monkey imitation. Other films whose titles alone promised a similarly wacky approach included *Theodora Goes Wild* (1936), *The Mad Miss Manton* (1938), *Nothing Sacred* (1938) and the last in particular delivered with slugging matches between stars Fredric March and Carole Lombard.

In Frank Capra's comedies, eccentricities were also upheld as a sign of welcome individuality—particularly in the case of the entire family of *You Can't Take It with You* (1938) who have retired from the Thirties rat race and given up such oppressive measures as paying income tax. In other films, there was a serious side of showing how ordinary decent human beings could win the day against the killjoys and the corrupt, though as in the case of *Mr. Deeds Goes to Town* (1936), where an overnight millionaire (Gary Cooper) is put on trial for philanthropically wanting to give his fortune away, the odds were stacked so heavily against him as to give little comfort to a more thoughtful spectator. The honest senator of *Mr. Smith Goes to Washington* (1939) got into such serious straits pitting himself against the corrupt party machine that the film hardly qualified as a comedy despite much humorous warmth of observation between players James Stewart and Jean Arthur. In the earlier *It Happened One Night* (1934), however, the mood was entirely light as reporter Clark Gable introduced runaway heiress Claudette Colbert to piggy back riding and other simple pleasures, and even earlier in *Platinum Blonde* (1931) the director showed with great charm how to conduct the pursuit of happiness and be true to oneself in depicting a reporter's flirtations with high society before he settles down to a happy life with an ordinary but devoted girl reporter.

Cary Grant was subjected to much the same strain in trying to marry into a stuffy rich family in the utterly enchanting and deeply moving *Holiday* (1938), ultimately rescuing his *fiancée*'s sister from her stifling surroundings (a beautiful performance by Katharine Hepburn). George Cukor directed it from a script by Donald Ogden Stewart and Sidney Buchman based on the Philip Barry play.

Cary Grant's comedies

Cary Grant was also the star of two memorable comedies with a similar plot situation of a husband trying to reclaim his ex-wife before she marries into the quiet life offered by a dumb beau (portrayed both times by Ralph Bellamy). Leo McCarey's *The Awful Truth* (1937) also starred Irene Dunne and had a sensitivity of touch and warmth of mood more open than that of Cukor in *Holiday*, as well as more elaborate slapstick sequences. Earlier McCarey had directed *Ruggles of Red Gap* (1935), a classic of comedy in which an English butler (Charles Laughton) learnt that a man need not remain subservient in the American democracy.

The second Grant comedy was *His Girl Friday* (1938), an ingenious re-working of the drama *The Front Page* (1931) with Grant skilfully and ruthlessly campaigning to reclaim the affections of Rosalind Russell against a hectic background of journalism and political corruption. But its director, Howard Hawks, made the humour of his *Bringing Up Baby* that same year more painfully basic in stripping the dignity of his Cary Grant character, a sheltered academic, to shreds in the paws of a zany, confusion-spreading Katharine Hepburn and her baby leopard.

The Thirties was a rich decade for comedy and in no sense a period of mourning for the redoubtable achievements of the Twenties. Its best films were never mechanical but usually warmly understanding of the individual and sympathetic to his quirks, affirmative about the opportunities for happiness in an often depressing world; and even the poorer comedies gained much from the rich number of supporting players like Edward Everett Horton, Charlie Ruggles, Charles Butterworth, Franklin Pangborn, Margaret Hamilton (to mention a few) who popped up to lend their own deft line of humorous observation to the proceedings. *aje.*

Hollywood in the Thirties did not begin the gangster film— its antecedents go back to Feuillade and Griffith—but it did establish the rules of the *genre* which persist today. Warner Brothers, devoted to gritty urban realism, set the fashion for films on the low life of American cities, and although some of the period's finest gangster dramas—Josef von Sternberg's *Underworld* (1927) and *Thunderbolt* (1929)—pre-dated it, Warner's *Little Caesar* (1931, *dir* Mervyn LeRoy) marks the beginning of real public awareness of organised crime and its myths.

THE GANGSTER FILM

The period was propitious. Chicago's half-admired gang boss Al Capone had been jailed in 1931, and by 1933 the federal authorities, given sharper teeth after the Lindbergh case, were close to destroying the rural bank robbers. In December 1933, prohibition was repealed, wiping out the gangs' richest source of revenue, and 1934 saw the death of "Ma" Barker, "Pretty Boy" Floyd, John Dillinger and the Barrow gang. A public that had adulated the more colourful bank robbers queued to re-live their exploits in films often written by ex-newsmen who had covered the original.

Prohibition was a prime film subject. George Hill's *The Secret Six* (1931), Victor Fleming's *The Wet Parade* (1932), John Adolfi's *Midnight Taxi* (1928) and dozens of others showed the mechanics of the trade, though Raoul Walsh's *The Roaring Twenties* (1939), with Humphrey Bogart and James Cagney as bootleggers graduating to more ambitious crime as times changed, related prohibition to the gangs' rise and fall. Liquor king Capone also provided the model for *Little Caesar, The Secret Six* and the period's finest film of gangland, Howard Hawks's *Scarface* (1932), Paul Muni portraying the Chicago boss with vulpine relish in a script by ex-newsman Ben Hecht.

Hollywood discovered crime everywhere. Big business was represented as a seat of greed and extortion in *Quick Millions* (1931, *dir* Rowland Brown), *Smart Money* (1931, *dir* Alfred E. Green) and, with more humour, in Mervyn LeRoy's *High Pressure* (1932). Crime penetrated politics (*Bullets or Ballots,* 1936, *dir* William Keighley), high society (*Three on a Match,* 1932, *dir* Mervyn LeRoy), the cab industry (*Taxi,* 1932, *dir* Roy del Ruth), boxing (*Kid Galahad,* 1937, *dir* Michael Curtiz), trucking (*Racket Busters,* 1938, *dir* Lloyd Bacon) and most human activities.

Often glee in violence was balanced by an honest description of how a corrupt society manufactures its criminals. William Wellman's *The Public Enemy* (1931) and *Wild Boys of the Road* (1933), Curtiz's *Angels with Dirty Faces* (1938), Lewis Seiler's *Dust Be My Destiny* (1939) and William Wyler's *Dead End* (1937) underlined social responsibility for crime. George Hill's *The Big House* (1931), LeRoy's *I Am a Fugitive from a Chain Gang* (1932), Lloyd Bacon's *Invisible Stripes* (1939) and Howard Hawks's *The Criminal Code* (1931) showed prison as a force for corruption, not reform.

Although crime drama glamorising the gangs remained a staple part of the field, the growing power of the FBI led to films praising the efforts of the police. Alexander Hall's *I Am the Law* (1938) and William Keighley's *G-Men* (1935), the latter with Cagney cast against type as an incorruptible force for good, represented the best of them, while M-G-M's *Crime Does Not Pay* series of shorts touted police omniscience and fortitude.

Later in the Thirties, comedies parodied the outdated gang mentality, an anachronism in a world adjusting to nationally syndicated larceny and respectable criminal personalities. Akim Tamiroff was an almost comic gang boss in *King of Gamblers* (1937) and *Dangerous To Know* (1938), both directed by Robert Florey; Edward G. Robinson played a double role in John Ford's *The Whole Town's Talking* (1935) as a mild clerk masquerading as gang boss; and in *The Amazing Doctor Clitterhouse* (1938, *dir* Anatole Litvak) was a society physician who took over a mob as a research project. *Brother Orchid* (1940, *dir* Lloyd Bacon) showed Robinson's hiding out in a monastery during a gang war, then turning to religion full time. "Flip" private detectives— Warren William as Perry Mason, William Powell as Philo Vance and Nick Charles, "The Thin Man"—further mocked lumbering gang thugs in Warner and Metro thrillers.

The period supported a group of actors who became permanent inhabitants of the film underworld. George Bancroft of *Underworld* and *Thunderbolt* was a burly menace in *Ladies Love Brutes* (1930), *Angels with Dirty Faces* and others. George Raft flipped a coin in *Scarface,* remained for years in a series of double-breasted menace roles, then entered the real world as professional gambler and underworld *habitué.* Humphrey Bogart, smouldering and pitiless, James Cagney, "feisty" and vicious, Edward G. Robinson, tough and intelligent, not to forget the gangsters below them: ratty Allen Jenkins, brutal Joe Sawyer, amiable Frank McHugh, furtive George E. Stone, sturdy Lyle Talbot, sturdier Barton MacLane, dapper Marc Lawrence, saintly "Father" Pat O'Brien and the gangs' scruffy auxiliary, Frankie Darro and the Billy Halop/Leo Gorcey "Dead End Kids." Their faces, once quintessentially depraved and menacing, seem almost friendly beside the mindless violence of the modern world. *jb*

Horror and the supernatural entered the film almost as soon as the film entered the cinema. Circa 1893 Edison produced a picture of the execution of Mary, Queen of Scots, under one minute in length, showing the actual decapitation, with the blood-dripping head falling in the dust. Frankenstein's monster appeared in an Edison one-reeler of 1910, played by Charles Ogle, and *Dr. Jekyll and Mr. Hyde* in 1908. The first real horror school, however, flourished in the febrile atmosphere of postwar Germany, the most famous example being *The Cabinet of Dr. Caligari* (*Das Kabinett des Dr. Caligari,* 1920). It was notable for its distorted expressionist settings and its claustrophobic atmosphere of madness and terror. Though a dead end, however brilliant, in the development of the film, it contained most of the ingredients of later horror film formulae—mad scientist, zombie, walking dead, defenceless white-draped girl.

Other important films of the period were the two versions of *The Golem* (1914, directed by Paul Wegener and Henrik Galeen; 1920

THE HORROR FILM

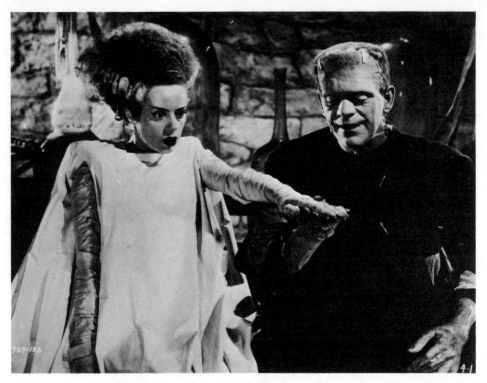

Elsa Lanchester and Boris Karloff in THE BRIDE OF FRANKENSTEIN

by Wegener and Carl Boese); two versions of *The Student of Prague* (1913 by Stellan Rye and in 1926 by Henrik Galeen); the early Dracula film *Nosferatu* (1922), directed by F. W. Murnau; *Warning Shadows* (1924) by Arthur Robison; *Waxworks* (1924), an episodic film with one section based on Jack the Ripper, by Paul Leni. All these German productions were memorable for their louring atmosphere, their heavy-shadowed photography, their sense of isolation and madness and doom.

From Sweden came *Häxan* (*Witchcraft through the Ages,* 1922), a compendium of witches' lore directed by Benjamin Christensen who himself played a boisterous Devil. The film, hilarious and horrifying by turns, was recently reissued with musical accompaniment and a commentary by William Burroughs. In France, Abel Gance made a crazy scientist film, *The Madness of Dr. Tube* (*La Folie du Docteur Tube*), involving much use of distorted lenses, and in 1928 the first noteworthy adaptation of Edgar Allan Poe, *The Fall of the House of Usher* (*La Chute de la Maison Usher*), was directed by Jean Epstein. Notable examples from America were John Barrymore's famous portrayal of *Dr.*

Jekyll and Mr. Hyde (1920) directed by John S. Robertson, and *The Phantom of the Opera* (1925), by **Rupert Julian** (1886–1943), in which Lon Chaney's make-up was a horrific *tour-de-force*. **Tod Browning** (1882–1944), later famous for the Bela Lugosi *Dracula,* made an early vampire film with Lon Chaney entitled *London after Midnight* (1927). Chaney was to have played Dracula under Browning's direction, but died before production was started. In 1927 Paul Leni arrived from Germany and directed *The Cat and the Canary,* the best of three versions, despite some absurdities and feeble comic relief, and showing much of the director's German influence. He followed this with a series of interesting macabre films, all from the Universal Studios. This was really the start of the noted Universal horror cycle of the Thirties, which reached its fullest extent after the arrival of sound.

Before dealing with this, however, mention must be made of one of the earliest and most famous horror classics: in Denmark Carl Dreyer directed *Vampyr* (see Chapter Six).

From Universal, Browning's *Dracula* (1930) was a mixture of poetry (particularly in the first reel) and absurdity, with Bela Lugosi as a somewhat stolid vampire. Several more Dracula films followed, only one of which, *Dracula's Daughter* (1936) had any connection with the original creator, Bram Stoker. **James Whale** (1896–1957) came to Hollywood from Britain to make a film of *Journey's End,* and followed this in 1931 with *Frankenstein,* thereafter proving himself one of the great horror directors, despite the smallness of his output. *Frankenstein* was remarkable for its dignity of treatment, and for the sympathy it generated for the monster. Boris Karloff's portrayal fixed him for life in the world of the macabre, and remains the only one of seeming authenticity. In 1935, Whale followed and bettered this with *The Bride of Frankenstein,* arguably the best "monster" film yet made. Karloff further developed his moving characterisation, and there was an electrifying five-minute performance by Elsa Lanchester as the Bride. Karloff's last appearance as the monster was in *Son of Frankenstein* (1939), directed by **Rowland V. Lee** (*b* 1891). Thereafter both the original Dracula and the man-made monster declined into travesty. Other notable Universal pictures were James Whale's *The Old Dark House* (1932) and Tod Browning's extraordinary *Freaks* (1932), in which he used real circus "freaks" and turned the formula inside out by making the apparently monstrous beings sympathetic and admirable, while the apparently normal and beautiful only horrified.

Outside the Universal stable the most noteworthy American offerings of the period included *Dr. Jekyll and Mr. Hyde* (1932) directed by Rouben Mamoulian—by far the best version, with a superbly contrived "change" and a bravura performance from Fredric March; *The Mystery of the Wax Museum* (1932) by Michael Curtiz, an unfortunately "lost" picture, immensely superior to the 1953 3-D re-make, *House of*

Wax; and *The Most Dangerous Game* (1932) directed by **Ernest B. Schoedsack** (*b* 1893) and **Irving Pichel** (1891–1954) with Leslie Banks as the Count who, bored with hunting animals, turns to men for his victims. Schoedsack, together with Merian Cooper (*b* 1893), also created *King Kong* (1933), greatest of all prehistoric beast films. Kong himself was a magnificent and strangely lovable creation, animated by Willis O'Brien, famous special effects maker. *Son of Kong,* rushed out the same year to cash in on the first film's success, did not live up to the reputation of the original.

Karloff appeared in *The Mummy* (1932) directed by a famous photographer of German silents, **Karl Freund** (1890–1969) and Lugosi in *White Zombie* (1932) under Victor Halperin, both minor but interesting productions. They appeared together in 1934 in *The Black Cat* directed by **Edgar G. Ulmer** (*b* 1904), one-time assistant to F. W. Murnau, but the result was surprisingly tame. Tod Browning's later films, *The Mark of the Vampire* (1935), *The Devil Doll* (1936) and *Miracles for Sale* (1939), showed a decline, and he retired thereafter until his death in 1962. *ib*

Cecil Hepworth's studios at Walton-on-Thames

2. Britain

THE FIRST PUBLIC FILM PERFORMANCE in Great Britain, presented by Lucian Trewey on behalf of the Lumière Brothers, at the Regent Street Polytechnic on February 20, 1896, was in many ways the culmination of the work of two Englishmen: **William Friese-Greene** (1855–1921) and **Birt Acres** (1854–1918). The latter had filmed both the 1895 Derby and Boat Race, and produced numerous short subjects, both in Great Britain and Germany, up to 1900. However, Acres never fully realised the entertainment potential of the new invention, and it was left to his colleague, **R. W. Paul** (1869–1943), by trade a scientific instrument maker, to produce more ambitious films and also to accept much of the credit that rightly belonged to Acres. In 1899, Paul opened the first film studios in Great Britain at Muswell Hill, North London, and there, influenced by the work of Méliès, embarked on the production of a series of trick films. He retired from the industry in 1910.

The most concentrated area of filming at this early period was in Brighton; working here were G. A. Smith, James A. Williamson, Esme Collings and Alfred Darling. **George Albert Smith** (1864–1959) in 1896 devised his own camera, and by 1897 was producing his own films on the beach at Brighton or in his own back garden. These films included some of the earliest known trick films using double exposure, in particular *The Corsican Brothers* (1897), *The Fairy Godmother* (1898) and *Faust and Mephistopheles* (1898). Working in close association with G. A. Smith at this time was Alfred Darling, whose work as an engineer and camera designer benefited most of the early pioneers. In 1900, Smith joined the Warwick Trading Company, founded in 1898 by American Charles Urban. It was with Urban as his partner that Smith in 1906 patented the Kinemacolor 2-colour system, which remained in popular use up to the First World War.

James A. Williamson (1855–1933) was a chemist who ran a photographic business as a sideline. In 1896, he had bought a projector, and the following year started to produce his own films. With *The Big Swallow* (1901), Williamson introduced the tracking shot, and in the same year in *Fire!* were to be seen the rudiments of editing as Williamson used five consecutive scenes of varying lengths to tell the story of the rescue of a victim overcome by smoke from a blazing house. Little is known of Esme Collings, except that in 1896 he produced over thirty short-length films, none of which, unfortunately, are available for evaluation today.

Two other pioneers, whose works are of particular interest are **Arthur**

Pioneers

Melbourne-Cooper (1851–1961) and **William Haggar** (1851–1924). Melbourne-Cooper's Alpha Production Company at St. Albans produced films which were sold outright to other producers and distributors. In 1900, he filmed *Grandma's Reading Glass,* which is perhaps one of the first films ever to use the close-up; and in his 1907 *Dreams of Toyland* there is an outstanding example of early animation. Welsh fairground showman William Haggar made relatively few films compared to the other film-makers of the period. His *Life of Charles Peace,* however, filmed in the summer of 1905 at Pembroke Dock (North Wales), and based on the life of the notorious murderer hanged in 1879, is one of the most entertaining British films of the period.

Cecil Hepworth   Undoubtedly, the most famous of all early British films is *Rescued by Rover,* produced in 1905 by **Cecil Hepworth** (1874–1953) and directed by **Lewin Fitzhamon** (1869–1961). The film tells without the use of captions of the rescue of a kidnapped baby through the intelligence of Rover the dog, and contains both panning and low angle camera shots. So popular was *Rescued by Rover* that the story was filmed on three separate occasions as one negative after the other became worn out.

The son of a magic lanternist, Hepworth's career in the film industry dated from 1895. In 1897, he wrote *Animated Photography,* and by 1900 he was an established newsreel cameraman. In 1904, he founded the Hepworth Manufacturing Co. Ltd., and the following year he built the first of his studios at Walton-on-Thames. Hepworth was the first British producer to build up his own repertory company of players, and these included such popular British silent stars as Alma Taylor, Chrissie White, Stewart Rome and Henry Edwards.

His productions, all of which are interesting, but none of which are brilliant, include *Hamlet* (1913 with Johnston Forbes-Robertson), *The Cigarette Maker's Romance* (1913 with Sir John Martin Harvey), *David Garrick* (1917 with Sir Charles Wyndham), *Anna the Adventuress* (1920 with Ronald Colman) and *Alf's Button* (1920 with Leslie Henson). His great love of the English countryside shows in all his films, but never more than in *Tansy* (1921), which tells of the love of two farming brothers for a shepherdess, played enchantingly by Alma Taylor. *Comin' thro' the Rye,* first produced in 1916 and re-made in 1923 is the best remembered of all Hepworth productions. It was also the last film to be made by his own studios. Forced into bankruptcy, Hepworth found it difficult to work again—the British film industry that he had helped to build no longer needed him. The last years of his life were spent in the production of trailers for National Screen Service.

Florence Turner   One of the bright spots in the history of the British cinema came in 1913 when **Florence Turner** (1888–1946), who commenced her career as the Vitagraph Girl in 1907, came to Britain with her producer, Larry Trimble. Here she formed the Turner Film Company, based at the Hepworth Studios, and starred in a series of one and two reel comedies, and a number of feature-length romantic dramas including *East Is East* (1915, *dir* Henry Edwards, featuring Edwards and Edith Evans), *Far from the Madding Crowd* (1915, *dir* Larry Trimble, featuring Henry Edwards and Campbell Gullan), *The Welsh Singer* (1915, *dir* Henry Edwards, featuring Edwards and Edith Evans) and *My Old Dutch* (1915, *dir* Larry Trimble, featuring Albert Chevalier). She returned to the U.S.A. in 1916, but was back in Britain again in 1920, to remain until 1924. During this second period, she appeared in a series of minor productions, including *The Little Mother* (1921, *dir*. A. V. Bramble, featuring John Stuart) and *The Old Wives' Tale* (1921, *dir* Denison Clift, featuring Fay Compton). Florence Turner was without doubt Britain's most popular film star during the First World War, and her films were the most highly polished to be produced in Great Britain before 1920.

The most worthwhile British films of the Twenties came from four men; two of these men, George Pearson and Graham Cutts, were to

Betty Balfour and Ralph Forbes in REVEILLE, directed by George Pearson

fade into anonymity with the coming of sound. For the other two directors, Alfred Hitchcock and Anthony Asquith, the Twenties decade was to be merely a stepping stone to even greater triumphs.

George Pearson

The career of **George Pearson** (*b* 1875) in the film industry dated from 1914, when he gave up the secure occupation of a schoolmaster to become a scenario writer and director first for Pathe, and later for Samuelsons and Gaumont. His films during the period include *A Study in Scarlet* (1914, with Fred Paul), *Sally Bishop* (1916, with Marjorie Villis), *Kiddies in the Ruins* (1918, with Hugh E. Wright) and the "Ultus" series which had their origins in the French "Fantomas" serial and starred Aurele Sydney.

In 1918, Pearson formed his own company in partnership with T. A. Welsh, and went on to make some of the best British silent features commencing with *The Better 'Ole,* based on a wartime music hall sketch by Bruce Bairnsfather. Pearson's *Nothing Else Matters* in 1920 introduced Mabel Poulton (whose performances in Germaine Dulac's *L'Ame d'Artiste* and Adrian Brunel's *The Constant Nymph* are still worth recalling) and Betty Balfour. The latter was to become Britain's most popular film actress in the Twenties, and to star for Pearson in the "Squibs" films concerning the life of a cockney flower seller.

Pearson's finest work came in 1924 with *Reveille,* a study of the effects of war and the failures of peace on the ordinary people of London. Betty Balfour played the young mother of an illegitimate child, whose father was killed in the last week of the First World War, and who persuaded the two disillusioned ex-soldiers, Frank Stanmore and Stewart Rome, that the answer to the world's postwar problems lay not in a Communist-inspired revolution, but in teaching the children to create a better world. The final sequence, in which the principal characters observe the two minute silence, during which all British people remember the dead of the First World War, still remains unbearably moving today and shows the British silent cinema at its best.

Graham Cutts and Herbert Wilcox

The career of **Graham Cutts** (1885–1958) is closely linked with that of **Herbert Wilcox** (*b* 1892), for Wilcox was the producer of many of Cutts's earliest successes, including *The Wonderful Story* (1922), the film that first attracted the attention of the critics and public to these two men, *Flames of Passion* (1922) and *Paddy-the-Next-Best-Thing* (1923). The latter two films featured Mae Marsh, who was to be Ivor Novello's co-star in *The Rat* (1925), one of the most successful films of Cutts, both in Great Britain and the U.S.A. It was another Hollywood actress, Betty Compson, who starred opposite Clive Brook in Cutts's finest film, *Woman to Woman* (1923). A melodrama of a dancer at the Moulin Rouge, who sacrifices herself for the sake of her illegitimate son, the film was considered by Rex Ingram to have been one of the five greatest films ever made, and it also helped to gain the assistant director, Alfred Hitchcock, his first directorial assignment.

The name of **Alfred Hitchcock** (*b* 1899) must always be closely linked with the suspense film, yet of his nine silent features only *The Lodger* contains any real element of suspense. Although hampered by the acting of Ivor Novello ("He may be a bit queer, but he is a gentleman"), this story of a man whose actions lead him to be suspected of some particularly vicious murders and later to be nearly crucified at the hands of a mob intent on being both judge and jury, was the first true Hitchcock film.

Hitchcock's *début* as a director came in 1925 with *The Pleasure Garden,* filmed at the Emelka Studios in Munich. The melodramatic story gave little opportunity to the cast which included Virginia Valli and Carmelita Geraghty (both specially brought over from the U.S.A.), John Stuart and Miles Mander. However the critics realised that in Alfred Hitchcock they had discovered a director of whom great things could be expected. G. A. Atkinson, one of Britain's most respected film critics in the Twenties, commented, "Britain has discovered a young film producer of great promise. When Mr. Hitchcock is in a position to produce a drama entirely to his own liking, it is safe to prophesy that he will create a sensation." Mr. Hitchcock was not to be in this position until the coming of sound. His other silents were *The Mountain Eagle* (1926), *Downhill, Easy Virtue* (1927), *The Ring* (1928), *The Farmer's Wife* (1928), *Champagne* (1928), and *The Manxman* (1928). The latter featured Anny Ondra, who, with the voice of Joan Barry, was to star in Hitchcock's first talkie, *Blackmail,* produced in 1929.

Hitchcock was the son of an Essex shopkeeper; **Anthony Asquith** (1902–1968) had an entirely different family background. His father was Prime Minister of England from 1908–1916, and he was educated at Winchester and Balliol College, Oxford. As Forsyth Hardy has said, "With his scholarly background, Asquith brought to the cinema a passionate interest in craftsmanship. He saw the film as a medium of infinite possibilities and he was determined to exploit as many of them as he could."

Asquith entered films in 1926 with British Instructional Films. It was this company that gave him his first opportunity to direct (in association with A. V. Bramble) with the 1928 *Shooting Stars.* Asquith directed only two other silent films, *The Runaway Princess* and *Underground,* both made in 1928. His next film, *Cottage on Dartmoor,* produced in 1929, was released with a synchronised soundtrack. He achieved greatness with the coming of sound, yet Asquith had loved silent films; in 1948 he wrote, "To me they had become a self-subsisting medium."

Film production in Britain during the Thirties can be divided into two categories: the good quality, well-made films, which gained an international release, and the "quota quickies." The latter were produced in order to meet the requirements of the 1927 Cinematograph Act, which stated that a certain percentage of films shown in cinemas had to be British productions. Many pioneer directors from the silent era were reduced to working on these "quickie" pictures, none of which would cost usually more than £1 per foot to produce, including negative costs.

Alfred Hitchcock made a triumphant transition to talkies with *Blackmail* (1929), which *Close Up* described as "the most intelligent mixture of sound and silence we have yet seen." His next production, *Juno and the Paycock,* however, was far from satisfactory. Sean O'Casey's play was entirely unsuitable for filming, and Hitchcock failed completely to understand the emotions running through the piece, and completely ruined Juno's final soliloquy by tasteless cutting from Juno to a statue of the Virgin Mary to the window, and by the addition of superfluous sounds such as machine gun shots. Today, the film stands out only as a testament to the acting ability of Sara Allgood as Juno.

All Hitchcock's other British productions contained elements of suspense with which his name has become synonymous, with the exception of *Waltzes from Vienna* (1933) and *Jamaica Inn* (1939). The two films made immediately prior to *Jamaica Inn* show Hitchcock at his best: *Young and Innocent* (1937, U.S. title *A Girl Was Young*) and *The Lady Vanishes* (1938). Nova Pilbeam is delightful in the former as the chief constable's daughter who believes in the innocence of a suspected murderer. The comedy sequence with Basil Radford and the garden gnomes is a brilliant example of Hitchcock's understanding of the need for comedy in the best suspense thrillers. Comedy played a very important part in *The Lady Vanishes* with Naunton Wayne and Basil Radford as a couple of typical Englishmen abroad. The film was the culmination of Hitchcock's experiments with tension and suspense, and was undoubtedly very much responsible for his being offered a contract in Hollywood by David O. Selznick in the summer of 1939. With his departure to Hollywood, Britain's loss was very much America's gain.

Anthony Asquith had already used a short talkie sequence in *Cottage on Dartmoor* (1929), but his first full talkie did not come until 1931, when *Tell England* was released. The film proved to be a brilliant testament to the horrors of war, and was likened by many critics to *All Quiet on the Western Front* and *Journey's End.* Asquith made only six other films during the Thirties—he was not a prolific director, preferring to choose his subjects carefully—*Dance Pretty Lady* (1931), *The Lucky Number* (1933), *Unfinished Symphony* (1934), *Moscow Nights* (1935), *Pygmalion* (1938) and *French without Tears* (1939). The most important of these films was *Pygmalion,* the first major attempt to film George Bernard Shaw, and for his production Asquith used some of the finest talent available: Wendy Hiller and Leslie Howard

in the leading roles, Harry Stradling as lighting cameraman, David
Lean as editor, and with music composed by Arthur Honegger. The
film confirmed Asquith as one of Britain's most important directing
talents, and it is very much to his credit that he refused all offers to go
to Hollywood.

Asquith's *Moscow Nights* was produced by **Alexander Korda** *Alexander*
(1893–1956), one of the British cinema's two creative producers (the *Korda*
other is Sir Michael Balcon). Hungarian-born Korda formed London
Films in 1933, with the help of his two brothers Zoltan and Vincent
and scriptwriter Lajos Biro. In the same year he directed Charles
Laughton in *The Private Life of Henry VIII*, which established Korda
as this country's leading producer and director, Charles Laughton as a
major star, and the British cinema as being capable of producing films
with an international appeal. Between the years 1933 and 1948 Korda's
London Films produced some of the best British entertainment films
ever made; films such as *The Rise of Catherine the Great* (1934, *dir*
Paul Czinner), *The Ghost Goes West* (1935, *dir* René Clair), *Things*

Charles Laughton in THE PRIVATE LIFE OF HENRY VIII

to Come (1936, *dir* William Cameron Menzies), *Elephant Boy* (1936, *dir* Robert Flaherty and Zoltan Korda), *The Spy in Black* (1939, *dir* Michael Powell) and *Anna Karenina* (1948, *dir* Julien Duvivier).

The English music hall provided a wealth of talent for the British cinema in the Thirties and beyond. Stars such as Will Hay, Arthur Lucan, George Formby, Gracie Fields, Flanagan and Allen, Frank Randle and Sydney Howard all went through an apprenticeship period in music hall.

British Comedy

Will Hay (1888–1949) began his music hall career before the First World War. His film career dates from 1933, but it was not until 1935, when he starred in *Boys Will Be Boys,* that he was able to develop fully his character of the seedy schoolmaster. The following year, he appeared in *Windbag the Sailor,* directed by William Beaudine, and it was this film that introduced two actors who will always be associated with Hay, Graham Moffatt as Albert and Moore Marriott as Harbottle. Hay's screen character, pompous, blustering, shy and always evasive, reached full maturity in 1937, with *Good Morning Boys,* directed by **Marcel Varnel** (1894–1947). Varnel directed some of the best British comedies of the Thirties and Forties, and as Basil Wright has pointed out, he was "the only pure comedy director we've ever had in this country, and he had a flair for expanding a stage turn and developing the essence of an artist like Hay without losing the essential value of his genius."

Together Hay and Varnel made some fine British comedies, which combined the qualities of the music hall with the wider scope offered by the cinema, films such as *Oh Mr. Porter* (1937), *Convict 99* (1938) and *The Ghost of St. Michael's* (1941). With Hay's death, a fine tradition of British comedy disappeared.

Arthur Lucan (1887–1954) as "Old Mother Riley" with his wife **Kitty McShane** (1898–1964) playing daughter Kitty starred in over a dozen features during the Thirties, Forties and early Fifties. None were ever given a West End opening, none were ever reviewed by the critics, but all earned three to four times their cost of production. As David Robinson has pointed out, "one can credit in her nonsense a very affectionately observed caricature of the ignorance and strength of a back-street granny. Old Mother Riley's idle gossip, her fierce protective pride in her lovely daughter Kitty and her feeling for the smaller creature comforts—a chair, a fire, a shawl and a drop of gin taken as medicine—are true enough."

It was the North of England that produced these comedians, and to a large extent their films were more popular in the North than in Southern Britain. The only exceptions were the Crazy Gang members, whose vulgar, bawdy comedy was Cockney in its background and appeal. C. A. Lejeune was entirely wrong when she once complained that Britain's industrial North had more to it than Gracie Fields running around a Blackpool fun fair. Gracie Fields and the film to which Miss Lejeune was referring, *Sing as We Go, were* the North of England.

Sing as We Go represents the native British cinema of the Thirties at its best; chockfull of patriotism, pathos and tuneful songs, it may seem dated today. But one thing that has not dated is **Basil Dean's** (*b* 1888) direction. The final scenes in the film from the moments when Gracie Fields sings "Wonderful Love" to the final shots when she leads the workers back to the factory, waving a union jack and singing the title song are brilliantly handled. The montage sequences look like the work of an Eisenstein or Pudovkin, and the viewer is never allowed to become overwhelmed with emotion. The final shot of Gracie smiling up at the camera is interrupted by a fellow worker pushing her, and her angry retort, "Who do you think you're shoving?" The end title superimposed over a union jack and the words "This is a British picture" speak volumes. *as*

3. France

IN 1895 LOUIS AND AUGUSTE LUMIÈRE, bringing together the various developments of the pioneers described in Chapter Eleven, patented their first projector and showed, privately, their first film, *La Sortie des Usines Lumière*. Later the same year they gave the first public showing, including in the programme *La Sortie* and also *L'Arrivée d'un Train en Gare*, which caused a sensation and terrified the audience as the railway engine approached. They originated the newsreel by filming the French Photographic Society's Congress, and made what might be described as the first documentary—a series of four films about the Lyon fire brigade. The brothers held their first London performance at the Regent Street Polytechnic in 1896, and a few years later retired from production. They had specialised in the newsreel and documentary side of the cinema, and were not equipped to handle the fictional film in staged settings which was then rapidly developing.

In May 1897 the French cinema industry suffered a severe setback when a disastrous fire at a charity bazaar in Paris was allegedly started by a film show on the premises, owing to the inflammable nature of the celluloid stock. The bazaar was an important society occasion, and some two hundred people were burned to death. There was widespread and unreasonable (for the accusation was never proved) condemnation of the young industry. Fortunately, however, though the police imposed the severest possible safety regulations, there was no actual shutdown.

Two of the most important pioneering firms in France were those of Léon Gaumont and the Pathé brothers. **Gaumont** (1864–1946) started his career as an assistant to Alexandre Eiffel, the engineer responsible for the Eiffel Tower. After marketing an early moving picture system involving the use of glass plates he built up a flourishing business in the handling of both cinematograph apparatus and completed films. Later he became founder of the Gaumont studios and cinema circuit in Great Britain. His first film production was entitled *The Misadventures of a Piece of Veal* and featured the actress Alice Guy. In 1896 he developed a 60mm camera and projected a ballet picture at the Théâtre du Châtélet. He had already experimented with sound before the First World War, effecting a combination between phonograph and film in 1902. Our greatest debt to him in the art of the film, however, may well be his production of the Feuillade serials.

Rivaling Gaumont was **Charles Pathé** (1863–1957), who has been described as the Napoleon of the cinema. At the age of thirty he bought a phonograph and was soon visiting fairgrounds all over the country charging customers for listening to records. Soon afterwards he set up a shop in Vincennes, discovered the potentialities of the cinema, made up a camera with a partner, and went into competition with Lumière— his first film, in fact, being entitled *L'Arrivée d'un Train en Gare de Vincennes*. He built his own studio, and went into partnership with his brothers. The company produced films of every kind, including the first *Quo Vadis* (1902), which lasted twenty minutes and seems to have caused a good deal of unintended laughter. A business man rather than an artist, he was largely responsible for the rapid growth of the industry in France in the years before the First World War. Pathé films were sold throughout the world. In 1908, in the U.S.A., they outnumbered by 100 per cent all the home products of the American companies. In France, he began building his own cinemas and started the practice of renting rather than selling his films. The newsreel, Pathé Gazette, was probably the best-known in the world for many years.

GEORGES MÉLIÈS
There is no doubt that the imaginative genius of the period was **Georges Méliès** (1861–1938), justly regarded as the father of film art. For ten years before he came across the cinema he had been running a small theatre specialising in conjuring, founded by Robert Houdin, and from this suitable environment he brought to the film a love of fantasy and camera trickery combined with a vitality and a sense of impish—often satiric—humour that make his brief productions as fresh and entertaining today as when he originally created them. His first film, *Une Partie de Cartes,* appeared in 1896, and during the following twenty years he completed literally hundreds of short fantastic films of all kinds, writing the scripts, directing, designing the *décor* and costumes, overseeing the trick machinery and camerawork, and playing in them himself. His productions were generally divided into brief scenes, presented as if to an audience seated in the stalls facing the usual stage

A scene from Georges Méliès's 20,000 LEAGUES UNDER THE SEA

settings of wings, borders, painted backcloths and even a curtain. He created, in fact, the illusion of a theatre in which events only possible with a movie camera were presented. The two mainstreams of his output were fairy stories (*Cendrillon, Barbe-Bleue, La Fée Carabosse*) and futuristic tales after the style of Jules Verne but seen through the eyes of parody. Best known among these were *Le Voyage dans la Lune* (1902), *Le Voyage à Travers l'Impossible* (1904) which involved a trip to the sun, and *A la Conquête du Pôle* (1912). The last could be called one of the first monster films, containing an Abominable Snowman who emerges from a lake and begins to devour the band of explorers. He also made a number of historic re-enactments, one of which, *L'Affaire Dreyfus* (1899), caused a sensation owing to its committed attitude and was for a time banned in France. Others were *L'Explosion du Cuirasse* (1898), and *Le Couronnement du Roi Edouard VII* (1902). For a period his films were distributed by Pathé, but he broke with them when *Cendrillon* was cut from 2,000 to 900 feet.

Méliès's imagination, however, did not extend to the growing practical developments of the cinema. His camera was static; he rarely left the confines of the studio. Also, his business sense was limited. He shut his eyes to such mundane concerns, with the result that he was left behind in the race. Eventually he had to close down production, sell his studios and effects, and years later, in 1929, was discovered by a journalist selling toys and sweets in a Paris railway station. Despite his refusal, or inability, to move with the times, Méliès is one of the great figures of the early cinema, and this was recognised by his admission to the Legion of Honour.

Another notable name of the period was **Ferdinand Zecca** (1864–1947), originally engaged by the Pathé brothers to direct their new studios in Vincennes. Though he too at times made use of trickery and fantastic effects, Zecca's films as a whole formed a contrast to those of Méliès in their realism and freedom from studio confines, and also in a more mobile use of the camera. He made a number of low-life melodramas, such as *Les Victimes de l'Alcoolisme* (1902) and *L'Histoire d'un Crime* (1901), the latter starting a fashion for the film of violence, crime and the underworld that has lasted to this day. By contrast, one of his best known productions was the *Passion de Notre Seigneur Jésus Christ* (1902–5), inspired by contemporary chromolithographs and some 2,000 feet in length.

In 1908 a company known as the Film d'Art was inaugurated, in which Pathé had a part interest, to produce "prestige" films featuring famous theatrical personalities in famous plays—the first being *L'Assassinat du Duc de Guise* (1908), for which Saint-Saens wrote accompanying music. Other titles during the following two or three years included *Notre Dame de Paris, Les Misérables, Madame Sans-Gêne* (with Réjane), *La Reine Elisabeth* and *La Dame aux Camélias* (both with Sarah Bernhardt).

Well-known stage comedians also entered the growing industry, notably **André Deed** (1884– ?), who created a Pierrot-like character called Gribouille, and **Charles Prince** (1872–1933) whose screen personality was a sort of petit-bourgeois clown known as Rigadin. Both appeared in countless brief knockabout episodes.

Max Linder   Of much greater importance was **Max Linder** (Gabriel Levielle, 1883–1925), whose humour was considerably more sophisticated. He had worked in both the straight theatre and vaudeville before, in 1905, he was invited by Pathé to enter films. His first title was *La Première Sortie,* and over the next fifteen years he made a vast number of shorts such as *Max, Professeur de Tango, Max et le Quinquina, Max Toreador,* etc. His stock personality was that of a dapper, gay young man of independent means who got into various difficulties, and his story lines, though slight and often containing a good deal of slapstick, allowed him to develop a certain depth of character which extended through the series of separate films into a coherent whole. He wrote and directed nearly all his productions, and his style of playing was notable for a subtlety of touch, a significant use of small gestures and a sharp sense of timing which was unusual in the generally crude world of contemporary film comedy.

Chaplin has acknowledged his debt to Linder, and indeed the influence is obvious, but Linder never achieved the universality, the essential humanity of the greater comedian at his best. After the First World War he went to America and there made the three feature-length pictures by which he is remembered: *Be My Wife* (1921), *Seven Years Bad Luck* (1921) and *The Three Must-Get-Theres,* a parody of *The Three Musketeers* that brilliantly made affectionate fun of the swash-buckling Douglas Fairbanks costume pieces. He then returned to France to make *Au Secours!* (1924) and to Austria for *Le Roi du Cirque* (1925). His health had been failing for some time, and towards the end of 1925 he and his wife died tragically, apparently in a suicide pact. Linder had a special gift, which he shared with Chaplin, of building a whole sequence, even a whole film, round the permutations of one simple event or everyday mishap.

Prominent in the early French cinema was the crime serial. Its originator was **Victorin Jasset** (1862–1913), formerly a sculptor, whose first film was a Passion, *Le Vie de Notre Seigneur Jésus Christ,* based on a series of Tissot water-colours. He became known, however, for his series of *Nick Carter* adventures (started in 1908), and their success encouraged him to follow them up with adaptations of other popular serial stories such as *Balaoo* (1912) and *Zigomar* (1912). He was working on one such series, *Protéa,* at the time of his death in 1913.

His successor in this field was the much greater **Louis Feuillade** (1873–1925). One of the leading names in the early cinema, he began his career in 1906 with Léon Gaumont as a director of comic shorts, making special use of trick effects in natural settings, and building up from one situation a whole edifice of strictly logical absurdity. He was also responsible for two series featuring juvenile comics, *Bébé* (1910–12) and *Bout-de-Zan* (1914–17). In 1913 he worked on the first of his masterly crime series, *Fantômas,* a sequence of five films based on the adventures of a black-hooded arch-criminal invented by Pierre Souvestre and Marcel Allain, who had already written thirty-two novels about their character. Feuillade's inspiration was in placing the lurid activities of his protagonists against carefully realistic backgrounds of Paris and its environs. *Fantômas* was followed by *Les Vampires* (1915–16) in ten episodes, *Judex* (1917) in twelve episodes, and *La Nouvelle Mission de Judex* (1918), also in twelve episodes. Judex was not a criminal (the Minister of the Interior having protested about the enormous popularity of the criminal element in *Les Vampires*) but a righter of wrongs—a mysterious, dignified, slightly

Louis Feuillade

89

The closely-packed imagery of Feuillade's LES VAMPIRES

sinister and wholly captivating figure in black cloak and broad-brimmed black hat. Feuillade made numerous other films, *Tih Minh* (1918), *L'Homme sans Visage* (1919), *Barrabas* (1920), etc., but it is for *Les Vampires* and *Judex* that he will always be remembered. Both have been shown in recent years as mammoth films with all the episodes run together. His brilliance lies in his poetic combination of fantasy and reality, the sense of grandeur and doom with which he manages to invest the absurd events he depicts and the beauty, even today, of his black-and-white photography.

Jean Durand (1882–1946), a pupil of Feuillade, should be mentioned on account of his comedy series *Onésime, Calino* and *Zigoto* (made between 1909 and 1914). His influence can be seen in the work of both Mack Sennett and René Clair. Durand also produced a number of films about wild animals for his wife, who was a trainer.

The advent of the First World War had, inevitably, a cataclysmic effect on the cinema in France, and at first production came to a virtual halt. Gradually, however, as the months passed work was re-started.

Feuillade brought out his serials, Max Linder made a few films, the one constant being Rigadin, whose comedies seem to have been inescapable. At the same time new names were being brought before the public. Louis Delluc, then a writer and journalist, began to draw attention to directors for whom he saw a bright future, including **Léon Poirier** (*b* 1876 or 1884), **Jacques de Baroncelli** (1881–1951) and, in particular, Germaine Dulac and Abel Gance. Delluc himself was to turn director, notably of *Fièvre* (1921), a study of disillusionment set in a sailors' bar in Marseilles which foreshadows aspects of the French films of the Thirties. *ib*

The situation in the Twenties in France is a unique one in the history of the cinema; the search for new forms and new subject matter brought about by an extremely active *avant-garde* movement played an important part in stimulating the French film industry at a crucial time in its development, so that its legacy remained visible for many years afterwards. The movement was spearheaded by a growth in film criticism and the founding of a number of new magazines such as *Photogénie* and *Cinéma et Cie* which began a serious discussion of the cinema's relationship with other art forms, together with analyses of what film-makers were doing in other countries, particularly Russia, Germany and North America. There was an increased interest in the popular cinema, not only in Hollywood, but in the work of such film-makers as Feuillade, whose serials came to be valued very highly by critics. Specialised cinemas were opened, and there was a rapid growth in the *ciné-club* movement, which meant that the *avant-garde* could be given a wider showing so that a critical climate was created for their work. In this way, a number of patrons were prepared to back non-commercial ventures, and even commercial producers came to view *avant-garde* film-makers more favourably.

French avant-garde

The influence of the *avant-garde* first became evident in the commercial cinema itself between 1919 and 1923, although these films had very little commercial success. There had been a marked fall in production between 1919 and 1921, from 208 films to 163, due to the increasing dominance of Hollywood. Feuillade became artistic director of Gaumont Studios, and was responsible for opening its doors to a number of *avant-garde* film-makers. *La Fête Espagnole* (1919), directed by **Germaine Dulac** (1882–1942) and scripted by **Louis Delluc** (1890–1924), is generally acknowledged to be the first *avant-garde* film. Germaine Dulac's work is uneven; several of her films appear routine and purely commercial, among them *L'Ame d'Artiste* (1925) and *Antoinette Sabrier* (1927), but her best work marked her out as one of the major film-makers of the period. Dulac, strongly influenced by Freud's work in psychology, saw the cinema as a way of exploring the unconscious. *La Souriante Madame Beudet* in 1921 established her reputation and *La Coquille et le Clergyman* (1926), based on a script by Antonin Artaud, *L'Invitation au Voyage* (1927), based on one of Baudelaire's poems, and *Arabesque* (1929) were her most distinguished films. Louis Delluc was initially a playwright, novelist and film critic before beginning a career in the film industry which ended abruptly with his death in 1924. After scripting a number of films, he directed his first film, *Le Silence*, in 1920, which typified his approach to the medium. The film depicts a man waiting for a woman; he imagines he sees his dead wife whom he killed, believing her to have been unfaithful; when the girl finally arrives she finds he has killed himself out of remorse. The exploration of memory and imagination through the use of superimpositions was Delluc's major preoccupation, which he perfected in later films such as *Le Tonnère* (1921), *Fièvre* (1921), *La Femme de Nulle Part* (1922), and *L'Inondation* (1924); taken together they represented an important contribution to the development of the silent cinema. His attempt to study character in depth was aided by the outstanding performances of his wife, Eve Francis, who succeeded in imbuing all her roles with the fatalistic poetry that characterises Delluc's work in general.

Jean Epstein   Jean Epstein (1897–1953) was also a film writer and theoretician who entered the commercial cinema. His concern with the psychological possibilities of the cinema was similar to that of Delluc, and his early films, *L'Auberge Rouge* (1923) and *Coeur Infidèle* (1923) bore witness to this, and also displayed considerable technical ability, with skilful exploitation of the potentialities of the mobile camera. Epstein was basically a realist, with considerable feeling for landscape and atmosphere, which is particularly evident in *Coeur Infidèle,* with its impressively sordid low life scenes, and *La Belle Nivernaise* (1923), a moving evocation of French rural life. Epstein became increasingly interested in technique for its own sake, and abandoned his earlier approach, with such films as *La Glace à Trois Faces* (1927) and *La Chute de la Maison Usher* (1928), an adaptation of Edgar Allan Poe which obscured much of the psycho-analytical quality of Poe's world by depicting the Ushers as man and wife rather than brother and sister. *Finis Terrae* in 1928 witnessed a return to a more documentary approach which prefigured Neo-realism in its use of Breton peasants and fishermen as actors.

Marcel L'Herbier (*b* 1890), a poet and playwright, was not strictly part of the *avant-garde* movement, having entered the film industry in 1917 with *Phantasmes*. His early films such as the popular *Rose France* (1919) and *L'Homme du Large* (1920), based on a novel by Balzac, were romantic, almost sentimental in conception, the latter making full use of the landscapes of Brittany to achieve its effect. L'Herbier's most important films, however, indicated his strong interest in the *avant-garde. L'Inhumaine* (1923) brought together a tremendous number of outstanding talents of the day; a scenario by Mac Orlan, special music by Darius Milhaud, sets by Leger and Mallet-Stevens. *L'Inhumaine* was entirely abstract in conception, its cubist *décors* achieving a real sense of man at the mercy of mechanisation. *Feu Mathias Pascal* (1925) was based on Pirandello, whose world of fantasy L'Herbier made very much his own, with some extraordinary sets by Cavalcanti; the Russian actor, Ivan Mosjoukine, took the major role. With *L'Argent* in 1927, a film based this time on Zola, L'Herbier ceased film-making for ten years. Nevertheless, while his work was influential, though sometimes unpopular at the time, as the years have progressed his contribution can be seen as an important and crucial one.

ABEL GANCE

The work of **Abel Gance** (*b* 1889) stood in sharp contrast to L'Herbier's cerebral approach to the cinema. Gance's overriding obsession centred round technical innovation; as he once said, "The day of the Image has arrived." Gance entered the film industry as an actor, and later turned to writing scenarios. His first film *La Folie du Dr. Tube* (1916) in some senses prefigured *avant-garde* films of the Twenties; it was an experimental fantasy making use of distorting mirrors, but like so much of Gance's later work, its search for visual effects was often at the expense of any real depth. *J'Accuse* (1919) was remarkable for its extensive use of footage shot at the Front; an anti-war film built around a rather sentimental story, *J'Accuse* ends with an extraordinary scene in which the dead rise up from the battlefield, which Gance contrasts with the Victory Parade at the Arc de Triomphe, by using a split screen. *La Roue* (1923) was based on a similar narrative structure of two men in love with the same girl, and depicted life in the railway yards. It was remarkable for its innovational use of rapid, rhythmic cutting to achieve an intensity of effect. Like *J'Accuse* it displayed an extraordinary technical bravura marred by an underlying *naïveté* which characterised Gance's work in general. However, Gance's true *forte* was the epic film, and the monumental *Napoléon* (1927) showed this. *Napoléon* makes use of every technique of the cinema, from hand-held camera to cinemascope and stands as Gance's outstanding achievement. His use of polyvision, the screen split into three, for the sequence depicting the Italian campaign was quite outstanding and his technique was later developed into Cinerama. Gance also even experimented with 3-D and colour in this film, but his revolutionary innovations were seen by producers as potentially harmful to the industry, and *Napoléon* was consigned to the vaults.

Jacques Feyder

Another director worthy of mention was the Belgian **Jacques Feyder** (1888–1948), who began a career in the film industry as an actor and later as an assistant to Gaston Ravel. His first film was *L'Atlantide,* based on the novel by Pierre Benoit. His most interesting films of the period were *Crainquebille* (1923) and *Thérèse Raquin* (1928), in which he achieved considerable psychological depth to his characters with a highly inventive and expressive conception of *mise-en-scène*.

René Clair (*b* 1898) alternated between making *avant-garde* shorts and commercial features with similar preoccupations. His first film, *Paris Qui Dort* (1923) owed much to Georges Méliès in its exploration of fantasy. His short, *Entr'acte,* which he made a year later, with a scenario by Francis Picabia, caused considerable scandal when it was first shown; it depicted the exploration of a man's fantasy, using free association of images. *Le Fantôme du Moulin Rouge* (1924) and *Le Voyage Imaginaire* (1924) both display Clair's marvellous sense of the absurd, which always contains harsher undertones. *La Proie du Vent* which he made in 1926 stands out as an uncharacteristic film, which may be accounted for by the fact that it is a literary adaptation. With *Un Chapeau de Paille d'Italie* (1927), however, he returned to the world of *Entr'acte;* originally a theatre farce, Clair transformed it into a balletic burlesque fantasy, full of wit and invention. *Les Deux Timides* (1928) was an excursion into popular romance, with some exquisite scenes of French rural life, but Clair's insistent use of technical tricks in this context seems out of place. Clair clearly played an important part in shaping the cinema of the Twenties; however, many would contend that his major contribution was still to come.

The most important aspect of the French *avant-garde* was the direct influence it had on the commercial cinema. However, there were films which were made with no commercial aim in mind. Man Ray's *Le Retour à la Raison* was probably the first of these, which was originally shown at a Dada demonstration in 1923. Man Ray was a photographer, and his aim was to free the mind from rational logic. His other films,

Looking up at a ballet dancer, in René Clair's avant-garde film.
ENTR'ACTE

Emak Bakia (1926) and *L'Etoile de Mer* (1928) were experiments in free association and an attempt at a pure cinema. The painter Fernand Léger made *Le Ballet Mécanique* in 1925 with Dudley Murphy, and Marcel Duchamp made *Anémic Cinéma* in 1928. Henri Chomette made *Jeux des Reflets de la Vitesse* (1926) and *Cinq Minutes de Cinéma Pur* in 1926. **Alberto Cavalcanti** (*b* 1897), a Brazilian, who was later to have an important part to play in the documentary movement in England, introduced the spirit of *avant-garde* into documentary in *La P'tite Lili* (1928). cj

French Cinema in the Thirties

René Clair

The early years of sound in the French cinema were particularly marked by the comedy successes of **René Clair,** who had already established his maturity as an artist with *Un Chapeau de Paille d'Italie* in 1927. Exploiting with great invention the possibilities offered by sound, the advent of which he had initially viewed with some distrust, Clair made in quick succession *Sous les Toits de Paris* (1930), *Le Million* (1931), *A Nous la Liberté* (1931), *Quatorze Juillet* (1932) and *Le Dernier Milliardaire* (1934). Then he was lured to Britain by Alexander Korda to make *The Ghost Goes West* (1935) and, with the intrusion of the war, thirteen years passed before he completed another film in France. Clair's films of the early Thirties, his most fertile and inventive period, are all within the boundaries of comedy, but their range is still wide. With the aid of a team of very talented collaborators, notably the designer Lazare Meerson and photographer Georges Périnal, and a "stock company" of actors, Clair conjures up his own world of gentle humour and farcical misunderstanding while still stamping on each film a distinctive tone. *Sous les Toits de Paris* paints a warm and delicate picture of the little people of Paris, living on the fringes of crime and violence. The slightly self-conscious toying with sound and image of this film gives way in *Le Million* to a fully elaborated integration of chase plot and musical accompaniment. While *Le Million* is deliberately artificial (the chorus of tradespeople and the absurd contrivances of the opera), *A Nous la Liberté* strikes a new note of social awareness and mild social satire. Its ending, when the two heroes leave the world of big business for the carefree existence of the tramp, recalls both the innocent revolt of Vigo's *Zéro de Conduite* and the anarchy of Renoir's *Boudu Sauvé des Eaux*.

Clair, who had been making films since 1923, provides one instance of the continuity of the French cinema. The early Thirties also saw the end of the *avant-garde* movement with which he had been associated in his early days (*Entr'acte*, 1924, from a script by the dadaist Francis Picabia). The Vicomte de Noailles's patronage allowed the two most interesting and revolutionary later works of the movement to be produced. In 1930 **Luis Buñuel** (*b* 1900) followed up the scandal of *Un Chien Andalou* with a sound film *L'Age d'Or,* a bitter vision of civilisation littered with obscenity (the cloacal obsessions), blasphemy

Scene from Clair's A NOUS LA LIBERTE

(Christ as a sadistic sex murderer) and a spirit of uncompromising revolt. *Le Sang d'un Poète* (1930–32), directed by **Jean Cocteau** (1889–1963), used many surrealist procedures to conjure up its essentially personal vision of death's attraction for the poet. Twenty years later Cocteau was to re-work the same themes in *Orphée,* but in the late Thirties his more immediate concern was with the theatre. Buñuel too, experiencing exile and neglect, had to wait many years before he could again work with comparable freedom and control. Continuity with the silent film of a different kind is provided by the careers of such veterans as Marcel L'Herbier and Abel Gance, but generally speaking their work was of less importance. Gance, for instance, was largely limited to remaking his silent film successes—*Mater Dolorosa* (1917 and 1932), *Napoléon* (1927 and 1934), *J'accuse* (1918 and 1938)—and most of his grandiose projects went unrealised.

Guitry and Pagnol

While Clair's early films of the Thirties are sound films but not "talkies," the possibilities offered by the recording of dialogue attracted several notable authors from the theatre, among them **Sacha Guitry** (1885–1957) and **Marcel Pagnol** (*b* 1895). Guitry, son of the great actor Lucien Guitry and uncrowned king of the boulevard theatre, was author of about one hundred and thirty plays, and most of the dozen or so films he directed in the Thirties were simple transpositions of theatrical texts. The strength of these films lay in the writing and actors rather than in the direction, but with one film at least, *Le Roman d'un Tricheur* (1936), Guitry did contribute to film technique. With its dissociation of word and image, this film is a forerunner of some of Resnais's more ambitious work of the Fifties. The success in the cinema of Marcel Pagnol is also paradoxical. Pagnol is really a literary figure, author of some of the most striking theatrical successes of the Twenties and member of the French Academy since 1946. In the early Thirties he was the most outspoken advocate of filmed theatre and initially his interest lay in putting before the public excellent versions of his plays, acted by casts dominated by great actors like Raimu. It was in this spirit that Pagnol produced his celebrated trilogy *Marius* (1931, *dir* Alexander Korda), *Fanny* (1932, *dir* Marc Allégret) and *César* (1936). In the Thirties Pagnol built his own studio near Marseilles and, using the resources of the Provençal landscape to the full, produced a series of wonderfully acted films—*Angèle* (1934) and *Regain* (1937) with Fernandel, and *La Femme du Boulanger* (1939) with Raimu—which achieved a unique fusion of theatrical dialogue and open-air setting.

During these same years **Jean Renoir** (*b* 1894), son of the painter, *Jean Renoir* was pursuing a career which had begun with eight silent films—among them the brilliant *Nana* (1926). The Thirties—a period during which Renoir made in all some fifteen films—is the richest period in this great director's abundant *oeuvre*. His work during the years 1930–34 is uneven but lays the foundation for his later international success. The first need was to establish the confidence of producers and this he did with *On purge bébé* (1931), a farce made in just three weeks, one for scripting, one for shooting and one for editing. In this film Renoir worked with the actor Michel Simon, who also made a great contribution to *La Chienne* (1931) and *Boudu Sauvé des Eaux* (1932). Both these splendidly amoral tales were shot on location and in mood mix realism and caricature. Simon is superb both as Legrand, the little bank clerk who murders his faithless mistress and allows her lover to be executed for the crime, and as Boudu, who rewards the man who saves his life by seducing both his wife and his mistress. The two films reflect the sense of anarchy of the period in the glorification of the figure of the tramp. During these years Renoir also made adaptations of Simenon (*La nuit du Carrefour*, 1932, with his brother Pierre as Inspector Maigret) and Flaubert (*Madame Bovary*, 1934, with Valentine Tessier), but his most interesting work is *Toni* (1934). This story of the passions and crimes of migrant workers in the south of France, for which Marcel Pagnol served as producer, used non-professionals and

Renoir in the Thirties. Above left: the prisoners in LA GRANDE ILLUSION. Above right: the death of Batala in LE CRIME DE MONSIEUR LANGE. Opposite page: Marcel Dalio shows one of his musical boxes to Renoir himself in LA REGLE DU JEU

real settings in a manner that in some ways anticipates Italian neorealism.

Jean Vigo The early Thirties also witnessed the tragically short career of **Jean Vigo** (1905–1934). Vigo had already made a silent study of Nice, *A Propos de Nice* (1929), and a short documentary on the swimming champion Jean Taris, when he began work on a forty-seven minute film *Zéro de Conduite* (1933). Here, in his portrait of a repressive school system countered by a schoolboy revolt, Vigo was able to draw on his own boarding school past and on attitudes inherited from his father, a noted anarchist murdered in prison. The film leavens its precise observation with humour and caricature, but was authentic and powerful enough to be banned for a dozen years by the censor. After the world of children, Vigo turned to the problems of adult relationships. The feature length *L'Atalante* (1934) shows the relationship of a young bargee and his wife, their love, quarrels and misunderstandings. Again Vigo is able to achieve a unique poetry out of a synthesis of realistic detail (life on the barge) and fantastic exaggeration (the figure of the mate played by Michel Simon). Vigo's touch is deceptively simple, but it loses none of its power with the years. Vigo died soon after the opening of *L'Atalante,* which was mutilated by producers and

dubbed with an irrelevant popular song. Vigo, with a total output of about three hours of film, is now rightly seen as one of the very greatest of French directors and his influence has been a continuing one.

Jean Grémillon (1901–1959), another man of enormous talent, could not find a place for himself in French feature production. His first sound film, *La Petite Lise* (1930), was a critical success but a commercial failure. He was condemned to make uninteresting, routine films and eventually had to go abroad, first to Spain and then to Germany, to continue his career. He returned to France in 1939 to make *Remorques* from a script by Jacques Prévert with Gabin and Michèle Morgan, but the outbreak of war interrupted the production and it was not completed until two years later. While Grémillon was looking abroad for work, French studios were filled by an influx of refugees from Nazi Germany. Pabst, Lang, Siodmak, Litvak, Wiene all made French films in the Thirties (some of them while on their way to Hollywood), but the only exile whose films enjoy much critical esteem today is **Max Ophuls** (1902–1957). Ophuls came to France in 1933 to remake his remarkable *Liebelei* as *Une Histoire d'Amour* and remained in France until 1940 with only brief trips abroad to make *La Signora per tutti* (1934) in Italy and *Komedie om Geld*

Grémillon,
Ophuls

(1936) in Holland. His French films of the period are largely romantic melodramas of beautiful but unhappy women: *Divine* (1935), *La Tendre Ennemie* (1936), *Yoshiwara* (1937), *Sans Lendemain* (1939), *De Mayerling à Sarajevo* (1940). With the German invasion he left France for the U.S.A. and when he returned in 1950 it was to make a far more striking series of films on similar themes.

Jacques Feyder   In the mid-Thirties the French cinema underwent one of its periodic crises with a lack of confidence by producers and the loss of two of its leading directors (Clair and Vigo). Indeed Bardèche and Brasillach, writing their *Histoire du Cinéma* in 1935, conclude, somewhat melodramatically, that in that year "something quite important happened: the French film industry practically disappeared." In fact, in 1935 the French cinema was on the brink of one of its richest periods. To compensate for the loss of Clair was the return of **Jacques Feyder** (1885–1948), who had been one of the masters of the French silent cinema and had worked in Hollywood with Garbo. In the space of two years Feyder made three films which re-established his European reputation: *Le Grand Jeu* (1934), *Pension Mimosas* (1935) and *La*

Medieval Flanders re-created in Jacques Feyder's LA KERMESSE HEROIQUE

Kermesse Héroïque (1935). For these films Feyder assembled a brilliant team led by the scriptwriter Spaak, designer Lazare Meerson and assistant Marcel Carné and including his actress wife and inseparable companion Françoise Rosay. The contribution made by **Charles Spaak** (*b* 1903), who had previously worked with Feyder on *Les Nouveaux Messieurs* in 1929, is most interesting, for the late Thirties were a time when writers, particularly Spaak, Jacques Prévert and Henri Jeanson, began to play a dominant part in French production. The brilliantly acted *La Kermesse Héroïque*, a farcical plea for cowardice set in Sixteenth century Holland, has a brilliant visual style based on the paintings of the Flemish masters and marks the summit of Feyder's career. In 1937 he was tempted to London by Korda to make *Knight without Armour,* then went to Munich to make *Les Gens du Voyage* (1938). *La Loi du Nord* was begun in France in 1939 but interrupted for three years by the outbreak of war, and Feyder was able to make only one other film—*Une Femme Disparaît* (1941, in Switzerland)—in the last eight years of his life.

The late Thirties saw Jean Renoir achieve new heights with an incredibly varied selection of films. Unlike Feyder and Carné he did not collaborate consistently with a single writer and often he served as his own scriptwriter. For *Le Crime de Monsieur Lange* (1935), however, he had an excellent script by **Jacques Prévert** (*b* 1900), then at the beginning of his career. This story of a group of workmen who take over a printing firm after the supposed death of their crooked boss reflects the new mood of France. With the Popular Front a new sense of commitment has replaced the happy anarchy of *Boudu.* The workman hero Lange, who kills the crook when he returns to re-claim the firm, is "tried" by a group of his social equals, not by the authorities. The social meaning of the film is clear, but as in so many Prévert films the most striking figure is the villain, played with great relish by Jules Berry. Renoir himself was never a Communist but found himself caught up in the left-wing atmosphere of the time, even to the extent of making *La Vie est à Nous* (1936), an explicit piece of propaganda for the Communist party. The same year he made one of his most memorable films, *Une Partie de Campagne,* an exquisite love story based on a Maupassant tale which is redolent with the atmosphere of Impressionist paintings and contains some homages to Renoir's father. *Une Partie de Campagne* was left incomplete and not released to the public until 1946, for Renoir had meanwhile taken up a new subject. *Les Bas-Fonds* (1936), an adaptation of a Gorky novel written with Charles Spaak proved, however, to be an inconclusive work though offered good opportunities to actors like Louis Jouvet and Jean Gabin. More impressive was *La Grande Illusion* (1937), also written with Spaak, Renoir's most polished and disciplined work of the period. In terms of the film, war is the great illusion and the true path that of solidarity and internationalism. But looked at in retrospect, the film seems very naïve in this sense, harking back nostalgically to a cavalry officer's view of the First World War. What does remain remarkable is the acting of the central trio, the commandant Eric von Stroheim and the two French officers Pierre Fresnay and Jean Gabin. *La Marseillaise* (1938) was closer to the spirit of *Le Crime de Monsieur Lange,* having been financed by public subscription and made as a co-operative effort. A hymn to the revolution of 1789, it brings into the open the patriotism latent in *La Grande Illusion.* Renoir had always been fascinated by naturalist literature and one of his best known silent films had been an adaptation of Emile Zola's *Nana.* For his second film of 1938 he turned to Zola again to make *La Bête Humaine,* starring Jean Gabin and Simone Simon and with a small part for the director himself. The background details of the railwayman's life were given as much weight as the tragic passion itself and add greatly to the impact of the film.

In the months beween Munich and the war Renoir reached the climax of his career with *La Règle du Jeu* (1939), a virtual synthesis of all his aims and ambitions in the Thirties. For this film he enjoyed total artistic freedom, being his own producer, director, scriptwriter and actor. Breaking with the naturalism of his previous films he found a new style in the plays of Marivaux and Musset. The optimism of the days of *Le Crime de Monsieur Lange* has gone completely: Renoir paints a picture of a hierarchical society, of masters and servants where sincerity is the supreme social crime. By telling a frivolous story of frivolous people Renoir contrives to sum up a whole age and society. With the aid of a loose script and the systematic use of improvisation he is able to follow his characters as they group and re-group during a stay in the country, ostensibly devoted to hunting and arranging a masquerade. *La Règle du Jeu,* a complete *film d'auteur,* was far ahead of its time. Mutilated by producers and distributors it was a complete financial flop and had to wait twenty-five years for release in its original version. With the outbreak of war Renoir worked briefly in Italy on a project subsequently completed by his assistant, then went to Hollywood to continue his career there.

Julien Duvivier   Another director who had worked since the silent days but came to the fore in this period was **Julien Duvivier** (1896–1967), a thoroughly professional film-maker whose silent films had occasionally been ambitious but seldom wholly successful. With the advent of sound he made a notable study of a child, *Poil de Carotte* (1932), a first version of which he had directed in 1925. But out of a total output of nearly seventy films, the most interesting are three he made with Jean Gabin in the years 1935–37. These were *La Bandéra* (1935), a tale of the Foreign Legion, and *La Belle Equipe* (1936), a story of five unemployed workers who win a lottery, both written with Charles Spaak; and *Pépé-le-Moko* (1937), a strikingly successful gangster film.

The latter was scripted by **Henri Jeanson** (*b* 1900), a man who enlivened many routine films of the period with incisive wit. All three works are marked by a profound pessimism about human nature which also finds expression in *Un Carnet de Bal* (1937), the film which initiated the vogue for films comprising a number of distinct sketches. This was a form of film-making with which Duvivier achieved further success during his wartime exile in Hollywood.

The precise mood of the period—a sense of fatalism enveloping a pair of doomed lovers in a studio-contrived drably poetic urban setting—is also to be found in the work of **Marcel Carné** (*b* 1909). Carné had made a silent documentary on the Parisians' weekend resort *Nogent Eldorado du Dimanche* (1930) and worked as assistant to Clair and Feyder before making his first feature, *Jenny* (1936), at the age of twenty-seven. Carné was the most brilliant young director of the period and by the age of thirty he had made five features including two recognised everywhere as masterpieces, *Quai des Brumes* (1938) and *Le Jour se Lève* (1939). In both Jean Gabin and his mistress are confronted by a hostile environment and opposed by malevolent but picturesque villains (Michel Simon in the first film and Jules Berry in the second). Superbly acted, the films owed much to Carné's team of collaborators, notable among whom were the designer Alexandre Trauner and the composer Maurice Jaubert. In *Quai des Brumes* and *Le Jour se Lève* too, a unique fusion is achieved of Carné's technical precision and black fatalistic outlook on the one hand, and the writer Jacques Prévert's sense of anarchic poetry and basically optimistic populism on the other. Something of the same effect, but in a very muted form, is found in *Hôtel du Nord* (1938), which was scripted by Henri Jeanson, while the Carné-Prévert *Drôle de Drame* (1937) is perhaps the most remarkable comedy of the period, with an all-star cast including Louis Jouvet, Michel Simon and Jean-Louis Barrault.

The achievements during the late Thirties of the directors Feyder, Renoir, Duvivier and Carné, together with their principal writers (Prévert, Spaak and Jeanson), represent one of the golden ages of the French cinema. This was a period when the French cinema was widely considered the most important in the world and when it exercised a lasting influence, both on Italian neo-realism (the early work of Visconti, for example) and on the British cinema (the Forties work of Carol Reed). But with the outbreak of war in 1939 all this was swept away as production was disrupted and many of the principal film-makers were driven into exile. *ra*

Marcel Carné

4. Italy

E VEN BEFORE THE LUMIÈRE SCREENINGS in Paris, **Filoteo Alberini** received a patent (November 1895) for his home-constructed film camera and projection apparatus. In 1905, Alberini founded the firm of "Cines," in conjunction with Santoni. Their productions became very important later on. Alberini was also responsible for the first Italian feature of interest, *La presa di Roma* (1905). It was filmed in the open air against painted backgrounds. The second film capital was Turin. The producer Arturo Ambrosio shot several documentaries with his cameraman Roberto Omega. In 1908 the former typographer Luigi Maggi launched the huge series of Italian spectacular films of the period, with his vast production of *The Last Days of Pompeii* (*Gli ultimi giorni di Pompei*). When Cines began to compete with Itala-Films around the same time, **Giovanni Pastrone** (1882–1959), also known as Pietro Fosco, developed into the most important director of the early silent era. As early as 1907, with *Napoleono,* and above all with *Giulio Cesare* and *Enrico III* (both 1909), he was using real locations, and this set his work apart from the fabricated reconstruction of Zecca's epics in France. *The Fall of Troy* (*La caduta di Troia,* 1910) made use of elaborately designed model buildings as well as some eight hundred extras. The imagery of such early epics inspired later productions in the same *genre,* such as those directed by Griffith and DeMille in Hollywood.

Early Blockbusters   In 1912, Cines tried to conquer the world market with Enrico Guazzoni's *Quo vadis?* (from the novel by the Polish writer, Henryk Sienkiewicz). Yet two years later Pastrone's *Cabiria* surpassed even this. The immensely influential, exuberant poet Gabriele d'Annunzio wrote the titles for *Cabiria* and added to its subsequent prestige. In some respects Pastrone was decades ahead of neo-realism; using a dolly, he moved easily among his massive sets, giving the story an impression of authenticity. Though not an editor, Pastrone cut the film in such a way as to give it a kind of flowing rhythm. *Cabiria* was without doubt the forerunner of all blockbusters.

There were other interesting aspects of the Italian film industry between 1910 and 1920. Mario Caserini launched Lydia Borelli as a model vamp in *Ma l'amor mio non muore* (1913). The great tragedienne, Eleonore Duse, appeared in only one film (*Cenere,* 1916). Historical importance should also be attached to Nino Martoglio's *Sperduti nel buio* (1914), a slice of Neapolitan life brought to the screen with a vivid, unvarnished realism long before the more famous films of

Visconti, De Sica, or Rossellini. Giulio Bragaglia, inspired by the futuristic experiments of the writer Marinetti, shot the only early *avant-garde* movie of importance. It reached Paris and Berlin during the Twenties. The First World War put an almost complete end to the early flowering of Italian cinema. Mussolini's rise to power caused some of the better directors to emigrate, while others like Guazzoni (*Cesare Borgia*, 1920), Caserini, Pastrone, and Baldassare Negroni (*Chimere*, 1920) found their early success too much to maintain.

Not until the coming of sound was there a revival in Italian production, whose propaganda importance was eventually recognised by the Fascist *régime*. The semi-nationalised companies were organised into some kind of shape by the prominent writer Emilio Cecchi. **Mario Camerini** (*b* 1895) revealed his talent on the threshold of the sound period with *Rotaie* (1928), while **Alessandro Blasetti** (*b* 1900) inaugurated a second period of film realism in Italy with *Sole* (1929). Walter Ruttmann came as a guest from Germany to shoot the visual poem on steel, *Acciaio* (1933). Blasetti's *1860* (1934) brought to epic life the birth pangs of the Italian state under Garibaldi.

Fascist censorship came down hard on the liberal and pacifist inclinations of film directors and writers by insisting on productions with "heroic" nationalist themes, such as *Vecchia guardia* (1934, *dir* Blasetti), *Scipio Africanus* (1937, *dir* Carmine Gallone), and *Il grande appello* (1936, *dir* Camerini), which justified the attack on Abyssinia. But while the ruling ideology was glorified in the cinemas, opposition was forming among students, centred on the newly-established film school in Rome, "Centro sperimentale di cinematografia." There were also theoreticians at work like Luigi Chiarini, Umberto Barbaro, and later Pietrangeli (all teachers), who gave an aesthetic foundation to the movement that was to develop into neo-realism.

Mario Soldati (*b* 1906), in *Piccolo mondo antico* (1940) and *Malombra* (1942) took refuge from political realities by following the literary tradition of Antonio Fogazzano, while Augusto Genina (1892–1957) glorified the intervention of the axis powers in Spain and the victories of the North African campaign in *L'assedio dell Alcazar* (1940) and *Bengasi* (1942). Thus the Italian cinema offered Mussolini its final attempts to justify imperialism. *hpm*

5. Germany and Austria

U P TO 1913 the development of the cinema in Germany was meagre, compared to the spectacular progress of the French film. The most important personality of this early, archaic period was **Oskar Messter** (1866–1943), an inventor and the first film producer, in the modern sense of the term. Messter perfected the invention of the "Maltese Cross," a device for the jerky transportation of the film strip. From 1897 onwards he made and screened newsreels, using his own unique apparatus. In the same year he had built his own studios, where he started to make historical costume dramas, even though they only lasted a few minutes. Between 1900 and 1910 he devoted himself to experiments that combined film and phonograph; these early, even if technically still rather crude sound films he termed "sound images."

Yet as an industry the German cinema was nothing before the First World War, and no artistic figure of importance appeared. The true history of German film began in 1913, when Max Mack's *Der Andere* was made from a play by a famous stage writer, Paul Lindau. The theme dealt with a Dr. Jekyll and Mr. Hyde story; the principal player was Albert Bassermann, one of the most famous theatre actors of the day. At one blow this film seemed to push the cinema forward towards its status as an art form. The second important production of 1913 was Stellan Rye's *The Student of Prague (Der Student von Prag)*, with Paul Wegener in the lead. This film anticipated several themes and traits that were to characterise the German cinema in its most important phase—the Twenties: the inclination towards the ghostly and sinister, the preoccupation with morbidity, with demoniac power, and with the will of Fate, which, personified in a mighty tyrant or satanic adversary, overcomes the hero and drags him into the abyss. Siegfried Kracauer, whose book *From Caligari to Hitler* is still the best history of the German cinema prior to 1933, wrote of *The Student of Prague* and the theme of double identities in this film: "*The Student of Prague* introduced to the screen a theme that was to become an obsession of the German cinema: a deep and fearful concern with the foundations of the self."

Paul Wegener (1874–1948) and **Henrik Galeen** (18?–19?) shot another film, in 1915, which is equally well affiliated to the expressionism and romanticism of the early German cinema: *Der Golem,* the screen version of a medieval legend, in which Rabbi Loew in Prague brings to life a statue made of clay, which then turns into a monster. Unfortunately, this first Golem film has been lost; Paul Wegener's second Golem film, *Der Golem, wie er in die Welt kam*

(1920) is still in existence. It is particularly fascinating because of its angular and pointed *décor* by the art director Pölzig.

The economic prosperity of the German cinema dates from about 1917. In that year, the most important German production companies merged, supported by the German imperialist government, which was anxious, on account of the war, to use film as a propaganda tool, into a massive enterprise, the "Universum Film AG," Ufa for short. The Ufa was to become during the Twenties (and up to 1945) the major German production firm.

After the end of the First World War, the German cinema rose to extraordinary heights. Because of the inflation raging in the aftermath of war, it proved possible to offer German films at prices that discouraged competition from abroad. At this time, the amount a German film grossed in Switzerland was sufficient to recoup its production costs. By 1922 this economic miracle had reached its peak; 474 features were produced in Germany, a number never again achieved and surpassed at the time only by the U.S.A.

The peak of expressionist cinema: THE CABINET OF DR. CALIGARI

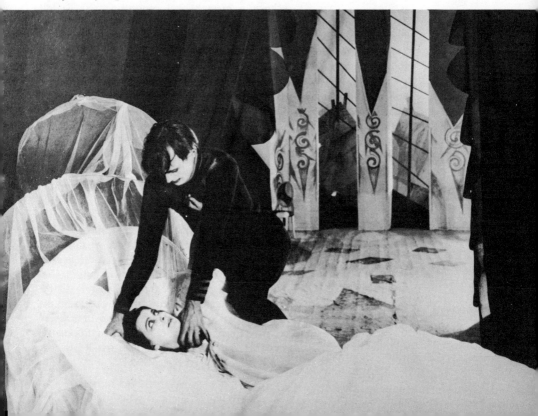

The classical era of German cinema was introduced by a work that at the same time was the signal for a new expressionistic style of film-making: *The Cabinet of Dr. Caligari (Das Kabinett des Dr. Caligari,* 1920, *dir* Robert Wiene, *script* Carl Mayer, Hans Janowitz). The film tells of a number of unexplained murders. The friend of a murdered student is investigating the crime and comes across a fairground exhibitor, who uses his somnambulist model, Cesare, to prophesy the future. As it turns out, the exhibitor is also the director of a mental home, who, fascinated by the phenomenon of somnambulism, gives criminal orders to the subdued Cesare. Finally the director of the asylum goes mad. Some critics, among them Kracauer, felt that through this construction, by which order in the world seems to be restored, the original conception of the film was distorted. Yet *Caligari* is not really disturbing because of its story. It is the expressionistic style of the narration that counts, and this style is also dominant in the framing story. Oblique, angular *décor,* pointed rooms, triangular windows, and unnatural shadows surround the actors and create a nightmarish atmosphere. The trees resemble skeletons, the roofs of the houses seem to reach into the sky, and the shadows of objects are painted directly onto the floor by set designers. The actors themselves adjusted to the expressionistic style by over-emphasising certain gestures and reactions, "by trying to achieve a metaphysical conception," as Rudolf Kurtz, a contemporary critic, wrote.

A number of other films made in Germany during the early Twenties, tried to pursue the expressionist style as shown in its purest form in *Caligari.* The most interesting was *From Morning to Midnight (Von Morgens bis Mitternachts,* 1920, *dir* Karl Heinz Martin), which was based on a play by Georg Kaiser. Here, the *décor* seemed even less pronounced and was limited to drawn and painted indications and lines. Also to be recognised as expressionistic films were Robert Wiene's *Genuine* (1920), *Raskolnikoff* (1923), and *Orlacs Hände* (1924), as well as Paul Leni's *Waxworks (Wachsfigurenkabinett,* 1924). Yet elements of expressionism can also be noted in other German films of the Twenties, particularly Jessener's *Hintertreppe,* Gerlach's *Vanina* (1922), Murnau's *The Last Laugh (Der letzte Mann,* 1924), and Lang's *Dr. Mabuse the Gambler (Dr. Mabuse der Spieler,* 1922). In many of these movies, however, expressionism was no more than a pictorial element grafted onto a story that was not suited to this style.

It has often been pointed out that the German films of the expressionistic period had a preference for cruel and tyrannical figures. The fact that these films reflected a fascination for the image of the Superman has also been stressed. This is certainly true, if one examines the most significant films of the period. The criminal doctor in *Caligari,* Fritz Lang's Dr. Mabuse, the Golem, the people shown in *Waxworks* (Harun al Rashid, a demented Ivan the Terrible, Jack the Ripper)—

in these and other leading personalities of the German film a dual feeling of fear and fascination developed towards the tyrant. This can be traced to the more realistic films of the late Twenties and the beginning of the Thirties, and is connected to the basic sense of resignation towards the forces of Destiny that runs through many German films of the time and is expressed in such works as Lang's *Der müde Tod* (1921).

Carl Mayer (1894–1944), the scriptwriter of *Caligari,* was one of the most important figures in German cinema of the Twenties. Although only active as a writer, he left his stamp on many vital films. Mayer was primarily linked to the "art films" movement, which dates back to the start of the decade. The "art films" for which he wrote the scripts—*Hintertreppe,* Lupu-Pick's *Scherben* (1921), and *Sylvester* (1923)—aimed at a strict unity of place, time and action. Their heroes were not specific personalities: Mayer preferred to call them "*the* Man," "*the* Mother," and so on. The "art films" abandoned many of the linking sub-titles so frequently used in silent cinema. They wanted to tell a story that could be understood visually without further explanation. Most of them were concerned with pessimistic, lower middle class dramas (a maid commits suicide after her *fiancé* is murdered by a jealous admirer—*Hintertreppe*); a railway worker kills his superior because he has seduced his daughter (*Scherben*); a man commits suicide because he cannot choose between his quarreling wife and mother (*Sylvester*). On the surface, the "art films" were more realistic than the expressionist productions; they also used real landscapes for their action (e.g. *Scherben*). Worldly objects are charged with a symbolic meaning in these "art films"—clocks, doors, windows appearing frequently in this way. They constitute a closed world, from which the hero cannot escape and in which his destiny is played out remorselessly.

Another type of German film in the Twenties that also elevated real objects to a symbolic significance was the "street film." The most outstanding example of the *genre* was Karl Grune's symbolic drama *Die Strasse* (1923). Here the fruitless efforts of a lower class figure to break free of his environment were given prominence. A young man, while his mother is preparing soup, strays into the "street," leaves his home and goes "outside" through various adventures until, cured of his dangerous desires, he returns home to weep bitterly in his mother's lap. The image of the street is decoratively stylised and given a mythical emphasis. The "street" represents a glittering and subversive contrast to the familiar pattern of the lower middle class world, and the negativism of *Die Strasse* can be found in many other films up to Bruno Rahn's *Dirnentragödie* and Joe May's *Asphalt* (1929).

There are certain undeniable common traits in the German films of the Twenties. Most of them were shot in an artificial studio world,

Lubitsch

showed a preference for romantic, unrealistic themes, and relied on lighting as their chief means of expression. It was also a cinema of *auteurs,* who left a definite stamp on all their films. **Ernst Lubitsch** (1892–1947) was the first of these important film-makers. After starting his career as an actor in comedies, he began to specialise during the early Twenties in historical costume dramas, among which should be mentioned *Madame Dubarry* (1919), *Anna Boleyn* (1921), and *Das Weib des Pharao* (1922). Basically, Lubitsch was not keen, as Lang was, to create a splendid display of mass action and power in his historical films. He was keener to stress the psychological pressures at work on his individual personalities, so that the story could be interpreted in the light of private grievances and opinions. Thus, in *Madame Dubarry,* the French Revolution is primarily due to the lover of Madame Dubarry, a guard at the Royal Court who is jealous of Louis XV because he has made Madame Dubarry his mistress. Lubitsch's grotesque distortion of historical events is made valid by his lively and inventive direction, his imagination, the rhythm of the individual scenes, and by the remarkable irony he brought to his work, a quality he developed later in America where it was known as the "Lubitsch touch." Lubitsch also shot a few comedies, such as *Die Puppe* (1919), *Kohlhiesels Töchter* (1920), and *Die Bergkatze* (1921), which was distinguished by its wit and sense of parody. *Die Puppe,* an ironical inversion of the E. T. A. Hoffmann theme of a girl's being changed into a doll, also contained anti-clerical and anti-authoritarian undertones. In 1922 Lubitsch went to Hollywood, and adapted himself to the American scene as no other German director managed to do— except perhaps Lang, and Lang's style had already been established in Germany, whereas Lubitsch only found his really in Hollywood.

The work of **Fritz Lang** (*b* 1890) continues to appeal to audiences at film societies and clubs, and its enduring quality may in part be due to Lang's choice of gripping themes, to his virtuoso direction, but also to the films' very marked stylisation, which gives them a formal attraction. As one French critic put it, Lang's films have a "metaphysic of architecture." Originally an architect himself, Lang wrote scripts between 1916 and 1920 for Otto Rippert and Joe May, and in 1919 he directed his first film, *Halbblut.* In the same year followed the portmanteau spy series *Die Spinnen,* which because of its baroque fantasy (in the tradition of Louis Feuillade's serials) exerts a fascination even today. *Der müde Tod* (1921), like *Dr. Mabuse the Gambler* (*Dr. Mabuse, der Spieler,* 1922), can be classified as a "tyrant film." In *Der müde Tod,* a young girl demands that Death should return her lover to her; but only when she sacrifices her own life is she reunited with him. Involved in the basic story are three fairy-tale episodes from China, Venice, and Baghdad. In this film it became clear for the first time that Lang was able to develop some extraordinary pictorial effects from his stylised architecture (e.g. when he places Death against an enormous wall that extends out of frame, or on a staircase leading to the Infinite, which is entered through a narrow, dark gateway). *Dr. Mabuse* tells of an ingenious master criminal who dreams of becoming ruler of the world, and by means of his hypnotic powers is able to achieve his ends. Later Lang shot a sequel under the title of *The Last Will of Dr. Mabuse* (*Das Testament des Dr. Mabuse,* 1933), and after the war yet another film on the same theme, *The 1000 Eyes of Dr. Mabuse* (*Die Tausend Augen des Dr. Mabuse,* 1960), again in Germany. *Dr. Mabuse the Gambler* contained another typical Lang *motif*— the fear of claustrophobia. Time and again in Lang's films people find themselves locked in a room and unable to escape while threatened. At the end of *Dr. Mabuse,* the criminal is trapped in his own hideout; in *M,* the hunted murderer tries to escape from an enclosed attic. Such situations are also found in Lang's American films (e.g. in *Fury*).

Lang continued the romantic legendary approach of *Der müde Tod* in his two Siegfried films, *Siegfrieds Tod* (1923), and *Kriemhilds Rache* (1924). He translated the classical German saga into a world of ornamental stylisation, in which moments of bathos (the artificial dragon killed by Siegfried in the forest, the idyllic *tête-à-tête* of Siegfried and Kriemhild under a blossoming tree) alternate with compositions

Peter Lorre as the child-killer in Fritz Lang's M

of great force, particularly where the architecture and *décor* are concerned. But these elaborate compositions of Lang's are not beautiful for their own sake; they illustrate and highlight the idea of an almighty Destiny that runs its inexorable course and to which everyone must submit. Of particular interest is the clash between an intriguing form and a reactionary content—in *Metropolis* (1926), a film produced by Ufa at enormous expense in the hope of winning an international audience. *Metropolis* is a "Utopia" film, showing a split between the upper and lower layers of a city of the future; while the *élite* disport themselves pleasantly in paradise gardens on the upper level, gangs of slaves have to work in subterranean dungeons, at the command of a huge Moloch machine. But the son of the city's ruler falls in love with Maria, a girl from the lower world, and thus, in the film's words, the heart overcomes the difference between the brain and the hand.

As ridiculous as this absurd story may seem, so impressive and imaginative are the scenes of the lower world—the slaves trotting metronomically from shift to shift—that one has the impression of direction, movement, and camera angles all working in intimate harmony, as one does in Fritz Lang's later films.

M (1930) is the most remarkable of all the movies Lang shot before leaving for the U.S.A. It reflects the realism which had begun to percolate the German cinema. In M Lang tells of a psychopathic child murderer (based on an actual man in Düsseldorf), who is hunted down, not by the police but by an army of beggars and is indicted at a kangaroo trial until the authorities arrive at the last moment. Several montage sequences suggest a parallel between police methods and those of the criminal underworld. As a result, the film has often been regarded as a denunciation of incipient Fascist methods in Germany, although this was perhaps never intended by Lang. These themes become more marked in *Das Testament des Dr. Mabuse* (1933), a film that was disapproved of and banned by Goebbels (this was the chief spur behind Lang's decision to leave Germany). Lang's work is notable for its realistic characterisation, its constant experiments with sound and image, and its fine construction.

While Lang was a director of strong storylines and a master of epic scenes, **Friedrich Wilhelm Murnau** (1889–1931) was important for his subtle blending of realism and fantasy, which sometimes leaned towards the weird and the sinister (as in *Nosferatu*). Most of the films he made between 1919 and 1921 have been lost. *Nosferatu—eine Symphonie des Grauens* (1922) has become a classic among horror films. Based on Bram Stoker's *Dracula*, *Nosferatu* was the first in a seemingly endless series of vampire movies, although the aesthetic refinement of this early Murnau masterpiece has never been surpassed by subsequent films in the *genre*. The special characteristic of Murnau's method is the horror that emerges from familiar, everyday surroundings. *Nosferatu* was shot mainly on location, but Murnau added a sinister dimension to the various scenes by his use of camera angles and stylistic compositions. In contrast to the ghostly world of the vampire Nosferatu, who remains aloof in his decaying castle, the world of the estate agent Hutter is described as normal and typically lower class, so that a French critic, Charles Jameux, has put forward the intelligent argument that the antagonists Hutter and Nosferatu are really two sides of one and the same personality.

Carl Mayer wrote the script of *The Last Laugh* (*Der letzte Mann*), which Murnau shot in 1924, and Karl Freund was responsible for the camerawork. Not only is the film impressive by virtue of its use of light and shade and free-wheeling camera movements; it is also distinguished by the social relevance of its story. The aged hall porter in a grand hotel is suddenly deprived of his uniform; his world collapses;

Murnau

Emil Jannings (right) as the degraded victim of Murnau's THE LAST LAUGH

his prestige and authority have disappeared. The film starts by observing the routine world of the big hotel, and gradually develops into a kind of nightmare, and Murnau invests the street, the tenements with their backyards and scolding women, and the hotel itself, with a dreamlike force. A happy ending was tacked onto the film whereby the porter becomes the heir to a fortune, but this seems unsatisfactory and arbitrary, not confirming the pessimism of the major part of the film.

Murnau's later films in Germany followed various literary trends: *Tartuffe* (1925), and *Faust* (1926). This was partly due to Ufa's determination to present "great" and "noble" themes in their productions for commercial reasons. This offered Murnau a chance to show his skill at working with light, shade, sets, and actors' movements. In *Tartuffe* the main plot was a film within a film, a brilliant conception at the time. *Tartuffe* also contained elements of social comment and was a fascinating study in contrasting personalities. Against this, *Faust* was more concerned with interesting pictorial compositions similar to those in *Nosferatu*. In 1926 Murnau left for Hollywood and, using the German author Sudermann as a source, shot *Sunrise*, the last high peak of German silent cinema.

Pabst   The development of the career of **G. W. Pabst** (1885–1967) parallels the development of German cinema up to 1933. Pabst is the typical director of the late Twenties, a period that has been identified with the term "new realism," Pabst's first film, *Der Schatz* (1924) was still under the influence of expressionism. Yet already in *The Joyless Street/Street of Sorrow* (*Die freudlose Gasse*, 1925), he was veering towards realism, with his bitter description of the economic misery caused by the inflation after the First World War. *Secrets of a*

Soul (*Geheimnisse einer Seele,* 1926) was a dramatised instructional film about psychoanalysis, based on the theories of Freud, and remains memorable by virtue of its dream sequences; a sense of disorientation is achieved not merely by *décor* and lighting as in early German silents, but also by technical devices such as multiple exposure.

In *The Loves of Jeanne Ney* (*Die Liebe der Jeanne Ney,* 1927), from a story by Ilya Ehrenburg, *Pandora's Box* (*Die Büchse der Pandora,* 1929), and *The Diary of a Lost Girl* (*Das Tagebuch einer Verlorenen,* 1929), the true style of Pabst became apparent—a style which, although it used the traditional methods of the German silent cinema, applied them in a new way to expressionism. There is no metaphysical overtone, no double meaning in Pabst's films. His sequences are built up from close-ups and points of detail; this accounts for their liveliness and fluency, qualities not achieved by any other German director of the time. But Pabst's attention was focused too closely on superficial objects, at least in his silent films, and he was unable to place his melodramatic and sentimental themes in a true perspective. But his style was undoubtedly responsible for the extraordinary screen radiance of Louise Brooks, who played the lead in both *Pandora's Box* and *The Diary of a Lost Girl.*

Pabst took a major step forward with the coming of sound. The three films he shot between 1930 and 1931 are very important. *Westfront 1918* (1930) is one of the most appealing and yet uncompromising anti-war films in cinema history. It dealt with the fortunes of four young infantrymen in the First World War, and Pabst resisted the temptation to glamorise the fighting. One of the most impressive features of *Westfront 1918* is its description of conditions at home, away from the Front. With a single shot (e.g. people queuing in front of a shop) Pabst could relate more than others could through elaborate action scenes.

The Threepenny Opera (*Die Dreigroschenoper,* 1931), the screen version of Brecht's stage play, achieved notoriety when Brecht announced his disapproval and sued the production company. It is true that Pabst's stylised, romantic vision tends to bury the polemical ingredients of the stage version. Because of a "veto" by Brecht's widow, the film has not been shown for several years in Germany.

Kameradschaft (1931) was Pabst's most politically committed picture. Taking a mining disaster at the German-French border as his example, Pabst showed how international solidarity among the workers could overcome nationalistic prejudice. In a very beautiful, if admittedly somewhat rhetorical sequence, Ernst Busch as a German miner organises with his colleagues a rescue team to help the trapped French miners, even though he is opposed by the management.

After a spell in the U.S.A., where he could not settle down, Pabst returned to Austria and finally to Germany, where, alone of the great German silent directors, he made two films under the Hitler *régime*: *Komödianten* (1941) and *Paracelsus* (1943), which, although based on historical fact, could be seen as emphasising the authoritarianism and nationalism common to Nazi cinema.

Realistic Trends before 1933
One of the most interesting phases of German film history is the period 1929 to 1933. As a result of the international depression, and the social tensions that came from mass unemployment, a few German directors—Piel Jutzi and Slatan Dudow in particular—laid the foundations for a realistic, critical, and politically committed cinema of the future, which attempted to rouse an audience into action rather than lull it with dreams and illusions. Unfortunately, this tendency was cut off in its prime by the events of 1933. Of course, realism was already apparent some years earlier in movies like Walter Ruttmann's documentary *Berlin, Rhythm of a City* (*Berlin, die Sinfonie einer Grossstadt,* 1927). The idea for a feature-length documentary struck Carl Mayer after he had been persuaded by *Battleship Potemkin* to abandon the traditional outline of the feature film. He wrote the script, and **Ruttmann** (1887–1941), who had worked as an experimental filmmaker, edited hundreds of shots of daily life in the capital into a cross-section of the city's people and places. There was no story or plot in the conventional sense, and Ruttmann held the film together by adhering to a rigid time schedule—moving forward from dawn to night. Although many individual sequences and shots are still admirable, one has to admit that Ruttmann gave only a superficial glance at the city itself, and that he was more fascinated with abstract movements and rythmical sequences *per se.*

Still, *Berlin* stimulated the production of more documentaries, and

116

four young film-makers, later to make a name outside Germany (Robert Siodmak, Fred Zinnemann, Billy Wilder, and Edgar Ulmer), followed in Ruttmann's footsteps with an unpretentious, but very successful, feature documentary about the Berlin of their time: *People on Sunday* (*Menschen am Sonntag*, 1928). The actors in the film were amateurs, and it was shot on location. The theme was the Sunday adventures of four young Berliners, average citizens with fairly undistinguished personalities. Although *People on Sunday* did not have any political axe to grind, it achieved more and came closer to the life of ordinary folk than many a more obvious "problem film." This was due primarily to its casual observation, its improvisation, and its satirical style.

Piel Jutzi (1894–19?) made a stronger attempt at social criticism with his remarkable film, *Mutter Krausens Fahrt ins Glück* (1929). It told of the fate of an old working woman who, plunged in misery because of her son's becoming a criminal, decides to commit suicide. Jutzi described the appalling living conditions of the tenement blocks and backyards where "Mother Krause" lived, and also criticised the outmoded moral standards to which she adhered. There was a sub-plot running parallel to the main story, which showed the daughter of "Mother Krause" joining the labour movement with her boy friend and taking part in street demonstrations.

Jutzi tried to pursue this approach with his sound film, *Berlin Alexanderplatz* (1931), based on the novel by Döblin. Here too fictitious action was combined with documentary material. But the pungency of the novel was somehow muted in the film version: the centre of the story was no longer the steam roller at Alexanderplatz, but the personality of Franz Biberkopf, who, in spite of crippling bad luck, does not lose faith in life, because "he has his heart in the right place." The film only convinced when it confined itself to straightforward description, and certainly not in its social and psychological pretentions.

The most significant achievement of the German film at this time *Dudow* was undoubtedly *Kuhle Wampe,* shot by the young Bulgarian **Slatan Dudow** (1903–1963) from a script by Bertolt Brecht. This was the only film which Brecht wrote and also acknowledged; it was also the only feature to appear under the Weimar Republic that openly expressed Communist sympathies. But apart from this, *Kuhle Wampe,* with its didactic approach, and its transfer to the screen of Brecht's alienation technique, established itself as a model for politically committed films of the future. *Kuhle Wampe* gave an acute picture of the despair of a Berlin working class family during the mass unemployment situation. When a young man commits suicide, the camera watches him first take off his wrist watch before slipping out of the window. This cold observation was something new in German cinema, and was promptly challenged by the censors of the time. The film was prohibited at first completely and then released with certain parts removed. Later on, *Kuhle Wampe* described the evicted family's move to a primitive housing estate, caricaturing the mentality of the workers with unerring skill. It was a film without visual pretentions or pyrotechnics, and yet despite this, the use of stylised music by Hanns Eisler, the well-judged "breaks" in continuity, and the occasional political song all emphasised that this was not reality but rather a *constructed* reality that was meant to provoke the spectator rather than make him identify with the characters.

Another famous German film of the early sound period was made from a literary antecedent: Josef von Sternberg's *The Blue Angel* (*Der blaue Engel,* 1930). As in the case of *Berlin Alexanderplatz,* it can be said that the screen version almost betrayed its original (*The Blue Angel* came from a novel by Heinrich Mann entitled *Professor Unrat*). The sharp critical comment of Mann's book was missing from Sternberg's film. The conclusion was sentimental, even sloppy, and one still identifies with the tragic end of the teacher, whereas in the novel he was ridiculed. But the merits of Sternberg's film are different. He knew how to evoke an atmosphere, to produce subtle tensions, and to surround his principal actress **Marlene Dietrich** (*b* 1902) with a glittering, erotic aura. The confidence of his style was admirable, but *The Blue Angel* was really not typical of the German cinema of 1930. Sternberg was still responding to certain expressionist traits from the films of the early Twenties.

The Hitler Period

The seizure of power by the Nazis in 1933 put an abrupt end to the best traditions of the German cinema under the Weimar Republic. There began a dark epoch of conformism and lies, under the ruthless command of Hitler's propaganda chief, Goebbels, who relished his hold over the film industry. Non-Aryan directors were forbidden from working in the studios. A "Chamber of Film" controlled all members of the film world. Censorship was extended to all stages of production, from working script to finished film, and of course the censors would only permit truly "National Socialist" sentiments to be expressed. In later years Goebbels exercised more and more control over production, in particular the newsreels, which were one of the most important features of Nazi propaganda. But even features were personally encouraged or banned by Goebbels.

Nevertheless the Nazis did not have to effect too big a change in the outlook of the German cinema, because since 1930 several "heroic" and "patriotic" films had appeared, working ideologically in favour of the Third Reich. In this respect the series of films about Frederick the Second, the Eighteenth century King of Prussia, loomed large, for they exalted militarism and authority, and thus were continued during the Nazi period. As forerunners to the Nazi cinema prior to 1933, there were *Das Flötenkonzert von Sanssouci* (1930, *dir* Gustav Ucicky), war films like *Die letzte Kompanie* (1930, *dir* Kurt [Curtis] Bernhardt), and *Dawn* (*Morgenrot*, 1933, *dir* Ucicky), as well as the "mountain films" by Luis Trenker—*Der Rebell* (1932), and *Berge in Flammen* (1931). These "mountain films," with their sentimental mystique and their heroic characters, were a specifically German *genre*, with an innate link to Fascism.

The Nazis' first move was to produce films that directly glorified the Hitler movement. Thus in 1933 *Hitlerjunge Quex* (*dir* Hans Steinhoff), *SA-Mann Brandt* (*dir* Franz Seitz), and *Hans Westmar* (*dir* Franz Wenzler) were made. But gradually the Nazis realised that indirect propaganda could be more effective. Already in 1934 any portrayal of Hitler's party and its meetings was forbidden in feature films (for Leni Riefenstahl's documentaries, see below). From then on, feature production went in two main directions: on the one hand, a flood of worthless, escapist comedies and drawing-room dramas appeared, the main function of which was (after the outbreak of war) to distract the German people from reality; and on the other hand a series of "ambitious" (and more obviously propagandist) epics were produced, glorifying great leaders, criticising other countries or races, and by their anti-Semitist views preparing for the mass extermination of the Jews.

Harlan

The star director of the Hitler period was **Veit Harlan** (1899–1964), who was adept in a variety of *genres*. In *Der grosse König* (1942), he glorified Frederick the Great and justified war; analogies between Frederick and Hitler were quite clear; in the final scene Frederick sat in a cathedral while an organ played the "Deutschlandlied." Harlan shot one of the most infamous films of this period or any other, with *Jud Süss* (1940). With every emotional and rhetorical means at his disposal, Harlan inflamed the audience's hatred of the Jews, who were described as having ruined Germany. The film was a fable, set in the past, but the cry for mass murder expressed in *Jud Süss* was unmistakable. In 1945 Harlan made *Kolberg,* another historically distorted film that tried to justify an already lost war.

Another director of Nazi propaganda cinema was Hans Steinhoff; in *Ohm Krüger* (1941), he glorified the historical leadership of the Boers at the expense of the British, who were caricatured and blamed for torturing innocent Boer women in concentration camps. There were some visual echoes of *Battleship Potemkin* in this film, and it was well known that Goebbels had been impressed by Eisenstein's work and had encouraged German film-makers to copy his example. But a National Socialist *Potemkin* could never be, and never was made.

Leni Riefenstahl

Even today some critics praise the documentaries of **Leni Riefenstahl** (*b* 1902) for their apparently aesthetic quality. Her films have a special place in the cinema of the Third Reich. *Triumph of the Will* (*Triumph des Willens,* 1934), her record of the Reichsparteitag in Nuremberg, was the propaganda film *par excellence;* it was born from the director's total identification with the "spirit" of the National Socialist movement, and raised it to an extraordinary aesthetic level. Every camera movement, every composition, evokes the intoxication of a mass occasion, in which the individual is nothing and the crowd is all. It is impossible to separate the aesthetic and political aspects of Riefenstahl's work, as some observers have done. On the contrary, every technical device in the film was there not for itself but for the justification of a monstrous political ceremony, the Parteitag, whose real point is not shown in *Triumph of the Will.*

Riefenstahl's two-part film about the Olympic Games of 1936, *Olympiade, Fest der Völker—Fest der Schönheit,* had several parallels with *Triumph of the Will.* Sport is celebrated as a mystical, even religious phenomenon. This is underlined by a weak prologue: at the start of *Triumph of the Will* Hitler appears from the clouds, and in the beginning of *Olympiade* the pillars of the Acropolis do so too. The commentary continually speaks of "Fights" and "Victories." A stylised camera technique converted even the events themselves into a kind of ritual, and the frequent introduction of shots of Hitler himself leave no doubt about the National Socialist sympathies of the director; one has the impression from the film that the Games were held solely for Hitler's benefit.

There was hardly any film opposition to Nazism in Germany, as there was to Fascism in the Italian industry. There were a few hopeful signs during the Hitler *régime,* such as Helmut Käutner's film version of a Maupassant story, *Romanze in Moll* (1943), and the tugboat drama *Unter den Brücken* (1945), the last film made before the collapse of the Third Reich, and one that faintly recalled the French realist pictures of the Thirties. But these were drops in the ocean compared to the thousand and more mainly propaganda films produced in Germany between 1933 and 1945. *ug*

AUSTRIA   Even before the invention of film (generally taken to imply the year 1895), Austrians were concerned with the projection of "living images" —and many registered patents indicate their importance: the "Lebensrad" (Wheel of Life) or Stroboskop of Simon Stampfer (1833), the "Projektions-Stroboskop" of Franz von Uchatius (1845), the "photographische Dialyt" (Ortoskop) for snapshots (Joseph Petzval, 1854), made by Voigtländer in Vienna, were significant if elementary steps towards the development of cinematography.

Yet the practical history of film in Austria begins—as in most other European countries—with the first screening of the "Cinématographe Lumière" in Vienna (March 20, 1896 at the Graphische Lehr- und Versuchsanstalt, Westbahnstrasse), after which more public showings

Michael Kertesz (Curtiz) directed DIE SKLAVENKÖNIGIN in Austria, in collaboration with Arnold Pressburger

followed. Around 1900 Karl Juhasz, Austria's first "film dealer," acquired a film apparatus (operated with lime light) and founded a touring cinema. Others followed his example. In 1903 the first permanent cinema, known as the Munstedt-Kino, was opened in Vienna's Prater, and by 1910 there were ten cinemas. Imported films from abroad, mainly from Pathé, were the staple fare of these houses, and Pathé opened its first Austrian distribution office in Vienna in 1908.

Around 1906 the photographer Louis Kolm began the production of short films (documentaries) in his attic studio (Wipplingerstrasse 16), where the first Austrian feature was made in 1908, entitled *Step by Step* (*Von Stufe zu Stufe, dir* Heinz Hanus). Apart from Kolm's "Erste Österreichische Kinofilm-Industrie," which in 1910 was remodelled as the Österreichisch-Ungarische Kino-Industrie," it was Earl **Alexander Kolowrat** (1886–1927), nicknamed "the film Earl," who, with his studio in Pfraumberg, "Sascha-Filmfabrik," became the real pioneer of the Austrian cinema. He established the studio in Pfraumberg in 1910 and in 1914 he also set up in Vienna.

The first Austrian feature films were still strongly influenced by literature and the theatre. Stage plays were filmed and stage actors, like

121

Alexander Girardi in *The Millionaire Uncle* (*Der Millionenonkel,* 1913), performed in them. Not until the beginning of the First World War did a tremendous surge forward in Austrian films take place, for the import of films from hostile foreign countries was then forbidden. In 1916 the first film studio was established in Vienna (Sievering), built by Alexander Kolowrat and his "Sascha-Messter-Filmgesellschaft," and during the same year the patriotic epic film *Vienna in War* (*Wien im Krieg*) appeared. Apart from such topical themes, exemplified in *Dream of an Austrian Reservist* (*Der Traum eines österreichischen Reservisten,* 1915), there were still literary films, adapted from such folk poets as Anzengruber, Raimund, Nestroy—even Ibsen's *Ghosts* was filmed in 1918—, as well as the much favoured "soul and love dramas" like *Letter from a Dead Woman* (*Der Brief einer Toten,* 1917, with Fritz Kortner) and *Don Juan's Last Adventure* (*Don Juans letztes Abenteuer,* 1918, with Magda Sonja). But all these works were of only moderate artistic importance.

Golden Age   After the war the Austrian cinema took a great step forward. New production companies were founded, new studios built, and in certain years over a hundred features were completed, so that one could really refer to a "Golden Age" in Viennese film production (commercially, at least, if not artistically). The prime initiator of this boom was again Alexander Kolowrat, whose "Sascha-Film-AG" tried to secure a world market for their films and turned out several gigantic epics (mostly historical in theme), following the example set by Italy and the U.S.A. These were produced at enormous expense and with huge casts on the Laeser mountain outside Vienna. They included *The Prince and the Beggar Boy* (*Prinz und Bettelknabe,* 1920), based on Mark Twain's book; *A Sunken World* (*Eine versunkene Welt,* 1922); *Sodom and Gomorrah* (*Sodom und Gomorrha,* 1922, in two parts); *Young Medardus* (*Der junge Medardus,* 1923), adapted from Schnitzler; and finally *The Moon of Israel* (*Die Sklavenkönigin,* 1924), from the novel by Rider Haggard. Kolowrat's collaborators on these films were Karl Hartl, Michael Kertesz (later Curtiz), Gustav Ucicky, Alexander Korda, Ladislaus Vajda, the actors Fern Andra, Maria Corda, Lily Damita, Lucy Doraine, Agnes Esterhazy, Anny Ondra, Ossi Oswalda, Nils Asther, Willi Forst, Theo Shall, Walter Slezak, Michael Varkonyi, and many others, who were to become famous later on the international film scene.

Another company, which also specialised in spectacular productions, was the Vita-Film-AG, established in 1919, with its own studio—the largest in Vienna—at the Rosenhügel (completed in 1923). Among their films was a *Samson & Dalila* (1922), and a beautiful version of *The Tales of Hoffmann* (*Hoffmanns Erzählungen,* 1923). But the company went bankrupt at the beginning of the inflation period, and the severity of the financial crisis resulted in cheaper productions and a strong flow of Austrian film-makers to other countries. In this atmosphere, only a few works of significance were made. They included *The Hands of Orlac* (*Orlacs Hände,* 1925, *dir* Robert Wiene, starring Conrad Veidt), *Der Rosenkavalier* (1926, *dir* Robert Wiene, starring Huguette Duflos, Carmen Cartellieri, Paul Hartmann and Michael Bohnen), *Pratermizzi* (1927, with Nita Naldi, Anny Ondra, and Ingo Sym), and *Café Electric* (1927, with Marlene Dietrich and Willi Forst). The coming of sound brought a swift end to this "Golden Age."

In retrospect, it can be seen that the Austrian silent film did not create a firm, individual image; nor did it influence the development of film art. Only a few worthwhile or interesting films were made and yet from them certain names grew, names like Erich von Stroheim, Josef von Sternberg, Fritz Lang, G. W. Pabst and others, who were to become renowned from Berlin to Hollywood.

With the arrival of sound, the crisis in the Austrian industry grew worse. "Sascha-Film" had to change with the times and merged with "Tobis-Klangfilm" to become "Tobis-Sascha-Film." Eventually the firm bought the disused Vita-Studio and from 1933 onwards produced all its films there. Although the first Austrian sound picture was already shot in 1930—*Money in the Street* (*Geld auf der Strasse, dir* Georg Jacoby)—the new phase only began in 1933, when Willi Forst made his *début* as a director with *The Unfinished Symphony* (*Leise flehen meine Lieder*). This period can be regarded as the most fruitful and most artistically important in Austrian cinema. Films of international stature appeared, such as Forst's *Maskerade* (1934, with Paula Wessely and Adolf Wohlbrueck), Erich Engel's *Riding School* (*Hohe Schule,* 1934, with Rudolf Forster), *Vaudeville* (*Vorstadtvariete,* 1935, with Luise Ullrich), Walter Reisch's *Episode* (1935), Willi Forst's *Burgtheatre* (1936, with Werner Krauss), Karl Hartl's *The Emperor's Candlesticks* (*Die Leuchter des Kaisers,* 1936, with Heinz Rühmann), Carl Froelich's *The Great Big Follies* (*Die ganz grossen Torheiten,* 1937, with Paula Wessely and Rudolf Forster), and Geza von Bolvary's *Magic of Bohemianism* (*Zauber der Boheme,* 1937, with Jan Kiepura and Martha Eggerth)—all films with particular "Austrian" themes, produced with polish and above-average *mise-en-scène.* These films were frequently distinguished at the Venice film festival, already then in existence.

When Austria came under the German Reich in 1938, independent Austrian film production was at an end. The extant companies were united under the heading of "Wien-Film-GmbH" in 1939, and were classified as part of the German Ministry for Propaganda. The popularity, however, of the "Viennese film" image caused the Minister to use Wien-Film for the manufacture of gay, musically inspired films with a specifically Austrian flavour and so between 1938 and 1945 several pictures were shot in the enlarged studios, quite different in

Austria Speaks and Sings

subject matter from other Nazi productions. Thus *Immortal Waltz* (*Unsterblicher Walzer,* 1939), *Vienna Tales* (*Wiener G'schichten,* 1940), *Hotel Sacher* (1940), Willi Forst's *Operette* (1940), *Vienna Blood* (*Wiener Blut,* 1942), and Geza von Bolvary's *Schrammeln* (1944) were made—and also one of the most notorious political films of the Third Reich, *Homecoming* (*Heimkehr,* 1941, *dir* Gustav Ucicky, starring Paula Wessely). But apart from this Wien-Film was almost a centre of secret resistance to the political unification, the tenets of National Socialism, and the preservation of Austrian "character." All this can be discerned in films whose artistic level is still undisputed. *gd*

Paula Wessely and Adolf Wohlbrück in MASKERADE

6. Scandinavia

OTTOMAR ANSCHÜTZ'S "Schnellseher" had already been to Stockholm over eighteen months before the Lumière programme made its appearance in Sweden (Malmö, June 28, 1896). The first film to be produced in the country was *Komische Begegnung,* a sketch by Max Skladanowsky, the German showman; but the pioneer Swede was **Ernest Florman** (1862–1952), a court photographer who began as a film reporter. In August 1897 he produced two short farces, *Byrakstugan* and *En akrobat har otur.* **Charles Magnusson** (1878–1948) was the key figure in the development of a national cinema. It was due to his efforts and to his enlightened policy at the head of Svenska Biografteatern (later to become Svensk Filmindustri) that Sweden established a film tradition while other countries, such as Norway and the Netherlands, failed to do so. Studios were built; technical standards were taken to an exceptionally high level (notably by **Georg af Klercker** [1877–1951] at his Hasselblad Studios outside Göteborg, where some of the most underrated of Swedish silent pictures were made). As a result of this, Sweden was able to survive a bad crisis in the Thirties and still make a creative comeback with directors like Sjöberg, Bergman, and Mattsson.

The richest phase of the silent era in Sweden was between 1914 and 1920. Two directors, **Victor Sjöström** (1879–1960) and **Mauritz Stiller** (1883–1928) were pre-eminent and have remained so in all later assessments. But they were not alone, and apart from af Klercker in the west of the country, there were several other directors of value at work in the Lidingö studios in the suburbs of Stockholm—**Ernst Dittmer** (1890–1941), **Anna Hoffman-Uddgren** (1868–1947), and **Konrad Tallroth** (1872–1926). The atmosphere was one of enthusiasm and prolificness. "There were times when the head office hardly knew more of what we were doing than the title of the picture," recalled Sjöström, "and anything called budget meeting or budget did not exist." Many films were shot on location, and the presence of mountain and pastoral landscapes gave a dimension of authenticity and elemental persuasiveness to films that might otherwise have been as stiff and portentous as contemporary efforts from Germany and Italy. Writers like Selma Lagerlöf, Ibsen, and Strindberg found their books snapped up by the film companies and converted into passionate screen dramas. The younger directors of the Sixties have attacked the traditional cinema for its lack of social engagement. True, Swedish films have rarely been radical (the work of Hampe Faustman always excepted); they have been much more concerned with the plight of the

SWEDEN: THE PIONEERS

125

Elegant comedy from Sweden: Mauritz Stiller's EROTIKON

individual and his conscience when confronted by a hostile environ-ment and a cynical society. There have been few Swedish comedies to stand comparison with those of Hollywood or France. If the Swedish cinema is by no means always a gloomy cinema, it is only occasionally free of serious overtones. Metaphysical dilemmas; the role of Destiny; the insignificance of human life and effort: these have been the com-mon factors linking one generation of directors to the next.

But Stiller, born in Helsinki of Russian descent, did manage to face the concerns of his time with a satirical eye. Comedies like *Love and Journalism* (*Kärlek och journalistik,* 1916) and *Thomas Graal's First Child* (*Thomas Graals bästa barn,* 1918) were full of visual gags that were never overstressed to the point of burlesque. They were elegant and fast-moving, and their players (Karin Molander and Victor Sjöström the best of them) went about their comic business with a relish and spontaneity that must in large measure have been due to Stiller's direction. A more famous Stiller film, *Erotikon* (1920), made a considerable impact in its era because of its *risqué* dialogue and its sumptuous "production values" (the Opera in Stockholm was filled with eight hundred extras for one scene alone). But it has lost its freshness with the years and should not be regarded as the masterpiece that many film histories claim it to be.

There was also another side to Stiller's talent. He made some very

Victor Sjöström (at right) in his own THE PHANTOM CARRIAGE

important epic films such as *Sir Arne's Treasure* (*Herr Arnes pengar,
1919*). This was adapted from a novel by Selma Lagerlöf and set in the
reign of Johan III during the Sixteenth century. The conflict between
good and evil, so marked a feature of the Swedish cinema, was here
given potent expression as the Scottish mercenaries, led by Sir Archie
(Richard Lund), escaped from prison and involved in their flight the
frail and innocent figure of Elsalill (Mary Johnson). Set-pieces like
the burning of Sir Arne's mansion (later to be surpassed by Stiller in
a magnificent fire sequence in *The Atonement of Gösta Berling*) were
blended successfully with moments of fantasy and introspection, just
as they were in a lesser known but in many ways just as stirring Stiller
film, *Gunnar Hede's Saga* (*Gunnar Hedes saga, 1922*), again based on
a story by Selma Lagerlöf.

The daily round of pastoral life and physical labour, usually associated
exclusively with Sjöström's work, was boldly caught by Stiller in *Johan*
(1921), a tale of banked-up passion showing a handsome stranger—
a familiar figure in Swedish films—fleeing by boat with a farmer's
wife. Stiller's technique and psychological perception were not so impressive in *The Atonement of Gösta Berling* (*Gösta Berlings saga,
1924*), which has unfortunately achieved a kind of embalmed emi-
nence as the "swansong" of the Golden Age of Swedish cinema. Ram-
bling, episodic, and extravagantly played, the film lacked the outdoor

authenticity of the best Swedish pictures and even the famous chase across the ice was spoilt by crude back projection and agonised close-ups of Lars Hanson's Gösta. This epic adaptation of Selma Lagerlöf's novel did, however, introduce **Greta Garbo** (*b* 1905) to a wider public, and shortly afterwards she went to Germany to play in Pabst's *The Joyless Street/Street of Sorrow,* and thence to Hollywood, in company with Stiller.

Victor Sjöström's work did not have the lissom expertise of Stiller's. It was ponderous, solemn, and doughty. But no film-maker before him had integrated landscape so fundamentally into his work, or conceived of nature as a mystical as well as a physical force in terms of film language. He was an established stage actor when, in June 1912, he was telephoned one evening by Charles Magnusson, who invited him to join Svenska Bio. Thus began a partnership that was to continue for over a decade before Sjöström, like Stiller, was attracted by Hollywood offers. He made over forty features during this time, but most of them were destroyed in the severe fire that swept through the Lidingö studios in the Forties. His first major film was probably *Ingeborg Holm* (1913), which still survives. Its social relevance was acute. Loopholes in the Poor Law regulations enabled speculators in forced labour to buy children from destitute women, and the fate of Mrs. Holm was typical. There was a stern anger in Sjöström's approach to his subject, and he did not hesitate to use scenes of hardship and sentimentality to convince his audience of the injustices of the system.

A true pantheist, Sjöström was fascinated by Ibsen's *Terje Vigen* (*A Man There Was*), about the fisherman who pierced the English blockade during the Napoleonic Wars and found his wife and child dead from starvation on his return from prison. In 1917 his film version of the poem was released, with Sjöström himself as Terje, brandishing his fists at his adversary the sea. This extraordinary vision of man's essential loneliness was evoked in *The Outlaw and His Wife* (*Berg-Ejvind och hans hustru,* 1918), where the predicament of Berg-Ejvind and the woman he loved was expressed through the landscape of Iceland (where the picture was shot). Alone in these natural tracts, leading a life of rigour and simplicity, human beings took on a dignity that was to infuse later Swedish films like *The Bread of Love* and *The Seventh Seal.*

Bucolic subjects continued to attract Sjöström, and *The Girl from the Marsh Croft* (*Tösen från Stormyrtorpet,* 1917) contrasted the life of the girl from the mountain cottage with that of the landowner's son in the valley below. The minor characters were convincing, as always in Sjöström's cinema, whether brawling in a tavern or making remarks during a court-room interrogation. They also played an imposing part in *Thy Soul Shall Bear Witness/The Phantom Carriage* (*Körkarlen,* 1921), Sjöström's version of Selma Lagerlöf's moral tale about the

Ingrid Bergman and Gösta Ekman in INTERMEZZO

drunken rascal whose soul is removed by Death's wagoner on the stroke of midnight on New Year's Eve. But the sophisticated style of the film, with Julius Jaenzon's camera achieving ghostly effects, overcame the psychological deficiencies of the affair. Here was the first Swedish film that seemed aware of the limitations of silence and determined to surmount them (when Holm is summoned by the coachman, he puts his hands to his *ears,* not his eyes).

Sjöström's career in Hollywood produced at least one masterpiece (*The Wind,* see Chapter One), but he did not really settle in America, and returned to Sweden in the autumn of 1928. Stiller was on his deathbed. The Swedish cinema was at a low ebb and remained so during the Thirties, but Sjöström lived to see a revival in the Forties and to take an active role in it as "artistic director" of Svensk Filmindustri during the war years. He continued to act in major films, and in 1957, three years before his death, he played the finest part of his career—Isak Borg in Bergman's *Wild Strawberries*.

The Thirties were a bad time for the Swedish cinema. Frivolity was the keynote of most of the films produced during the decade, although in fairness to directors like John W. Brunius and Gustaf Edgren it should be emphasised that their work urgently needs re-appraisal. Many of the films have disappeared or were burnt in the Lidingö fire. What can be said with confidence is that no major director flourished during the Thirties. **Alf Sjöberg** (*b* 1903) had shot a brilliant silent picture, *The Strongest (Den starkaste)* in 1929 and thereafter had been barred from the studios. Frustrated, he devoted his talents to the theatre. Stiller was dead. Sjöström had virtually retired from direction (except for *Under the Red Robe,* made in England in 1937). Only **Gustaf Molander** (*b* 1888) continued to turn out worthwhile entertainments such as *Swedenhielms* (1935) and *Intermezzo* (1936), which launched Ingrid Bergman on her international career as a romantic actress, and Molander was also responsible, earlier in the decade, for the first Swedish talkie of stature, *One Night (En natt,* 1931). But few of the 250 odd features produced in Sweden during the period were aimed at an international market. They were only for domestic consumption like, for example, the Danish films of the Fifties. In 1936 there was a meeting in Stockholm to protest against the poor quality of these "Pilsner" films, but it was not until the outbreak of the Second World War that standards improved.

Probably the most significant development of the Thirties was on the commercial level. Since the early years of the century Svenska Bio (Svensk Filmindustri from 1919 onwards) had dominated the production field. In the Twenties this predominance had become a virtual monopoly. But in 1930 Gustav Scheutz founded Europa Film, a company that was assured a firm future by its highly popular series of comedies—especially those starring Edvard Persson—and is still active today. In 1938, Terra Film and Sandrew Film were launched. Now at last there was a choice for the film-maker with ideas other than pandering to the taste of the masses. Marmstedt at Terra gave many opportunities to **Hasse Ekman** (*b* 1915, son of the great stage actor Gösta Ekman) during the Forties, and later he produced some of the most outspoken of Ingmar Bergman's early films. **Anders Sandrew** (1885–1957) was one of the portal figures of the modern Swedish film industry. He put Rune Waldekranz in charge of production, and for thirty years Sandrews have matched the success of Svensk Filmindustri with pictures such as *Miss Julie,* winner of the Palme d'Or at Cannes in 1950, and Bergman's *Sawdust and Tinsel. pdc*

In Denmark, the period up to 1920 was dominated by entertainment films with few pretensions—thrillers, melodramas, romances, comedies —and only one or two directors aspired to the perfection of film language that Stiller and Sjöström sought in Sweden. August Blom made a screen version of *Atlantis* (1913), from Gerhard Hauphmann's novel about a disaster at sea; **Holger Madsen** (1878–1943) was something of a stylist, judging by accounts of *Opium Dreams* and *The Spirits* (1914). But **Benjamin Christensen** (1879–1959) was the greatest of these early Danish film-makers and the least known of the world's major directors. *The Mysterious X* (*Det hemmelighedsfulde X*, 1913) was already a mature work, its pictorial effects as impressive as those of Stroheim in *Foolish Wives* some eight years later. His *Witchcraft through the Ages* (*Häxan*, 1922) was made in Sweden. In many respects this dissertation on the supernatural derived its style from medieval painters—Dürer, Bosch, Cranach, Breughel—while its spirit was unmistakably Nordic. The film was a gallery of terrifying tableaux: obscene and barbaric experiments, lusty devils appearing to ravish their victims, deformed old women (recruited from a hospice in Copenhagen). Christensen's subsequent career was rather an enigma—a period in Germany, five films in Hollywood, among them the wickedly funny and imaginative thriller, *Seven Footprints to Satan* (1929), and then back to Denmark until his death.

Apart from Dreyer (see below), the occasional talent emerged. Detlev Sierck (later, and better, known as Douglas Sirk) went to Germany to begin his career because at the close of the Twenties the Danish cinema relapsed into frivolous comedies of the kind that also predominated in Sweden.

Most of the great Scandinavian artists have couched their work in a religious or certainly metaphysical framework, whether or not they themselves have been believers. Like Ingmar Bergman, **Carl Theodor Dreyer** (1889–1968) was brought up in a strict Lutheran family, and this background more than anything else caused him to meditate on death, solitude, and sacrifice in his films, each of which had significance. From an early age, Dreyer was interested in the arts, and particularly in architecture; he began his career as a journalist. Then from 1913 onwards he was a title writer and editor at Nordisk Films, responsible for several adaptations a year.

Although Dreyer's silent films outnumber those he shot during the sound period, only *The Passion of Joan of Arc* has become famous. His first picture was *The President* (*Praesidenten*, 1920), a typically sentimental picture of the period save for Dreyer's introduction of a flashback (then rare) and, as he recalled, "for the first time, I took, to play old people, *old* men and *old* women." *Leaves from Satan's Book* (*Blade af Satans bog*, 1921) was an attempt to improve on *Intolerance*, Dreyer treating four stories separately instead of linking them together as Griffith had done in his film.

Some of his silent pictures were made outside Denmark. His third movie, *The Parson's Widow* (*Praesteenken*, 1921) was a bright and

understanding comedy that caught the mood of the Norwegian countryside, and was shot on location in the style of Victor Sjöström's
bucolic films. In Germany, Dreyer came under the influence of the
expressionist movement, and *Mikaël* (1924) was one of his most impressive achievements. Here for the first time the even pace and intimacy that were to distinguish his finest work were discernible. A film
about the artist's role in life, and the essential sympathy between
master and pupil, *Mikaël* took place in huge, grey rooms, every shot in
harmony with the whole. Dreyer's method of observing his characters'
faces from a variety of angles as they spoke gave the film an intensity
beneath its superficial calm. Benjamin Christensen played the ageing
painter-sculptor in *Mikaël*.

As a result of his anti-bourgeois study of manners, *Thou Shalt Honour
Thy Wife* (*Du skal aere din hustru*, 1925), Dreyer was invited to
France to make a film of his choice. He proposed three subjects, dealing
with Marie Antoinette, Catherine de Médicis, and Joan of Arc, and after
long discussions the last was selected by drawing matches. Forty years
after it was made, *The Passion of Joan of Arc* (*La Passion de Jeanne
d'Arc*, 1928) is probably among the five most familiar silent films. The
intimacy of the style is extraordinary (the action outruns the projection
time by only a tiny amount). Figuratively speaking, Dreyer lays bare
the soul of Joan. Only when a soul is confronted by death, he appears
to say, are its true richness and nobility revealed. Every gesture, every
slow-running tear is minutely regarded. The camera *sympathises* with

Joan, and one feels that Falconetti sacrificed herself utterly to the part. (Like Bresson's leading players, Dreyer's heroines seldom played a major role again). The long interrogation scenes are theatrical in appearance but not in tone. The enormous close-ups become symbolic: the faces of the inquisitors, some bloated, some emaciated, are scrutinised in such detail that they convey an abstract impression of intolerance. The final segment of the film, as Joan is burnt at the stake, was more dynamic in movement than the rest and showed that Dreyer could accelerate the pace when he really needed to.

For both Joan, in her interrogations, and David Gray, in his nocturnal walks in *Vampyr* (1932), life is a dark and sinister reverie. Both characters are very much shut off from their natural environment. Although shot on location in France, *Vampyr* was the most Teutonic of Dreyer's films. On one level it was naturalistic; on another it was weird and dreamlike. Patently set in the present (the flour mill in which the villainous doctor is suffocated looks quite modern), *Vampyr* still has an eerie, timeless quality. David Gray (played with almost ridiculous stuffiness by the Baron de Gunzberg, who helped to finance the picture) wanders about in curiously deserted, misty surroundings that call to mind the underworld of classical mythology—and the harvester who tolls the bell for the ferry is surely on the banks of Lethe. The ghost-like photography of *Vampyr* came from an error during the first days of filming. A false light was projected on the lens of the camera; when Dreyer and Rudolph Maté, the director of photography, saw the rushes, they decided that they should capitalise on the mistake, and, as Dreyer said, "Henceforth, for each take, we directed a false light on the lens by projecting it through a veil, which sent the light back to the camera." The whites and greys of *Vampyr* more than compensated for the clumsy acting and tangled plot. *pdc*

The other Scandinavian countries have made a more modest contribution to the cinema. In Norway the emphasis from the first was on distribution rather than production. Eventually the government recognised the cultural value of film, and a tax of ten per cent was taken from the box-office receipts on imported pictures. But even so, productions of merit were rare, and the most striking effort of the early years, *The Dangers of a Fisherman's Life* (*Fiskarlivets faror*) was directed by Julius Jaenzon, the great Swedish cameraman. Surprisingly, this drama of a sailor's son drowning before his parents' eyes was shot not at sea but on a protected stretch of water at Frognerkilen.

The first Norwegian film studio was built in 1936 at Yar, in the Oslo suburbs, although for a decade or so before this the firm of Kristiania Film had begun to produce on a steady scale. A pioneer director in this prewar period was **Rasmus Breistein** (*b* 1890), whose work ranged from seafaring films like *Miss Faithful* (*Junfru Trofast,*

Norway

1921) to *Life* (*Liv*, 1934), and *The Golden Mountain* (*Guldfjället*, 1941). Two other personalities asserted themselves: **Leif Sinding** (*b* 1895), who had a certain feeling for bucolic drama in films like *A Mountain Adventure* (*Fjälläventyret*) and an eye for the box-office in the first Norwegian screen musical, *Fantegutten* (1932); and **Tancred Ibsen** (*b* 1893), who, after a spell in Hollywood as a scriptwriter for Metro, established himself in Norway in 1931 with the first Norwegian talkie, *The Great Baptism* (*Den stora barnedapen*) and then proceeded to make a number of films in Norway and Sweden. *pdc*

Finland   Although film-makers of note have been born in Finland (Mauritz Stiller and Gustaf Molander, to name but two), the country has produced only one internationally known director (Jörn Donner). As in Norway, the early cinema was lethargic, with exhibitors only interested in importing foreign product. Even today, a Finnish film has to be seen by one in ten of the five million population if it is to be a big success. There were several documentaries of a competent standard, but it was not until 1919 that two stage actors, Erkki Karu and Teuvo Puro, founded the first significant Finnish film company—Suomi Film. Both men began directing, specialising in bucolic, pastoral themes. When sound films came on the scene, the Finnish industry found it difficult to cope with the innovation, and the situation only improved in 1934, when a consortium (Suomen filmiteollismus) was established and soon produced an average of a dozen pictures each year. Leading film-makers of this period included Risto Orko, Valentin Vaala, and Nyrki Tapiovaara. *pdc*

7. Eastern Europe

SOVIET CINEMA, which set the film-making world by its ears during its first great peak period between 1925–30, was established nearly two years after the Revolution, when the industry was nationalised in August 1919. But it was not a case of starting from scratch. Some two thousand full-length feature films had been produced in Russia between 1907 and 1917; these represented, on the one hand, a heritage of skill and experience and on the other a challenge to the young, revolutionary film-makers who wanted to break clean away from old traditions and to create a new language of the cinema.

The bulk of these pre-Revolution films, heavily influenced by German, French, Belgian and British companies which were set up in Moscow, were trite commercial farces or highly commercialised dramas of no lasting artistic value. But there were some important and highly successful adaptations of literary classics—early examples of a tradition that has been carried through into the Seventies as a consistent and high-level feature of Soviet film-making. And there were examples of socially critical and stylistically experimental films which can be seen as forerunners of the early Soviet (i.e. post-Revolution) films.

The first Russian film theatre was opened by the Lumière brothers in St. Petersburg (now Leningrad) in May 1896, soon after the coronation of Czar Nicolai II, when film pioneers and businessmen from Europe and America had flocked to Moscow and St. Petersburg to take advantage of the colourful event. The seven film reports of this occasion shown at the Lumière Cinématographe are the earliest examples of Russian-based film-making. After its success in St. Petersburg the Cinématographe toured the Russian provinces, giving audiences their first glimpse of the new invention. During the turbulent years of the early Twentieth century, Russian audiences mainly saw French films, ranging from stereotyped Biblical epics to reportage of day-to-day events. In 1905 they were able to see an on-the-spot film report of the Potemkin mutiny, later immortalised on the screen by Eisenstein. It was a French company, Pathé Frères, which made the first Russian film, *Cossacks of the Don* (*Donskiye kazaki,* 1908, *dir* Maurice Maître). Other foreign companies quickly jumped on the band-wagon of its success, making films that appealed to Russian audiences by depicting colourful aspects of Russian life.

Although various amateurs had experimented with film-making no Russian professional emerged until 1907 when Alexander Drankov shot but only partially completed a stage version of Pushkin's *Boris Godunov.* By 1910 his output was so prolific that he became a major threat to his foreign rivals, with films carefully attuned to Russian taste, including screen records of Royalty and of Leo Tolstoy who at that time was the centre of political and religious controversy. Among his most popular early films was *Stenka Razin* (1908), a very romanticised account of the life of the legendary peasant leader. His flair for showmanship rather than serious film-making can be deduced from the titles of the wartime films produced by his company, such as *The Bloody Fortnight, Thirsty for Love* and *In the Claws of the Yellow Devil.*

Of much higher artistic value were the films made by the company of Alexander Khanzhonkov, which included many splendid screen adaptations of the classics as well as original films rooted in Russian tradition. Among the outstanding directors employed by Khanzhonkov and later, in some cases, by the company of another important producer, **Yosef Yermoliev** (1890–1962) were **Vasili Goncharov** (1861–1915), mainly known for his historical films, including the ambitious *Defence of Sebastopol* (*Oborona Sevastopolya,* 1911); **Yevgeni Bauer** (1865–1917), a brilliant director of contemporary subjects; **Pyotr**

Chardynin (1872–1934) who often dealt with epic themes, and **Alexander Volkov** (1885–1942). Another company with serious aspirations was that of Thiemann and Reinhardt which, although not Russian in the native sense, gave scope to many up-and-coming Russian directors. Among their most important directors were **Yakov Protozanov** (1881–1945) and **Vladimir Gardin** (1877–1965).

Protozanov, who had previously worked under Drankov and Kranzhonkov, was a prolific director who could bring distinction to a wide range of *genres* and who continued to make a steady contribution to cinema in the post-Revolution years. In 1913 he collaborated with Gardin on *Keys to Happiness* (*Klyuchi schastya*), a sentimental drama based on a best-selling novel, which proved to be the greatest box-office success of pre-Revolution Russia. One of his most important films in this period was a very attractive version of Pushkin's *Queen of Spades* (*Pikovaya Dama*, 1916).

The outstanding actor in the prewar period was Ivan Mozhukin (or Mosjoukine). Any film in which he featured was assured of a good public; he was the most sought-after actor of his day. Among the actresses, Vera Kholodnaya was the brightest and most talented star.

By 1910, there were some fifteen "Russian" companies, most of them branches of foreign companies, which flooded the market with costume dramas based on historical and Biblical themes. The outbreak of the First World War freed the Russian industry from foreign domination and native output became prolific. The productions were, in the main, (as has already been indicated through the work of Drankov), lurid and low-level dramas which sprang from, or perhaps compensated for, the tragic atmosphere of the times. An important exception— considered by the film historian Jay Leyda to be the most significant of all pre-Revolution films—was *A Picture of Dorian Gray* (*Portret Doriana Greya*, 1915), made by the great theatre experimenter **Vsevolod Meyerhold** (1874–1942) through the auspices of Paul Thiemann, after Thiemann's partner Reinhardt had been forced to leave the country because of rising anti-German feeling. Meyerhold's subsequent film under Thiemann, *The Strong Man* (*Silnyi chelovek*, 1917), based on the first novel of a trilogy by the Polish writer Stanislaw Przybyszewski, was a work of such striking realism and harsh cynicism that it was held up from release.

The outbreak of the Revolution in November 1917 ended Russia's participation in the war and many of the leading film personalities fled to Europe. Among them were Yermoliev, Volkov, **Viatcheslav Turzhansky** (*b* 1892), Protozanov, the actor Mozhukin, the actress Natalia Lissenko, and the brilliant animator **Wladyslaw Starewicz** (1892– 1965). Together with other fugitives from the Revolution, they formed a successful *émigré* film-making group in Paris. Protozanov returned to the Soviet Union in 1924.

The first Soviet film organisation was founded as a sub-section of the Ministry of Education on November 9, 1917—two days after the establishment of Soviet power. A film school was opened in Leningrad later in the year, and the following year a similar one was set up in Moscow. In August 1919, after a long and bitter struggle (in which the poet Vladimir Mayakovsky was deeply involved) between the young Soviet government and the commercial distributors, the industry was nationalised. With the country torn apart by civil war, devastated by foreign troops and ravaged by famine, the nationalised industry was not able to become very effective until 1922. It was in February of that year that Lenin made his famous remark to the Minister of Education, Anatoli Lunacharsky: "You are known among us as a protector of the arts so you must remember that, of all the arts, for us the cinema is the most important." This dictum, with some discussion about the significance of the words "for us," has been a guiding principle of Soviet production ever since.

In the early days of nationalisation, the studios were in an appalling state of disrepair and stocks and equipment were in desperately short supply. The first productions of the nationalised industry tended to be "agit-prop" productions designed to rally the people behind the new government, shot from scripts by, among others, Lunacharsky and Mayakovsky. Following pre-Revolution traditions, a number of screen versions of the classics were made in this period. **Alexander Sanin** (1869–1955), for instance, filmed a very successful *Polikushka* (*Polikushka*, 1919), based on a Tolstoy story, in the unbelievably harsh conditions of the winter of 1919–20, and *The Thieving Magpie* (*Soroka-vorovka*) in 1920. **Yuri Zheliabuzhsky** (1888–1955), cameraman of *Polikushka,* directed a screen version of Pushkin's children's story *Father Frost* (*Morozko,* 1924) which he followed with Pushkin's *The Stationmaster* (*Kollezhski registrator,* 1925). Also based on a literary work, but more experimental in concept was the screen version of Alexei Tolstoy's *Aelita* (1924) set on Mars and in the Soviet Union in the years 1919–20, and directed by Protozanov who returned to the U.S.S.R. from France in 1924. In each of his subsequent silent films Protozanov continued quietly and steadily to experiment with new ways of adapting literary classics for the screen, and in 1927 he made the first screen version of *The Forty-first* (*Sorok pervyi*). (A new version was made in 1956 by Grigori Chukhrai.)

One of the most popular films of the period which, although no masterpiece, has remained a favourite with children over many generations, was *The Red Imps* (*Krasniye diavolyata,* 1923) made in Georgia by **Ivan Perestiani** (1870–1959), about the adventures of a group of children during the Civil War.

In this transitional period, many film-makers were beginning to come to grips with contemporary subjects and to break away from traditional styles. **Abram Room** (*b* 1894), for instance, turned his back on the glamorised, commercial approach for *Bed and Sofa* (*Tretya maschanskaya,* 1924), a comedy highlighting the housing shortage, about a husband (played by Nikolai Batalov) who invites a friend to share a room which is already driving the wife to distraction because it is so small.

Many people were involved in the search for new approaches to cinema, but two pioneers in particular played a key part in laying the theoretical basis for the great burst of film creativity which reached its peak in the second half of the decade. They were the experimenter, theoretician and educationalist **Lev Kuleshov** (*b* 1899) and **Dziga Vertov** (1896–1954), who revolutionised the newsreel.

Kuleshov was only eighteen when he directed his first film, *Engineer Prite's Project* (*Proyekt inzhenera Praita,* 1918). He had already gained experience as a designer before the Revolution and he published his first theoretical articles in 1917. He led a group of cameramen and actors at the front during the Civil War, and afterwards set up a "workship" at which he and his fellow-enthusiasts studied film principles in the abstract, being unable to obtain any means of putting their theories into practice. Their first opportunity came in 1923, when they were given facilities to make the comedy *The Extraordinary Adventures of Mr. West in the Land of the Bolsheviks* (*Neobychainiye priklucheniya Mistera Vesta v stranye bolshevikov,* 1924). Through the character of an American tourist in Russia, it satirised the wild tales that were being circulated in the Western press about life in the young Soviet Republic. It was a major attempt to break away from traditional style and to establish certain elementary rules of cinema language. Despite some severe technical weaknesses, it was a great success, encouraging the group to carry its theories further in its second film, *The Death Ray* (*Luch smerti,* 1924–25), in which it tried to extend the action style of the best American and French adventure films by using the group's most advanced techniques. It was a failure, and the group was sharply criticised for its lack of ideology and for its emphasis on experiment for its own sake. But Kuleshov's theories, his experiments, and his practical work provided the basis on which Eisenstein and Pudovkin later created their masterpieces.

Dziga Vertov Vertov (born Denis Kaufman) fought as a conscript in the First World War. During the Civil War, he was chief newsreel cameraman with a partisan army. By the age of twenty-two he had become head of the cinema department of the All-Russia Central Executive Committee and it was in this period that, very much influenced by Mayakovsky's aesthetic approach, he developed his celebrated theory condemning "play-films" and establishing the camera as a "film-eye." "I am the film eye," he wrote. "I am in perpetual motion. I approach and recede from objects. I climb under them. I climb into them. I move

alongside the muzzle of a running horse. I barge into a crowd. I run before running soldiers. I fall on my back. I rise with aeroplanes. I fall and soar with falling and soaring bodies. . . ." In 1919 he formed a group of *avant-garde* enthusiasts called Kinoki (Film-Eye Group), and three years later began issuing monthly newsfilms, *Kino Pravda* (*Film Truth*), based on his revolutionary conceptions of newsreel reportage. Controversy raged sharply, but the films—twenty-three of them—were tremendously popular. He and his brother, Mikhail Kaufman, would roam the streets in search of subjects, which they shot with the new, hand-held cameras that were to regain popularity forty years later. Working from a damp, rat-infested basement, Vertov received material from cameramen stationed all over the Union. Here, with the help of his assistant, Yelizaveta Svilova, he built up his new-style newsreels—lively, immediate and unpredictable.

Because of shortage of stock, he was forced to include pre-Revolution footage; but this proved to be a blessing in disguise, for the contrasting juxtaposition of the old and new brought an additional dramatic quality to his films. In 1925, his two shorts about the death of Lenin, in the Kino-Pravda series, introduced a new element of emotional involvement that he developed more fully in the late Thirties.

Gradually the camera itself, the eye of the audience, became a kind of participant in the film. His most dazzling and controversial silent film was *The Man with a Movie Camera* (*Chelovek s kinoapparatom*, 1929), for which he indulged in every kind of virtuoso trick, earning the film a great deal of criticism as well as praise. Vertov's early films, his experiments and his theories were of key importance to the development of Soviet cinema, and, in particular, exerted a great influence on the subsequent work of Eisenstein.

Esther Shub (1894–1959) contributed to the development of the documentary in a quieter and more sensitive way, raising the art of newsreel compilation to new heights. Her five years in the cutting-room had provided her with a great insight into the meaning and potential of every frame. Through the most painstaking archive research and with a deep understanding of the dramatic effect of the juxtaposition of contrasting materials, she assembled fragments of old footage to compile forceful film chronicles of the past. Her best-known films are *The Fall of the Romanov Dynasty* (*Padeniye dinasti Romanovikh*, 1927) and *The Great Road* (*Veliky put*, 1927), based on newsreel footage from the previous ten years, which she made in honour of the Tenth Anniversary of the Revolution.

The year 1925 was the opening of a period of Soviet film-making so rich and dynamic that its influence was felt throughout the world and reaches forward to the present day. To understand its background, one must appreciate the atmosphere of the time. The young Soviet country, which had been devastated by war and famine, was at last beginning to become busily engaged in building its future. The entire country was bustling with idealism, activity and controversy. The intellectuals (minus those who had fled during and immediately after the Revolution) were fired with enthusiasm for the Revolution but had contradictory ideas about how best to work for it. Novelists, poets, painters and musicians were all experimenting and searching for forms in which to express the revolutionary concepts. It was no accident that the new ideas found their most powerful expression in the newest of arts—the cinema. And indeed, many of the dozens of highly talented and versatile film-makers who emerged in this period might well, in another era, have made their mark in other creative fields. The spectrum of masterpieces and near-masterpieces that emerged, revolutionary in content as well as in technique, were no mere propaganda pieces (as their detractors have, from time to time, suggested) but sprang from the very spirit of the times.

The 1925–29 period brought forth many famous names in Soviet cinema; greatest of them all were the three screen masters—Eisenstein, Pudovkin and Dovzhenko.

EISENSTEIN **Sergei Mikhailovitch Eisenstein** (1898–1948), born into a well-to-do family in Riga, displayed a talent for art at an early age. At the Petrograd Institute of Civil Engineering, where he studied architecture, he developed a deep interest in the life and work of Leonardo da Vinci; his interest in Freud helped to give him an insight into some of the undercurrents of human behaviour. As a volunteer in the Red Army during the Civil War, he organised an amateur theatre company among his fellow-soldiers. In Moscow after demobilisation, Eisenstein joined the workers' theatre movement, "Proletkult," the first experimental theatre of its kind (which owed much to the leadership of Meyerhold), as designer and director. The methods used by this group, including the staging of massive pageants, the re-enacting of recent history and the use of film in stage presentations, were important influences on Eisenstein's cinema work. A visit by the Japanese Kabuki Theatre, with its stylised traditions, was a further influence on Eisenstein's development. Arising from these experiences, he made his first film, *Strike* (*Stachka*), in 1924–25.

This was the beginning of his famous partnership with the brilliant and inventive cameraman **Edouard Tissé** (1897–1961) who worked with him on all his films (although only on the exteriors in *Ivan the Terrible*) and with **Grigori Alexandrov** (*b* 1903), who was co-director on all his silent films. It was during this period that Eisenstein developed in detail his principles of film construction—each shot representing a subjective view of the total sequence and montage (the linking of one shot to another) used not just as a means of going from A to B but as a dramatic force in itself. It was this approach that made *The Battleship Potemkin* (*Bronenosets Potyomkin,* 1925) such a startling film

The Odessa Steps sequence from BATTLESHIP POTEMKIN

experience in its time, influencing all subsequent film-making; and which keeps it alive to-day, as one of the masterpieces of world cinema. *Potemkin* was planned as a long film to be made in celebration of the twentieth anniversary of the unsuccessful 1905 Revolution. But the single episode—the mutiny of the sailors on the battleship; the mounting anger of sailors and civilians when a young sailor is shot; the mowing down of the crowds by the White Guards in the famous Odessa steps sequence—gradually absorbed all Eisenstein's attention. Its scenario grew in conception and detail during the actual shooting— a contrast with Eisenstein's later work, for which he planned every detail in advance, even down to the faces of the characters, for which he would seek actors who would match his sketches. Even Tissé's beautiful shots of mists were extemporised—an inspired use of a natural phenomenon which to a lesser cameraman could have spelt disaster.

Eisenstein's following film, *The Old and the New* (*Staroye i novoye,* 1929) was about the clash between the old and the new in the struggle for collectivisation in agriculture. Work on it was interrupted while the production team embarked on a race against time to make a film in celebration of the tenth anniversary of the Revolution. They took three months to complete *October* (*Oktyabr,* 1927) an explosive, polemical account of the key events that led to the Revolution, known in most countries as *Ten Days that Shook the World.* It was a bold and dynamic film, full of striking and dramatic action sequences culminating in the famous "Storming of the Winter Palace," their impact heightened by Eisenstein's brilliant use of montage. It was imbued with sardonic humour satirising the politicians who were trying to hold up the crumbling edifice of the old order, and intensely packed with symbolic references and visual puns. *October* was not liked in official circles, where Eisenstein was accused of "formalism"—an accusation which was to oppress him with increasing weight throughout the rest of his life.

The Old and the New (known abroad as *The General Line*) was the most personal of the Eisenstein films—a quiet, beautifully composed epic of the countryside, built around the experiences of a peasant woman who persuades some of her neighbours to join up their lands and form a collective farm. Their first investment is in a cream separator, and there is a memorable scene in which the peasants gather round their new acquisition, doubtful and suspicious at first, until the wonderful moment when the cream begins to drop slowly into the bucket.

After *The Old and the New,* Eisenstein, Alexandrov and Tissé set out for the West on a year's leave, including an abortive period in Hollywood. Plans for two films, *Sutter's Gold* and *An American Tragedy,* were wrecked, largely through the political cold feet of the Hollywood tycoons who had originally commissioned them. The scenarios, which can be read in Ivor Montagu's lively account of the trip, *With Eisenstein in Hollywood,* give an indication of what might have been

Angry argument in Pudovkin's STORM OVER ASIA

achieved. The three faced further disappointments when they left Hollywood for Mexico, to make a film depicting Mexican history, *Que Viva Mexico!*

PUDOVKIN

Vsevolod Illareonovitch Pudovkin (1883–1953) was a chemist from Moscow University until the First World War when he volunteered for military service and spent several years as a prisoner of war in Germany. He joined Kuleshov's workshop as an actor, and he had a role in *The Extraordinary Adventures of Mr. West.* But he became increasingly absorbed by Kuleshov's general teachings and in 1925 made his first film as a director, *The Mechanism of the Brain* (*Mekhanikha golovnovo mozga*), a straightforward documentary about scientific research, followed by a two-reel comedy *Chess Fever* (*Shakhmatnaya goryachka*). His three subsequent films, *Mother* (*Mat,* 1926), *The End of St. Petersburg* (*Konyets Sankt-Peterburga,* 1927) and *The Heir to Ghengis Khan* (*Potomok Chingis-Khan,* 1928) known abroad as *Storm over Asia,* put him among the forefront of world directors.

Pudovkin's appeal is more immediately emotional than Eisenstein's because he is more concerned with character and narrative; but his attack is equally forceful. He used mixed casts of professionals and actors, but he chose his professionals carefully, searching for actors whose backgrounds matched the roles they were to play and using the amateurs to add realism to the less demanding roles. Unlike Eisenstein, he did not use montage to build up a single experience from its different aspects, but cut swiftly from one action to the next, or from symbol to dramatic reality, propelling the narrative forward with tremendous pace and passion.

This technique gave *Mother,* based on the Gorky novel, its powerful emotional impact and heightened the bitterness of its tragic ending. At the beginning, the mother, movingly interpreted by Vera Baranovskaya, is leading a wretched and miserable life, beaten almost to stupefaction by her brute husband. Through the arrest and imprisonment of her son, played by Nikolai Batalov, she is seen proudly bearing the flag at the head of a workers' demonstration before being trampled to death by the cavalry as they ride the demonstrators down. Baranovskaya gave another memorable performance in *The End of St. Petersburg,* which was about an ignorant peasant lad who goes to St. Petersburg to look for work and, in the explosive atmosphere of the years preceding the Revolution, begins to understand his own role in the clash of political forces. Pudovkin placed his fictional drama against a broad canvas of historical events. His amazingly fast, sometimes almost subliminal, cutting pointed vivid social contrasts—between the aggressive equestrian statues of the city and the personal dramas developing in their shadows; between the excited bobbing of bowler hats as profits soar at the Stock Exchange and the wretchedness of the men on the picket line at the factory where the workers are on strike; between the nationalistic fervour of the middle-class civilians when war is declared and the sufferings of the peasant, now a soldier, in the mud and pain of battle.

The Heir to Ghengis Khan was a much more complex film, combining adventure, personal drama, political passion, symbolism and documentary reconstruction with flamboyant sweep. Its background is the clash between the White Army and Red Partisans on the steppes of Central Asia during the Civil War. It is about a young Mongol trapper who joins the partisans after a riot caused by a European trader who has cheated him over the sale of a valuable fur. When he is captured and shot by the Whites, they discover among his belongings an amulet proving him to be the direct descendant of Genghis Khan. Finding him still alive, they resuscitate him and present him to the local people as their new king. The ceremony goes quietly until the trapper recognises his valuable fur round the neck of the general's daughter. He grabs it; in the riot that follows, he smashes up the Ceremonial Hall and gallops back to the partisans, whom he leads to victory. This strong story, told with rich visual symbolism, made tremendously dramatic cinema.

DOVZHENKO   **Alexander Petrovitch Dovzhenko** (1894–1956), son of Ukrainian peasants, began his working life as a schoolteacher. A gifted artist, he

144

Still from Dovzhenko's pastoral master-piece, EARTH

later became a cartoonist on a newspaper. In 1925 he began writing scenarios and in 1927 he directed his first feature film, *The Diplomatic Bag* (*Sumka dipkurera*). The script was trivial and this routine spy story reflected little of the true Dovzhenko spirit. His next film, *Zvenigora* (1928), a collection of legends linked by the symbol of hidden treasure, displayed a wealth of experimentation, lyricism and fantasy surprises. Although it was not wholly successful, Dovzhenko himself accurately summed up its qualities as "a catalogue of all my creative possibilities." This potential found its first full expression in *Arsenal* (1929). Beginning with war and ending with the bloody suppression of a revolt among Kiev factory workers, it was a tragic film poem of the Ukraine. Epic in proportions, unshackled by story-telling devices, it flowed like a song, intensely personal, rich in emotion and revolutionary ardour.

Dovzhenko's work in the silent era reached its peak in 1930 with *Earth* (*Zemlya*), depicting the agricultural revolution—the conflict between the old peasant farming methods and the new collectivisation. The story itself is spare—a clash between the younger peasants of a Ukrainian village, who venture into the beginnings of co-operation by buying a tractor, and the kulaks, or rich peasants, who defend their boundaries against encroachment by the collective. A film of great lyricism and beauty, unfolded at the slow, rhythmic pace of nature, and enriched by Dovzhenko's deep feelings for the natural cycle of life and death, it is one of the masterpieces of world cinema and had a profound influence on the subsequent development of Soviet filming.

While Eisenstein, Pudovkin and Dovzhenko were the three cine "giants," each representing the highest peak of one aspect of Soviet

145

film-making, there were many other gifted film-makers of the period whose works have become world classics.

Among the most important were the young Leningrad film-makers **Grigori Kozintsev** (*b* 1905) and **Leonid Trauberg** (*b* 1902) who, like Eisenstein, had gained their first experience in the experimental theatre movement.

In 1921, Kozintsev and Trauberg had gathered a group of young enthusiasts around them and founded F.E.X. (Factory of Eccentric Actors), which aimed at bringing the principles of circus and music hall on to the traditional stage. Their stage productions aroused some antipathy among critics but attracted enough attention for them to be invited to make films. Their early screen productions made little impact; their first undoubted success was their eccentric version of Gogol's *The Cloak* (*Shinel,* 1926).

Their most striking contribution to silent cinema was *The New Babylon* (*Novyi Vavilon,* 1929), in which Pudovkin took a small acting role. A highly stylised and sharply sardonic drama, it was set in an elegant department store in Paris during the Paris Commune of 1871 and contrasted the styles of living and the political and national loyalties of the rich and the poor of the times. The directors invited **Dmitri Shostakovitch** (*b* 1906) to write a musical accompaniment, and thus the young composer made his first contribution to film music—the beginning of a long association with cinema based on the principle that musical score is neither an accompaniment nor a background illustration, but an integral part of the film.

Trauberg's younger brother, **Ilya** (1905–1948), who had worked as assistant on *October,* made *The Blue Express* (*Goluboi ekspress,* 1929), an exciting adventure story undershot with a political allegory in which the train symbolises China moving rapidly towards Communism and the class divisions in the train symbolises the political groupings.

Among those who adhered very successfully to the older traditions was the former actress **Olga Preobrazhenskaya** (*b* 1884) who had played in many of Protozanov's films before the Revolution and who had begun directing in 1915. Her *Women of Ryazan* (*Babi Ryazanskye,* 1927), deeply rooted in Russian peasant lore, told a sombre story in orthodox style but was remarkable for its warm and poetic evocation of the countryside and its people. **Boris Barnet** (1902–1965) also used a conventional approach for *The House on Trubnaya Square* (*Dom na Trubnoi,* 1928), a simple satire on satirical contemporary Moscow life, which was one of the best of his comedies.

Many noteworthy directors gained their early experience during this fertile period. **Yuli Raizman** (*b* 1903) worked with Protozanov before making his first major film *Penal Servitude* (*Katorga,* 1928), a strong but pessimistic account of an unsuccessful revolt in a Siberian prison camp in the early part of the century. **Friedrich Ermler** (1898–1967) and **Sergei Yutkevitch** (*b* 1904) made their *débuts* as directors and **Alexander Zarkhi** (*b* 1908) and **Yosef Heifitz** (*b* 1905) who had worked together as scenarists, began their long and fruitful directing partnership in 1929 with *Facing the Wind* (*Veter v litzo*).

Mark Donskoy (*b* 1901) who collaborated with Mikhail Averbach on *In the Big City* (*V bolshom gorod,* 1928), made his first independent full-length film *Fire* (*Ogon*) in 1930.

A strong group of creative directors was developing in the Georgian studios, led by **Nikolai Shengalaya** (1903–1943), **Mikhail Chiaurelli** (*b* 1901) and **Yefim Dzigan** (*b* 1898).

Mikhail Kalatozov (born Kalatozishvili in 1903), who was to become one of the leading figures in the "new wave" in Soviet cinema in the mid-Fifties, entered the film industry as a cameraman, and turned to direction in 1929. His *Salt for Svanetia* (*Sol Svanetii,* 1930), a harsh and impassioned exposition of the primitive conditions endured by an isolated community in the Caucasus, has been acclaimed as a masterpiece.

Founder of the cinema in neighbouring Armenia was **Amo Bek-Nazarov** (1892–1965).

Because of the relatively late arrival of sound techniques in Europe, Soviet film-makers were able to avoid most of the more obvious pitfalls into which the Hollywood companies, anxious to exploit the new development, had fallen. The film industry was in any case going through a massive reorganisation on a more centralised basis, with several new studios completed and others still under construction, and the transition from silent to sound pictures was integrated with the general changes that were taking place.

In 1928, Eisenstein, Alexandrov and Pudovkin had issued a joint manifesto about sound. They warned against the naturalistic use of sound and proposed that it should be used as a counterpoint to vision rather than its duplicate. But despite some notable achievements with imaginative use of sound, the general run of films inevitably became more naturalistic.

The first sound films were documentaries and none aroused more controversy than Vertov's *Symphony of the Donbas* (*Entuziazm* 1931). Vertov, excited by the new possibilities, exploited them to the full— some thought too fully—cutting the sound with the same dashing technique with which he cut the visuals. Three years later he produced his finest sound film, *Three Songs of Lenin* (*Tri pesni o Leninye*), a calmer and deeply felt film based on folk ballads sung by peasant women of the Ukraine.

Early experiments with "talkies" included Raizman's *The Earth Thirsts* (*Zemlya zhazhdyot* 1930), about the conflict between a group of young Communist engineers constructing a canal and the Bey of the district who does everything he can to obstruct them, and *Alone* (*Odna,* 1931, *dir* Kozintsev and Trauberg) about a young teacher from Leningrad whose first assignment is in the wilds of Altai. Both these films were sound adaptations of productions planned as silents. Then came *Road to Life* (*Putyovka v zhizn* 1931), the first to be conceived wholly in terms of sound. Based on a real-life experience, it is about a teacher who forms a settlement of wild youngsters who had lost their parents during the turbulent years of the revolution and the Civil War, and were roaming the streets and countryside in marauding bands. It is a film of enormous human appeal, full of lively incident and character interest, funny and touching at the same time. There are memorable performances in it from Nikolai Batalov as the teacher and from a Chuvash boy, I. Kryla, in the colourful and tragic role of the young delinquent Mustapha. It represented an enormous technical and artistic triumph for its young director **Nikolai Ekk** (*b* 1902).

After the first Five Year Plan was adopted in 1928 the whole energy of the Soviet people was devoted to a massive programme of industrialisation and reconstruction, and the newly-centralised film industry was closely geared to the overall plan. Special importance was attached to the cinema, and film-makers were offered better facilities than they had ever had before. Emphasis was placed on the need for films that would inspire people in their immense construction tasks. The officials at the head of the industry, however, were non-specialists who took a narrow and over-simplified view of creativity, and under their top-heavy influence many of the films about industrialisation tended to be schematic in conception and dogmatic in style. These characteristics were apparent in one of the most ambitious productions of the early Thirties, *Counterplan* (*Vstrechnyi* 1932), which investigated the personal problems and conflicts among workers engaged on a race against time to complete the construction of a gas turbine. The task which the directors, Yutkevitch and Ermler, set themselves—an analysis of the nature of collective work and the social relationships it involves—was too complex and led to a didactic approach. But there were some fine performances, and a musical score by Shostakovitch, the main theme of which has long out-lived the film.

The Vassilievs

Films that looked backwards to the Revolution and the Civil War were less burdened by problems of style. There was a move away from simple, generalised heroics, with emphasis placed on individual personality. The first major success in this direction was *Chapayev* (*Chapayev* 1934), made by **Sergei** and **Georgi Vassiliev** (1900-1959 and 1899–1946) a young directing team whose previous film *A Personal Matter* (*Lichnoe delo,* 1932) had dealt with a similar theme. It is an intimate and personalised study of Chapayev, a highly individualistic partisan fighter who became a leader of the Red Army. It is rich with humour and incisive little details of character and back-

148

ground and has an affectionate appreciation of human frailty. It was an immediate success with critics, public and authorities and remains one of the most popular Soviet films of all time.

Trauberg and Kozintsev also went deeply into character exploration with their *Maxim Trilogy*. This very perceptive trio of films, brilliantly shot by **Andrei Moskvin** (1901–1961) with music by Shostakovitch, is about a St. Petersburg labourer who becomes Minister of Finance. *The Youth of Maxim* (*Yunost Maksima*, 1935) shows how he becomes involved in the revolutionary movement before the First World War. In *The Return of Maxim* (*Vozvrascheniye Maksima*, 1937) he is seen as an experienced political worker and *The Vyborg Side* (*Vyborgskaya storona*, 1939) brings his story up to the period of the Civil War.

The popular films of 1936, both concerned with events in the Baltic region, illustrated divergent approaches to revolutionary themes. *We*

CHAPAYEV, one of the finest Soviet action films of the Thirties

from Kronstadt (*Miy iz Krondstdat, dir* Dzigan) is an account of the struggles of the Baltic Fleet during the Civil War and wars of intervention. It is a warm and spirited film, with some pleasing human touches, but the characters are lightly sketched in and their heroism is over-simplified. In contrast, *Baltic Deputy* (*Deputat Baltiki*), about a lonely, elderly professor who finds friendship among the Baltic Fleet sailors and is elected as their deputy to the Petrograd Soviet, was a highly personalised drama with a remarkable lead performance from **Nikolai Cherkasov** (1903–1966) who gained world fame through this role. It was directed by Zarkhi and Heifitz, who pursued a slightly similar theme in *Member of the Government* (*Chlen pravitelstva*, 1939) about a peasant woman on a collective farm, played by Vera Maretskaya, who becomes a member of the Supreme Soviet. This film is also notable for its striking central performance. Zarkhi and Heifitz continued to work together until 1953.

In more romantic mood were the films of **Lev Arnshtam** (*b* 1905) who had been in charge of sound recording on the Kozintsev-Trauberg film *Alone*. His *Girl Friends* (*Podrugi*, 1936) was a touching and lyrical account of the bond between three front line nurses, with a splendid lead performance from Zoya Federova. *Friends* (*Druziya*, 1938) depicted the gradual breaking down of old barriers and prejudices between peoples of different nationalities in the North Caucasus during the Revolution.

A particularly lively and attractive drama of the Revolution was Raizman's *The Last Night* (*Poslednayaya noch,* 1936) scripted by **Sergei Gabrilovitch** (*b* 1899).

Musicals were popular throughout the Thirties, especially those of Eisenstein's collaborator, Alexandrov, who began making films independently in 1934. *The Jolly Fellow* (*Veselye rebyata*, 1934; also known as *Jazz Comedy*), *Circus* (*Tzirk*, 1936), *Volga-Volga* (1938) and *Bright Paths* (*Svetlyi put*, 1940) were lively singing-and-dancing films with infectious humour, catchy melodies by Isaac Dunyevsky and attractive lead performances from Lyubov Orlova, who became Alexandrov's wife. The musicals of **Ivan Pyriev** (1901–1968) including *The Rich Bride* (*Bogataya nevasta*, 1938), *Tractor Drivers* (*Traktoristy,* 1939) and *Favourite Daughter* (*Lyubimoya devushka,* 1940) were based on more down-to-earth stories and had a simple, modest charm.

The pioneering work in the field of animation done by Starewicz in the pre-Revolution period was carried forward by **Alexander Ptushko** (*b* 1900) in his first full-length production, *A New Gulliver* (*Novyi Gulliver,* 1935), an ingenious and very entertaining political version of *Gulliver's Travels,* in which all the characters are "played" by puppets.

In the second half of the decade, a number of massive historical spectacles emerged, a trend which was initiated by Stalin. Among the earliest was *Peter the First* (*Pyotr Pervyi* Parts I and II 1937–8; *dir* Vladimir Petrov), rather stolid in general style, but with a striking title role performance by Cherkasov.

A significant film of the period was Ermler's two-part *The Great Citizen* (*Bogataya nevesta*, 1938–39) a highly political film dealing with inner-party conflicts and providing an "official" justification for the Moscow trials.

With the rise of Hitler, the spread of Nazism and the growing threat of war, several films of strong and passionate opposition to Fascism were made, among the best of which were *Professor Mamlock* (*Professor Mamlok*, 1938, *dir* Herbert Rappoport) and *The Oppenheims* (*Semya Oppenheim*, 1939, *dir* Grigori Roshal).

Despite the growing objective difficulties arising from the increasing political tensions at home and abroad, the talents of a number of directors who had gained their early experience and training in the silent era blossomed forth in the second part of the decade. **Mikhail Romm** (*b* 1901), who had been an assistant on *Men and Jobs* (*Dela i lyudi*, 1932, *dir* Alexander Macheret), directed his first film *Boule de Suif* based on the Guy de Maupassant story, in 1934. It won considerable acclaim but has tended to be overshadowed by two subsequent films, for which he is more famous, *Lenin in October* (*Lenin v Oktyabre*, 1937) and *Lenin in 1918* (*Lenin v 1918 godu*, 1939), both scripted by **Aleksei Kapler** (*b* 1904) with Boris Schukin as the first of the great screen Lenins. Yutkevitch also embarked on his series of "Lenin" films in this period, with Maxim Strauch as the great revolutionary leader in *Man with a Gun* (*Chelovek s ruzhyom*, 1938) and *Yakov Sverdlov* (*Yakov Sverdlov*, 1940).

Mikhail Romm

Sergei Gerasimov (*b* 1906), who had worked as an assistant and had been an actor in the Kozintsev-Trauberg films, emerged as a director deeply concerned with the theme of youth—which continues into the Seventies to be his main preoccupation. *Seven Bold People* (*Semero smelykh*, 1936) was about youngsters in the wilds of the Arctic; *Komsomolsk* (*Komsomolsk*, 1938), dealt with an industrial community built in 1932 by a team of young Communists, and *The Teacher* (*Uchitel*, 1939) was concerned with the problems of a dedicated young teacher who goes to work in an outlying village. Gerasimov's early associations with F.E.X. and his experiences as an actor helped to equip him for his exemplary screen work with actors.

The most important talent to flower in the Thirties was that of Mark Donskoy. In 1934 he collaborated with **Vladimir Legoshin** (1904–1954) in *Song of Happiness* (*Pesnya o schastye*), an attractive, good-natured story about the children of the Mari nationality in one of the regions of the Volga. Legoshin went on to make *Lone White Sail* (*Byeleyet parus odinoky*, 1937) a delightful story of a children's adventure during the Civil War, which was very popular at home and

Mark Donskoy

151

abroad. Donskoy began to prepare for his great *Gorky Trilogy,* the richest achievement of the late Thirties and among the finest productions in the whole history of Soviet cinema.

Based on the autobiography of the writer Maxim Gorky, the three films, *The Childhood of Gorky* (*Detstvo Gorkovo,* 1938), *My Apprenticeship* (*V lyudyaki,* 1939) and *My Universities* (*Moi universiteti,* 1940) teem with life and character and are full of robust warmth and humour. The bustling riverside scenes, the detail in the streets, homes and workplaces are testimonies to Donskoy's gift for total recreation of a bygone age. Among the many remarkable performances in them is the unforgettable portrayal of the earthy and strong-spirited grandmother by one of Russia's greatest actresses, Varvara Massaltinova.

The first of the three Soviet "greats" to experiment with sound was Pudovkin, with a drama of marital relationship that started out with the title *Life Is Beautiful* and after drastic revision was distributed as *A Simple Case* (*Prostoi sluchai,* 1932). It was not very successful at home and was released as a silent abroad. But between the making of the two versions he was able to start work on a new subject *The Deserter* (*Dezertir,* 1933) which embodied to the full his principle of sound as counterpoint to vision. He cut and composed the sound with the same swift, incisive editing techniques that he used for visuals to such forceful effect.

Its hero is a revolutionary who chooses to return to the struggle in Germany rather than to lead a cushioned life in the Soviet Union, and becomes involved in a dockers' strike in Hamburg. It is a film of striking beauty and great dramatic impact and its political passion was heightened by real-life developments in Germany. When Hitler seized power in 1933, the unit returned to the Soviet Union and completed the exteriors in Russian locations; the script was adapted to encompass the new situation.

The Deserter proved to be the last film which reflected Pudovkin's true individual genius. His subsequent works in the prewar period, *The Victory* (*Pobeda,* 1938), about the search for a pilot who is reported lost while on an experimental Arctic flight and *Minin and Pozharsky* (*Minin i Pozharsky,* 1939), a lavish production made in line with the trend for historicals, had excellent action sequences but lacked Pudovkin's characteristic depth of perception. His final film in the period was *Twenty Years of Cinema,* a documentary presenting the highlights of Soviet screen history, which he made in collaboration with Esther Shub.

Dovzhenko's first talkie, *Ivan* (1932), about the building of the Dneiper Dam, can be seen as the major Ukrainian screen contribution to the industrialisation period. Dovzhenko's lyrical vision raised it to the level of a poem of the romance of construction. Woven into it is an ingenious and comic psychological study of an anarchistic layabout peasant who is involved in the work. *Aerograd* (1935) was also about industrial construction—this time in the Soviet Far East. Returning to his native Ukraine, Dovzhenko directed what is undoubtedly the most magnificent of his sound films, *Schors* (*Schors*, 1935), in response to a suggestion from Stalin that he should make a "Ukrainian Chapayev." Although the life of its hero, a Ukrainian partisan, had many parallels with that of Chapayev, the film itself is totally different. It is a dynamic action film of massive scale, with great battles, hand-to-hand fighting, astonishing glimpses of ordinary life being carried on amid thunderous bombardment, and cavalry charges in the snow. Dovzhenko had taken part personally in many of the military and political actions he reconstructed for the screen. The film's autobiographic basis heightens the passion of its rhetorical style, which, like all the best Dovzhenko films, reflects the director's preoccupation with the twin but opposite forces of life and death. During the period immediately preceding the Soviet Union's entry into the war, Dovzhenko, like Pudovkin, worked in the documentary field.

The creative work of three of the Soviet masters, like that of lesser artists, was hampered, throughout the Thirties, by the growing weight of supervision from above—the fear of being accused of either "formalism" or "naturalism" or of deviation from the social and political perspective expected of them. None suffered more sharply in this respect than Eisenstein.

After his disappointments in Hollywood, Eisenstein and his team had gone to Mexico to make *Que Viva Mexico!* which he had conceived on an immense and complex scale as a six-part epic of living Mexican history and culture. After a quarrel between Eisenstein and his backers, the novelist Upton Sinclair and his wife, the film was withdrawn uncompleted from Eisenstein's hands. The two versions that were later put together by others—*Thunder over Mexico* (edited by Sol Lesser, 1932) and *A Time in the Sun* (Marie Seton, 1940)—gave an indication of the quality of what would almost certainly have been one of the great masterpieces of world cinema.

Returning with Alexandrov and Tissé to the Soviet Union in 1932, Eisenstein had to face more bitterness and frustration with the discovery that he was very much out of favour with the head of the newly-organised industry. Plans to film a comedy, *MMM*, and a film about the Haitian Revolution, *The Black Consul*, with Paul Robeson in a leading role, came to nothing. His consolation was an invitation to conduct a director's course at the Moscow Film School, where his remarkable teachings directly influenced an entire generation of film-makers.

He returned to the director's chair in 1935, to make *Bezhin Meadow* (*Bezhin lug*) only to face further frustrations. The scenario carried forward the theme of *The Old and the New*, depicting the struggle for collectivisation in the countryside through the conflict between the

members of a young collective and the traditional-minded rich peasants or kulaks who, together with their associates, plot to sabotage the harvest. It was to reach its dramatic peak through a tragic confrontation between a father, representing the old, and his young son, Stepok, representing the new. But criticism from above, on the grounds of its "formalism," dogged the production, which was started, stopped, restarted, and finally abandoned.

The negatives of the parts that had been completed were destroyed during the war. Surviving fragments and stills were painstakingly brought together in the Sixties, and a short film edited to indicate the narrative sequence was made by Yutkevitch and Naum Kleimann in 1967.

With *Alexander Nevsky* (*Aleksandr Nevsky,* 1938) Eisenstein raised the concept of the historical picture to new heights and regained his place as the leading creative figure of Soviet cinema. This epic of Prince Alexander, the leader of the people of Novgorod, whose armies fought and vanquished the Knights of the Teutonic Order, reached its climax with the celebrated "battle on the ice"—the whole of which, incidentally, was shot in a specially surfaced field near Moscow during a heat-wave. Its effectiveness was heightened by the magnificence of the camerawork, for which Tissé used special filters to achieve the wintery effect and slowed down the cameras to obtain the required rhythms of the fighting. Cherkasov's performance as Nevsky was monumental and Prokofiev's exciting musical score was an integral part of the film.

Eisenstein was in the initial stages of preparing his final masterpiece, the great historical tapestry of the birth of Russia as a unified nation, *Ivan the Terrible* (*Ivan Groznyi*), when the Soviet Union was invaded by the German army. *nh*

CZECHO-
SLOVAKIA

In 1898 a Prague architect, Jan Křiženecký bought a cinematograph in Paris two years after the first Lumière demonstrations, returned to Prague, made and projected the first film-strips in Bohemia —then part of the Austro-Hungarian Empire. This puts Czech cinema with the earliest pioneers. A small company was formed in 1908, feature production began in 1912 under improvised conditions, and though growth was rapid the infant industry was commercial with no attempt at large-scale co-ordination or methods.

The Czechs, Moravians and Slovaks making up Czechoslovakia had a long history of vassalage to powerful neighbours—Poland, Germany, Russia and Hungary. These pressures kept national feelings strong; regional folklore was embedded in literature, both Bohemian and Slovak—legends, ballads, songs, dances, heroes—these elements finding expression in cinema. Examples are: *Janošik* (1921, 1936, 1963), *Jan Hus* (1955) and *Jan Žižka* (1956).

*Early Period
to 1939*

A vast output of about 700 features by 1939 comprised newsreels, curious ephemera such as records of classical stage roles, serials, comedies and slapstick, melodrama, excusions into poverty or realism, and period pieces. *Janošik* (1921) dealt with the Eighteenth century Robin Hood-like Slovak hero-highwayman and was followed by *Koratovič* (1922), a similar figure. In the Twenties several important directors and cameramen emerged. **Karel Lamač** (1897–1952), in cinema from 1918 onwards, made some 265 films—also acting in some—ranging far afield in subject, and later working abroad in Germany, Holland, Paris, Austria and Hollywood. **Přemysl Pražký** (1893–1964) made fewer films as he was a director for stage and later, television, as well; but his *The Battalion* (*Batalion*, 1927) was an early and important literary adaptation. **Gustav Machatý** (1901–1963), who also directed abroad, was notable for *The Kreutzer Sonata* (*Kreutserova Sonáta*, 1926), with its elaborate sets incorporating *Art Nouveau* style and night exteriors suggesting Expressionism; and *Erotikon* (1929) which achieved much success abroad. **Martin Frič** (1902–1968) worked in films from 1922, made nearly ninety features, and his *Father Vojtech* (*Páter Vojtěch,* 1928) and *The Organist of St. Vitus* (*Varhaník u sv. Víta,* 1929), which used dramatic deep, rich shadows, both showed significant background atmosphere, social awareness and psychological studies increasingly apparent in the Twenties and Thirties. He wanted to become a pilot and flew one of the first biplanes in Bohemia, crashed and suffered such extensive leg injuries that he took up painting in hospital. This helped him as a poster- and scene-painter when he went

155

to work in the theatre, and later in films where his pictorial vision was distinctive. He was the first director to receive the Award of National Merit. Machatý's *From Saturday to Sunday* (*Ze soboty na neděli,* 1931) used a social theme, and his *Ecstasy* (*Extase,* 1933) with Viennese Hedy (Kieslerová) Lamarr achieved wide fame. **Josef Rovenský** (1894–1937), working from 1914 onwards, made *The River* (*Řeka,* 1933), a lyrical film that established one of the main streams of Czech cinema. He also acted in his own films.

Against his lyricism was the able, versatile improvisatory style with Frič as its chief exponent—his *The Revisor* (*Revisor*) appeared in 1933, as did *Dawn* (*Svítání*) by Václav Kubásek (1897–1964), a director and scenario-writer from 1919. Frič made a second version of *Janošík* in 1936 in Slovakia with **Paľo Bielik** (*b* 1910), actor, scenario-writer, and now *doyen* of Slovak directors in the title role—still a film worth seeing. Bielik was to make his own huge two-part colour version of *Janošík* in scope format in 1962–63. **Otakar Vávra** (*b* 1911) came to cinema in 1929 and began a third main stream of development by linking his films to poetry and literature. His *Virginity* (*Panenství,* 1937) and *The Guild of the Kutna Hora Virgins* (*Cech panen kutnohorských,* 1938) showed sensitivity and keen psychological perception, the latter film winning the Luce Cup at Venice in 1938. In this period Frič made a series of successful comedies using Jiří Voskovech and Jan Werich, intellectual and satirical stage comedians.

Early Cameramen   Some important cameramen in this early period are: **Jaroslav Blažek** (*b* 1896), with a large output from 1919 onwards; **Jindřich Brichta** (1897–1957), film historian as well as cameraman; **Karel Degl** (1896–1951), whose work started in 1916 and who later became instructor in photography at the Prague Film School (**FAMU**); **Otto Heller** (*b* 1896) who, starting in 1918 achieved an enormous list of films at home and abroad, with many important British titles; **Jan Stallich** (*b* 1907) whose father, Julius, worked on films from 1908, and who, himself, began in 1927, going on to become very important, working abroad, and then returning in Prague in 1946; and **Václav Vích** (*b* 1898), with a large output from 1922 onwards, doing much work in Italy, with a few films in U.S.A., Britain and Germany. *ld*

POLAND   Poland has a long history of film-making and can boast some early results in cinema engineering inventions. Apparatus designed by the young engineer **Kazimierz Prószyński** in 1894–96 was used soon after the turn of the century to produce several comedy shorts. The birth of the film industry is usually considered to date from 1908, with *Tony in Warsaw* (*Antoś w Warszawie*), a short feature starring a popular comedian, **Antoni Fertner.** A network of cinemas was soon established and by 1911 several companies had begun regular production of full-length films—mainly adaptations of literary classics featuring outstanding stage actors of the day.

The first studio was set up in 1920, two years after the restoration of the independent Polish State. Between the wars film production was mainly a matter for small-time speculation; companies making only two or three films would mushroom and then disappear. Of about 146 companies, only six made more than ten films each.

Among the best-known film personalities of the silent days were **Pola Negri** (*b* Appolonia Chalupek, 1897), the celebrated actress who later went to Berlin and Hollywood, **Ryszard Ordyński** (1878–1953), who was mainly concerned with adaptations from literature and the theatre, **Wiktor Biegański** (*b* 1892), the first director to break away from theatre styles, and **Ryszard Boleslawski** (1889–1937), who later made a name for himself in Hollywood. The prolific director **Aleksander Hertz** (1879–1928) was less notable for his technique than for his discovery and projection of the immensely popular actress **Jadwiga Smosarska** (*b* 1900), who reached the peak of her popularity in *Iwonka* (*Iwonka,* 1925) and *The Leper* (*Tredowata,* 1926).

With the coming of sound, the most successful director in the commercial field was **Jósef Lejtes** (*b* 1901) who achieved a high standard with films like *The Young Forest* (*Mlody las,* 1934) and *The Day of the Great Adventure* (*Dzień wielkiej przygody,* 1935) both of which gained international awards.

Three directors who began their film careers in the Twenties, **Aleksander Ford** (*b* 1908), **Leonard Buczkowski** (1900–1966) and **Eugeniusz Cekalski** (1906–1952) were of key importance in the establishment of postwar cinema.

Cekalski was one of a group of young directors, theoreticians and critics, including **Wanda Jakubowska** (*b* 1907), and **Stanislav Wohl** (*b* 1912), who, in 1929, founded the *avant-garde* film society START (Society of the Devotees of Artistic Film). They were joined in the early Thirties by, among others, the outstanding documentary-maker **Jerzy Bossak** (*b* 1910) and Ford. The Society's aim was to improve the artistic level and social content of cinema. Among films that sprang directly from its theoretical ideas was Ford's *Legion of the Street* (*Legion ulicy*) a touching story about Warsaw newsboys which, despite absence of stars and other customary box-office ingredients, became the most popular film of 1932. Ford's *Awakening* (*Przebudzenie,* 1934), which he made in co-operation with Jakubowska, about the independent life of three high-school girls after graduation, was so severely cut by the censor that it was rendered almost unintelligible. His *People of the Vistula* (*Ludzie Wisly,* 1936), made in collaboration with **Jerzy Zarzycki** (*b* 1911) was an important milestone. *nh*

In Hungary films were first shown in 1896, but the decisive year was 1912: by then the first studio, Hunnia, was completed, film was seen as a creative art, regular reviews appeared, and the first film

HUNGARY

157

magazine, *Pesti Mozi,* was founded. Production companies sprang up, mostly out of theatres; ninety per cent of films at this time were based on either plays or novels. By 1918 there were fifteen professional film directors in Hungary, including **Alexander Korda** (1893–1956), editor of *Pesti Mozi,* and then head of Corvin.

By the end of 1918 Korda was re-organising the industry, but in 1919 the government fell to the Communists, and from April to August, 1919, Hungary had the first ever nationalised cinema. It produced thirty-one films and made substantial reforms, but the harshness of the counter-revolutionaries accomplished the gradual collapse of the industry (no films in 1929), though critical theory flourished. Later, through indispensable subsidies, the government gained control of a reviving home production.

In 1931 the first two talking films were made, of which *Hyppolit the Butler* (*Hyppolit a Lakáj*) directed by **István Székely** (**Steve Sekely** *b* 1899), was an outstanding success. It offered characters, places, and accents that people recognised, and established Sekely as the most popular director of the Thirties. *sb*

YUGOSLAVIA   To understand Yugoslav cinema is to know that the country is divided into two alphabets, three languages, four religions, five nationalities (Slovenian, Croatian, Serbian, Montenegran, and Macedonian), six republics (the five nations plus Bosnia-Hercegovina), and over a dozen producing companies. Each company functions as a private enterprise within a Socialist system, with all the advantages and disadvantages of both.

Picture from Aleksić's INNOCENCE UNPRO-TECTED, which was later "exhumed" to glory by Makavejev

Still, the roots are common: the usual Lumière projections (1896),
followed by Lumière productions (e.g., *The Coronation of King Peter in Belgrade*), and finally (in 1905) a Macedonian photographer named "Monaki" purchased a camera and used it well enough to earn a reputation abroad. The first feature film was *Karadjordje* (1910), made by Jules Bairy for a French company and treating, fittingly enough, the first insurrection against the Turks. The Balkan Wars of 1912 were recorded both by Josip Halla of Zagreb and Slavko Jovanovic of Belgrade, and newsreels were common also during the First World War and after. Under the new monarchy a second feature film was shot, *Matija Gubec* (1919), by the "Yugoslavia D.D." company; but the company failed in 1925 due to the government's disinterest. Other individual efforts that merit some attention: Mihailo Al. Popovic's *With Belief in God* (1934), an epic on the Serbian people during the First World War; and Dragoljub Aleksić's *Innocence Unprotected* (1942), primitively shot and exhibited under the noses of the Germans during the Occupation. *rh*

Without taking into consideration the Lumière presentations of 1897
and the function of Vladimir Petkov's bioscope in 1903, the Bulgarian cinema began its history from 1908 when the first camera was imported and the first projection room erected to show continuous documentary programmes of everyday life and, more significantly, the Balkan Wars of 1912. The first full-length feature was a comedy, *The Bulgarian Is Gallant,* directed by and starring Vassil Guendov; it was exhibited in 1915 at Sofia's "Modern Theatre." Nothing of interest seems to have happened after the First World War due to the government's penchant for more lucrative foreign import, but many of these native, amateurish productions are lost. *dh*

8. Japan and Elsewhere

BOTH VITASCOPE AND LUMIERE devices reached Japan in 1897; interest was immediate and a market grew quickly. A cinema theatre was built in 1903; comprehensive audiences meant fairly high admission prices. Though film-making began at once, the content of the pictures was influenced by the public's fondness for the formal *kabuki* performances firmly anchored in the past—deriving from the feudal, Tokugawa period (1598–1867), and the *shimpa,* a romantic theatre form growing from the Meiji period (1868–1912). Subsequently, realism came with the *shingeki.* A curious restrictive practice hampered cinema development: the *benshi*—commentators or narrators sitting beside the screen telling the story. They came from the *kabuki* performances. Enormously popular, they held their function throughout the Twenties, despite early directors who had worked abroad and came home insisting that their films needed no *benshi*. The *oyama*, or female impersonator of the *kabuki*, was another link with the past. Some early films showed parts of *kabuki* performances or advertised *shimpa* productions (1899), even merging briefly into a marriage of *shimpa*-cum-cinema.

With tastes restricted to the past by the Japanese love of something familiar, the creative director emerged slowly. The popularity of the new medium caused an early growth of production companies, and these multiplied, forming a shifting, continuous pattern of competition and power up to the present time. Short films went abroad as early as 1905 but these were tiny excursions into native exotica. The first studio was built in Tokyo in 1908.

The first significant director was also a producer and theatre owner: **Shozo Makino** (*b* 1878). He discovered a *kabuki* player, **Matsuno-suke Onove** (*b* 1875) on stage from the age of six. Onove gathered other players and made films with Makino very quickly. Onove became a star and by 1913 the team made the first version of *The Loyal 47 Ronin* (*Chushingura*), a recurring favourite of *kabuki* and cinema. *Shingeki* realism, as *shomin-geki*, penetrated films in 1914 with *Katusha*, based on Tolstoy's *Resurrection*, and another Tolstoy adaptation, *The Living Corpse* (*Ikeru Shikabane*, 1917, *dir* Eizo Tanaka). As in *Katusha*, an *oyama* played the female lead: **Teinosuke Kinugasa** (*b* 1896), who became a prolific director from 1922 onwards. His *Gate of Hell* (*Jigokumon*, 1953), took the Grand Prix at Cannes in 1954.

In 1917 the first animated cartoons were made and the first attempts to use essentially cinematic and foreign techniques. In 1918 the innovation of actresses to replace *oyamas* occurred. The important novelist Junichiro Tanizaki was employed to write scripts. Some twenty of his books have been adapted for the screen. One of the earliest actresses was Haruko Sawamura, who appeared in the significant film, *Souls on the Road* (*Rojo no Reikon*, 1921, *dir* Minoru Murata and Kaoru Osanai). Murata was a lead-actor in 1918, and Osanai, who had studied with Stanislavsky and Max Reinhardt, was made head of Shochiku Cinema Institute—a pioneer of *shingeki*. This film of two inter-cut stories (one by Gorky), was of seminal importance with its essentially Japanese use of feeling instead of sharp story line. Other actresses to become stars were Sumiko Kurishima, extremely popular around 1924, and Yaeko Mizutani, who appeared in *Winter Camellia* (*Kantsubaki,* 1921, *dir* Masao Onove).

Kenji Mizoguchi

The first of the major names, **Kenji Mizoguchi** (1898–1956), graduated at a painting school and became a director in 1922. Painting ability and acting experience showed in his films, which sprang from literary sources. Ultimately a master of period drama, he was also important for his development of *shomin-geki*—showing life-as-it-is for

The impish children in Ozu's I WAS BORN BUT ...

common people with implicit criticism of the causes of unhappiness. His films became renowned for their pictorial beauty, and took several prizes, notably at Venice in 1952, 1953, and 1954, with *The Life of O-Haru* (*Saikaku Ichidai Onna*), *Ugetsu Monogatari*—an exquisite period piece compounded of life in the past, vivid action, and excursions into fantasy—, and *Sansho the Bailiff* (*Sansho Dayu*).

The catastrophic Kanto earthquake of 1923 meant rebuilding the film industry. Simultaneously reorganisation was applied; new names appeared. But 1925 saw the control of censorship unified under the Home Ministry, and this grew in bureaucratic power until government control was absolute by the outbreak of the Second World War. It was 1923 when **Yasujiro Ozu** (1903–1963) began as an assistant director. A consistent prize-winner in Japan, Ozu saw his work sent abroad only reluctantly since he, too, showed the realities of domestic life, with special emphasis on family relationships. This was felt to be too Japanese for foreign appreciation—which nevertheless followed. With careful preparation, a static camera set very near the ground, quietly beautiful compositions, and great control of his casts, Ozu produced a body of work distinguished for its homogeneity and dignity. Slow to use sound and colour, his whole career was measured and deliberate, but very important and close to the Japanese heart.

Yasujiro Ozu

Right at the end of the silent era a cameraman should be singled out: **Kohei Sugiyama** (*b* 1899), in films from 1922 outwards. His low-key photography was outstanding in Kinugasa's *Crossroads* (*Jujiro, 1928*), which with the same director's *A Page out of Order* (*Kurutta*

Ippeiji, 1926), set partly in a lunatic asylum, showing insanity from the patient's viewpoint, marked an important phase. In a long career he went on to photograph Kinugasa's *Gate of Hell* as well as to take the Cinematography Prize at Cannes in 1951 for Yoshimura's *Tales of Genji* (*Genji Monogatari*), the first Japanese novel, written by Lady Murasaki, *c* 1005, of which many screen versions have been made. Some prominent actors of the Twenties going into sound films were: Chiezo Kataoka (real name, Masayoshi Ueki), who started in 1917 and progressed to managing director of a film company; Ryunosuke Tsukigata, a graduate of Nikkatsu Studio school, making his *début* under Makino; Denjiro Okochi, in films from 1926; and Chojiro Hayashi, even more famous under his real name, Kazuo Hasegawa, who came from the *kabuki* theatre and enjoyed a long, immensely popular career, performing a dual role with bravura assurance in Ichikawa's *An Actor's Revenge*.

Yasujiro Shimazu (1897–1945) studied at Osanai's institute in 1920, was a pioneer of *shomin-geki* in the Twenties, and worked prolifically while training men like Gosho, Toyoda, and Kinoshita as assistants. Under his strict discipline they were well-grounded, and Kinoshita still follows the practice today with his assistants.

The Twenties ended with the first foreign exhibition of Japanese films in Moscow in 1929. Shigeyoshi Suzuki shot *What Made Her Do It?* (*Nani ga Kanojo o so Saseta ka,* 1930), in which a poor girl finally committed arson. This began a trend because it was the most successful box-office film of the silent era.

The Coming of Sound

The first Japanese talkie (record and film system) was made in 1927, but the first successful one (sound on film) was *The Neighbour's Wife and Mine* (*Madamu to Nyobo,* 1931), shot by **Heinosuke Gosho** (*b* 1902). Son of a wealthy father, Gosho graduated at Keio University, Tokyo, before directing in 1924. The most important phase of his career began in the Thirties. His films were drawn from major literary sources. His keen dramatic interest and expert craftsmanship created people very much in the round, placing him beside Mizoguchi (though he was less concerned with pictorial beauty), and Ozu (whom he surpassed in technical flexibility and complexity). *Everything That Lives* (*Ikitoshi Ikerumono,* 1934), *An Inn at Osaka* (*Osaka no Yado,* 1954), and *Four Chimneys* (*Entotsu no Mieru Basho,* 1953) are among Gosho's best work.

The Thirties saw a considerable expansion in the industry with 400 features in 1932 despite a strike organised by the *Benshi* who feared redundancy after Gosho's first talkie had been released. Then, as now, such a large output (rising after the war to 488 in 1965 and 442 in 1966) was marked by a dearth of scripts, many re-makes, and sharply varying levels of material.

Tomotaka Tasaka (*b* 1902), a director from 1926 onwards, came to prominence in 1938 when he made an important film about the Sino-Japanese war, *Five Scouts* (*Gonin no Sekkohei*, 1938) that was sent to Venice. He made many kinds of films, although his career was frustrated by many years in hospital following exposure to radiation in Hiroshima. He directed *A Pebble by the Wayside* (*Robo no Ishi*, 1938), which was adapted from a novel about a boy beset with hardship and deprivation. It was successful and re-made again and again. The boy was played by a child-actor, Akihiko Katayama, the son of **Koji Shima** (*b* 1901), an actor and then a director from 1939, making the first war film on location, in Malaya in 1943.

Tomu Uchida (*b* 1898) began as an actor in 1920, trained as assistant to Frank Tokunaga, and made his directing *début* in 1927. Invited to work in Manchuria in 1942, he later became a technical adviser in Communist China, returning to Japan in 1954. He progressed from period comedies to *shomin-geki* in the Thirties, and his sensitive, prize-winning *Earth* (*Tsuchi*, 1939) was made in a clandestine fashion while he turned out popular works for his company.

Two brief careers blossomed in the Thirties. **Sadao Yamanaka** (*b* 1907, killed in action in China, 1938) directed his first feature in 1932. His *Life of Bangoku* (*Bangoku*) of the same year established a series of period dramas, this one concerned with a *ronin*, or unemployed samurai. He won many prizes. Mansaku Itami became a director in 1928, also of period dramas, most of them starring Chiezo Kataoka, who had been popular in the Twenties.

Hiroshi Inagaki (*b* 1905) appeared as a juvenile lead in *Turkeys in a Row* (*Shichimencho no Yukue*, 1924, *dir* Mizoguchi), studied stage drama, and became a director in 1928. He helped to develop the period drama in the Thirties. In his extensive career he shot two versions of *The Life of Matsu the Untamed* (*Muho Matsu no Issho*, 1943 and 1958), both of which were excellent, the second, under the title *The Rickshaw Man*, winning the Leone d'Oro at Venice and achieving great popularity. He was another director who made features with roles for Kataoka; especially *The Sedge Hat* (1932).

Mizoguchi directed some fine period films in the Thirties, and with Shimazu and Gosho he turned to important novels for material. In 1936 he made two of his most impressive films, *Sisters of the Gion* (*Gion no Shimai*), and *Osaka Elegy* (*Naniwa Elegi*), both featuring Isuzu Yamada, one of Japan's best screen actresses.

Shiro Toyoda (*b* 1906), after an early interest in theatre, wrote film scripts and became Shimazu's assistant in 1925. Now a leading director, he too, was prominent in literary adaptations where his stage predilection produced a series of attractive performances from his small casts. His talent flowered still further in the Fifties. *ld*

The first film show in India was given by the Lumière brothers in **INDIA**

163

1896 in Bombay and there were immediate but not far-reaching attempts to make films locally. At the turn of the century, Hiralal Sen in Bengal was very probably photographing stage plays, but the credit for the first feature film is more universally given to D. G. Phalke in Maharashtra whose *Rajah Harishchandra* in 1913 began a long and adventurous career reflecting a strong urge towards presenting Indian mythology on the screen—a trend that persists to this day but has yielded the pride of place to more "modern" themes. The first talkie came in 1931 with Ardeshir Irani's *Alam Ara,* before the silent film had a chance to reach any abiding artistic merit, although Himangsu Rai and Frank Osten's long and fruitful collaboration did produce films like *Light of Asia* (1925—the year of *Battleship Potemkin* and *The Gold Rush*) four hundred prints of which were distributed all over the world and a command performance given before the King and Queen of England following its nomination in Britain as the Best Film of the Year.

Alam Ara included a dozen songs—a number which has stayed virtually unchanged in the vast majority of today's films. Apart from the operatic unreality decreed by the predominance of songs (and dances), the sound film introduced the language problem resulting in the independent establishment of cinemas in Hindi, Bengali, Marathi, Tamil, Telegu and Malayalam, later expanding to many other languages. Marathi cinema was prominent among these and strongly influenced by literary-dramatic traditions, like *Eternal Light* (*Amar Jyoti,* 1936), *Life is for Living* (*Admi,* 1939, Damle and Fatehlal's *Saint Tukaram* (*Sant Tukaram,* 1937) the first Indian film to win a Venice award. These and other productions made Prabhat Film Company of Poona a pioneering institution. Hindi cinema, later to become the all-India product, threw up Bombay Talkies, equally famous for its socially-conscious films like *Untouchable Girl* (*Achhut Kanya,* 1936) apart from Himangsu Rai's own *Karma* (1934) which continued his cooperation with Frank Osten from the silent days. The Thirties, reflecting the patriotic struggle for independence, also saw the Tamil cinema produce films like *Child Saint* (*Balyogini,* 1938) on the fate of Brahmin widows. *cdg*

SPAIN   The history of Spanish cinema has been strangely unrewarding for an industry that dates back to 1897 and ranks among the most productive in the world. But its provincial, folkloric tone was set in the earliest silent days and hardly wavered for half a century.

The first "significant" picture made in Spain was *The Damned Village* (*La aldea maldita,* 1929), by **Florian Rey** (1894–1962), but it was not followed by others of any real import, and the destructive Civil War of 1936–39 soon brought the industry virtually to a halt. After the war things took a predictable turn to the right and the national, with a series of heroic war films and such self-approving pieces as *Race* (*Raza,* 1941) by the popular **José Luis Sáenz de Heredia** (*b* 1911).

Changes in government policy only served to exaggerate this tendency and strangle the domestic industry. A nationalistic law requiring all foreign films to be dubbed gave the international product yet another advantage over the national, and the decision to link permits to import films with the production of Spanish films only encouraged the making of quicker and cheaper pictures. *wd*

Born on February 22, 1900, at Calanda in the province of Zaragoza, **Luis Buñuel** is the one film-maker of genius to have come out of Spain. While a student at the University of Madrid in the early Twenties, he became the friend of Salvador Dali and García Lorca and founded there the first Spanish film club. He went to Paris in 1925, a Paris much influenced by André Breton and the Surrealist movement. By enrolling at the recently established *Académie du Cinéma,* Buñuel met Jean Epstein and assisted him on *Mauprat* (1926) and *La Chute de la Maison Usher* (1928). Although interested in painting and busy writing poetry for Surrealist magazines, Luis Buñuel was discovering that the cinema was his medium.

With the help of some money given him by his mother, in 1928 Buñuel and Dali made *Un Chien Andalou.* Deliberately designed to create a scandal, the film became the prototype for all anti-bourgeois films. Its opening sequence is aggressively Buñuelian. A young man, Buñuel himself, stands on a balcony sharpening a razor. While some clouds drift lazily across the moon, the young man with dreamlike deliberation lifts the razor and slits the eyeball of a woman sitting beside him. The shock is inescapable. At the same time, the gesture is as elusive of interpretation as an image from a dream. Appealing subjectively to different elements in different people, it can have many meanings and stir up many feelings, none of which are easily related to the moral and rational way we have been encouraged to organise our lives. By such an effect, Buñuel wants to disrupt our complacency. He wants us to see the world in a different way. He is slashing our eyes as well.

Though important historically, *Un Chien Andalou* was too deliberately full of too many Freudian gags for the whole film to have the force of that opening moment. Far more successful was the film that Buñuel made next, again with some help from Dali—*L'Age d'Or* (1930). In this, the Buñuelian philosophy is already complete. Natural life seems founded on aggression (the scorpions), while civilisation is hopelessly torn apart by the urge to rebel felt strongly within the individual and the need to repress insisted upon forcefully by organised society. Buñuel's instinctual man seems trapped within this dilemma. Even when alone with the woman he desires, he cannot consummate his lust for her. Social conventions continue to intervene. Chairs trouble

LUIS BUÑUEL

Un Chien Andalou

L'Age d'Or

him and a statue gets in the way. He is thus left on his own by the end of the film, impotent in his rage.

If *L'Age d'Or* is as Freudian in conception as *Un Chien Andalou*, it possesses a far greater coherence and emotional power, largely through the accuracy and detail of Buñuel's observations of his fellow man. For Buñuel also possesses his documentary side, a side given powerful expression in his next film, *Land without Bread (Las Hurdes*, 1932). This deals with the impoverished Hurdanos who live in an arid region of Spain near the Portuguese border. For them in a different way, life seems hopeless. All the trappings of civilisation have passed them by. The irrelevance of our civilised assumptions about life is poignantly present throughout the film in the form of Brahms's Fourth Symphony— an ironic comment on our failure to deal successfully with the problem of poverty, a poverty that in this film seems unbearably extreme. If *L'Age d'Or* embodies a surrealist impulse so persuasively in realistic detail that it achieves at moments a documentary authenticity, *Las Hurdes* observes the starkness and misery of these people's lives with such feeling and insistence that it achieves a surrealist force. *ph*

Dead donkeys, prelates, and pianos in UN CHIEN ANDALOU

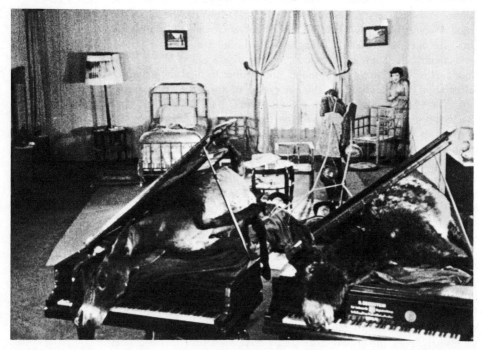

The history of film production in Canada is short and mostly undis- **CANADA**
tinguished. It is one long, frustrating chapter of plans made and never
realised, of studios opened and rapidly closed, of large sums of money
invested in brave ideas and ending in bankruptcy, of rogues and rascals
from abroad who prompted fancy schemes profitable to them and disastrous for Canada. Due to a combination of two factors—the country's
proximity to the U.S.A. and lack of initiative on the part of the government and investors—most of Canada's talented people left the country.
There was no work, and there was no government policy to encourage
and protect native production.

Canadian cinema has consisted largely of the travelogue and the
documentary. Travelogues were made as early as 1898 by Charles
Urban, for screening in Britain as an aid to "colonisation." From these
came the industrial film, and then the advertising short subject. The
only production that has remained constant over the years is that of
the documentary and the educational/industrial short.

The production of feature-length films has been wildly erratic and
not particularly noteworthy. Most "small" countries can point to some
films that became classics. If any were made in Canada, they were lost.
Most production seems to have been of the blatantly commercial kind,
designed to imitate Hollywood and to appeal to mass audiences. They
were made by American or British companies, or local individuals who
wanted to make a fast dollar. There has been hardly any attempt to
chronicle or keep track of Canadian films and film history, so much
has disappeared. At one time, cheaply made Canadian features qualified
as British quota pictures, until Britain ruled that such films must represent an expenditure of at least $150,000. The American producers then
found it cheaper to produce in England.

Among the players who appeared in Canadian features during the
Thirties were Rita Hayworth, William Gargan, Lyle Talbot, Wendy
Barrie and Toby Wing. The most fruitful years were the silent period
from 1919 to 1923 when producer Ernest Shipman turned out dozens
of entertainments such as *The Sky Pilot, The Man from Glengarry,* and
Blue Waters, working from offices in Winnipeg and Ottawa. But no
directors or personalities of any note came from this period. The history
books record only two films made before the Second World War that
seem to have lived on: these were *The Viking,* with Charles Starrett,
shot on location in 1930–31 in the Polar Regions by George Melford;
and Bruce Bairnsfather's *Carry On Sergeant,* made at Trenton, Ontario,
in 1928. It cost $500,000 and failed spectacularly as sound came in
at the very moment it was released. All the money invested was lost,
and Canadian film-making did not revive until the years following
the Second World War. (Flaherty's *Nanook of the North* is not really
considered as a Canadian film.) *gp*

GREECE   Film production in Greece dates from the early days of the cinema. In spite of pioneers like **Dimitris Gaziadis** (1897–1961), who produced, directed and scripted the first documentary (*Greek Wonder,* 1921), the first classical tragedy (*Prometheus Bound,* 1927), and musical comedies like *Apaches of Athens* and *Kiss Me Maritsa* (1930), Greek cinema failed to build up an entertainment industry and establish a national tradition. Torn apart by wars and political instability, the country only produced forty-seven features in the twenty-five years up to 1940, and these included nothing of distinction. *mg*

AUSTRALIA   Despite its geographic isolation, Australia has always been a film-going and film-making nation. In August 1896, a year after the first Lumière screenings in Paris, views of London Bridge and other scenes were screened in the Opera House, Melbourne. In September, travelling Lumière photographer Maurice Sestier arrived from India and shot harbourside scenes in Sydney. In November, he also shot the Melbourne Cup horse race, his film of which is the oldest surviving Australian motion picture.

In 1900, the Salvation Army Limelight Department under J. H. Perry produced *Soldiers of the Cross,* combining lantern slides, sermons and hymns with short film scenes of early Christian persecution and martyrdom. Other inspirational films followed, as well as more secular works. In 1906, theatrical *entrepreneurs* J. and N. Tait produced *The Story of the Kelly Gang;* running more than one hour, this is arguably the world's first feature film.

Literary   Local producers filmed such popular literary classics as *For the Term*
Adaptations   *of his Natural Life,* Marcus Clarke's drama of transportation, *Robbery Under Arms,* from the Rolf Boldrewood bushranging melodrama, and the story of the Eureka Stockade incident, a patriotic revolt during the gold rush. Like the story of Ned Kelly and his gang, these have been re-made frequently since, underlining the strong nationalism of the industry.

Up to 1920, the local market was well supplied with a diet of rural comedy, and romances of convict days, bushranging and outback life. During the First World War, patriotic dramas were popular. Major talents like producer/directors Raymond Longford and Franklyn Barrett emerged. Cameraman Arthur Higgins and actress Lottie Lyell showed world-class talent. Although inferior to Griffith, Wiene *et al,* these artists produced remarkable films. The team of Longford, Higgins and Lyell produced *The Romance of Margaret Catchpole* (1912) and *The Sentimental Bloke* (1919), and Barrett directed *A Girl of the Bush* (1920).

From 1920 to the Second World War, overseas competition hit under-capitalised Australian producers, who responded with stiff versions of stage successes and the familiar bucolic comedies and outdoor dramas. Location shooting in Australia's impressive landscape distinguished *For the Term of His Natural Life* and *The Adorable Outcast,* both directed in 1927 by American Norman Dawn, with spectacular Tasmanian coastal and Pacific Island backgrounds respectively.

Overseas domination of distribution and the lack of a quota system hampered production in the Thirties, but Charles Chauvel had varying success with *Moth of Moonbi* (1925), *Greenhide* (1926), *In the Wake of the Bounty* (1933) introducing local actor Errol Flynn, *Uncivilized* (1936), *40,000 Horsemen* (1941), *Sons of Matthew* (1949) and others. His impressive location shooting often balanced poor scripts and acting.

In the Thirties, the sole company of any size was Cinesound, in whose Sydney studios producer/director Ken G. Hall made rough comedies and outdoor dramas, interspersed with skilful versions of popular melodramas like *The Silence of Dean Maitland* (1934). Peter Finch, Shirley-Ann Richards, later successful in Hollywood as Ann Richards, and many other actors emerged from this studio, the closest Australia ever came to true film professionalism. Hall's vaudeville comedies are routine, but the forestry adventure *Tall Timbers* (1937) and *Smithy,* his biography of pioneer flier Charles Kingsford-Smith, show some skill. *jb*

Ken G. Hall

The first screenings in Switzerland took place almost simultaneously with those in Paris; they were held in Geneva in 1896 in the context of the international exhibition there. Thanks to the efforts of some early cinema owners, a modest domestic production developed, showing audiences events of local or regional importance (e.g. *Zürcher Sechseläuten, Winzerfeste in der Welschschweiz,* etc), billed as "living images."

SWITZERLAND

The birth of a real feature production programme only took place after the First World War. Such later celebrated directors as Robert Florey and Jean Choux (the latter in partnership with a very young Michel Simon) were at work in Lausanne and Geneva, as well as a well-known theatrical talent, Béranger. Bucolic themes, under the title of "Alpenfilme," were prominent (*La Croix du Cervin, dir* A. Gos; *Le pauvre village, dir* Béranger, not heard of again; and *Der Bergführer, dir* E. Bienz, with actors from the Basle stage). The Sunshine Corporation run by an American-Swiss named Harder produced around 1925 a vast historical film, *The Birth of the Swiss Confederation* (*Die Geburt der Schweizerischen Eidgenossenschaft*). In Berlin, Ufa concocted some "artificial" Swiss films, such as *Petronella,* from the novel by Jergerlehner.

However, during this silent period, the real "pioneer generation" of Swiss film-makers was established. The documentarist **Charles Duvanel** (*b* 1906) started the first local newsreel. The Polish-born **Lazar Wechsler** (*b* 1896) founded Praesens-Film AG, and produced

169

a series of fine travelogues—*This Is How China Lives* (*So lebt China*) etc.—in collaboration with the flying pioneer Mittelholzer and a cameraman named Berna. In 1933 Praesens began producing sound features.

The documentary developed considerably, much influenced by foreigners who worked temporarily in Switzerland—Eisenstein and Alexandrov, Tissé, Ruttmann, Cavalcanti, Hans Richter. The increasing distrust of Nazi Germany encouraged the production of a few patriotic films, among them *Landammann Stauffacher* and *Soldat Wipf.* More significant were such isolated and unusual expressions of talent as Leopold Lindtberg's *The Misused Love Letters* (*Die missbrauchten Liebesbriefe,* 1940), an affectionate yet critical reflection of the Swiss citizen's outlook, **Max Haufler's** (*b* 1910) screen version of Ch. F. Ramuz's *Farinet,* a highly personal work, and above all Hans Trommer's tightly-composed landscape film, *Romeo and Juliet in the Village* (*Romeo und Julia auf dem Dorfe,* 1941). **Trommer** (*b* 1904), working in Zürich, was here under the influence of the poetic realism of Renoir, and his film was poetic, moving, and authentic in feeling. Both Haufler and Trommer were confined subsequently to documentaries; they were perhaps the greatest unused talents of the Swiss film industry. *hpm*

9. Documentary and Animation

Robert Flaherty

R OBERT FLAHERTY (1884–1951) is perhaps the first great documentary film-maker. An American of Irish descent, brought up among trappers and Indians, he became an explorer and mining prospector in the far north of Canada and in his thirties secured financial support from a fur company, Revillon Frères, to make a film about the Esquimaux. His hour long *Nanook of the North* (1922) is made with intuitive understanding of their traditional struggle for food and shelter.

Nanook of the North had its forerunners in travelogues (a word first used in 1917 by Burton Holmes in America) and scenics. News and general interest films had been the first to be made and the medium was originally envisaged as a popular form of educational entertainment, but it was the fictional films which attracted the audiences and created a profitable industry and factual films were thereafter to be the Cinderella, fighting for screen time and dependent upon financial sponsorship. Despite these handicaps, factual film-making has developed rich and varied forms and techniques and influenced feature film-making.

Typical of early travel films were Hepworth's *The Date Industry in Egypt* (1909) and British and Colonial's *Seal Hunting in New-*

foundland (1912) but more impressive were the expedition films, notably from Cherry Kearton's and H. G. Ponting's *With Scott to the South Pole* (1911), followed by similar records of Shackleton's voyages. Scientific films were made from an early date. Fifty-four had been made before 1914 by **F. Percy Smith** (1880–1944) who left the Board of Education to devote himself to his hobby and with his own apparatus showed such things as *The Birth of a Flower* (1910). This field was to be developed in France in the late Twenties by **Jean Painlevé** (*b* 1902). Smith collaborated with **H. Bruce Woolfe** to make the *Secrets of Nature* series (1919–1933) and Woolfe in the Twenties was to pioneer educational film-making for schools at British (later Gaumont British) Instructional, working with **Mary Field** (1896–1968).

Woolfe's postwar films included *Zeebrugge* and *The Battle of Falkland and Coronel Islands* but the First World War saw from 1914 onwards a continuous stream of actuality films. Fighting was brilliantly covered by war cameramen, notably Malins, MacDowell, Tong and Jeapes, sent abroad by the War Office Topical Committee, which sponsored a series of war films. The subject matter and photography triumph over the poor editing in such films as *The Battle of the Somme* (1916) and *The Battle of Ancre and the Advance of the Tanks* (1917).

Travel, science, newsreel and compilation were thus to be among the beginnings of documentary. But the interpretation of the material and its editing were to be the key factors in its development. In 1926 John Grierson, reviewing Flaherty's film *Moana* in *The New York Sun*, coined the word "documentary," taking over the French word "documentaire" used to denote travel pictures. Grierson, a leading theorist and formative force was later to define documentary as "the creative treatment of actuality."

Apart from the inspired vision of an individual such as Flaherty an important influence was to be Soviet cinema where material of contemporary history was used in such films as Eisenstein's *Battleship Potemkin,* Pudovkin's *The End of St. Petersburg* and in Victor Turin's factual work, *Turksib* (1927) about the building of the Turkestan-Siberian railway, to be known particularly in Britain in a version prepared by John Grierson. Editing theory had first been developed in Russia by **Dziga Vertov** (1896–1954) who made the long *The Anniversary of the October Revolution* (1918), developed his Kino Eye theory ("a record must be kept and shown of all that happens around us"), wrote manifestos, formed a group (the *konoki*) and launched a weekly newsreel, *Film Truth (Kino Pravda).* Important for documentary in his development of editing techniques, Vertov's work is somewhat a *cul-de-sac* because he refused to develop emotion or attitude in his material.

A further influence was the Continental *avant-garde* movement allied to painting which led to aesthetic films about city life. In France the Brazilian ex-architect **Alberto Cavalcanti** (*b* 1897) with *Rien que les Heures* (1926) created an impressionistic view of a day in Paris but eschewed any real social analysis. In Germany **Walter Ruttmann** (1887–1943) made *Berlin, Die Symphonie einer Grosstadt*

Still from Ruttmann's documentary, BERLIN

(1927) with a fine regard for rhythmical movement, and Billy Wilder and Robert Siodmak collaborated on *People on Sunday* (*Menschen am Sonntag,* 1929) about four young men in Berlin on a day off.

In the U.S.A. Flaherty's naturalistic mode was sustained by Merian C. Cooper and Ernest B. Schoedsack in *Grass* (1925) a silent film of great beauty about a primitive tribe in Persia and *Chang* (1928), about a Laos native. *Grass* was sponsored by Famous Players-Lasky (Paramount) who also financed Flaherty's next film *Moana* (1925), an intimate study of South Sea islanders beautifully photographed by Flaherty in a pioneering use of panchromatic film. Flaherty then made two unimportant sponsored documentaries and went again to the South Seas to produce *Tabu* (1930), photographed by Floyd Crosby but predominantly the work of co-director F. W. Murnau. Flaherty was next to make *Industrial Britain* (1931) for John Grierson, *Man of Aran* (1934) a study of primitive community life made on an Irish island, and to travel to India to shoot material used in *Elephant Boy* (1937), a Korda feature.

The 1929 economic depression and the political unrest of the Thirties were to lead to the flowering of the British documentary school of social realist films. The key figure is the Scot, **John Grierson** (*b* 1898), son of a schoolmaster, who served in the Navy, graduated from Glasgow in social science, and returned in 1929 from America after studying the new science of public relations to become with Walter Creighton joint films officer to the Empire Marketing Board where the secretary, Sir Stephen Tallents had initiated a wide programme of public relations work. Creighton made the long *One Family* (1929) but it was the modest *Drifters* (1929) made by Grierson that was the success. A simple portrayal of the herring fishing industry and trawlermen at work, using Soviet editing techniques, this film is usually regarded as the start of documentary in Britain.

Grierson and British Documentary

Grierson brought over Flaherty but more importantly he built up a group of young film-makers who had social purpose in mind as much as aesthetic achievement. Leading names included Arthur Elton, Edgar Anstey, Basil Wright, Stuart Legg, John Taylor and Paul Rotha. The Empire Marketing Board was dissolved in 1933 but the film unit transferred to the General Post Office where Sir Stephen Tallents was first Public Relations Officer. Public relations work was begun by firms and other government organisations and commercial units established such as Strand (1935) and Realist (1937). In 1937 Grierson left the GPO to set up the advisory Film Centre.

Notable films of this period include Elton's *Aero-Engine* (1934), Rotha's *Contact* (1934), Evelyn Spice's *Weather Forecast* (1934), Basil Wright's *Song of Ceylon* (1935), John Taylor's *Dawn of Iran* (1935), Stuart Legg's *BBC—The Voice of Britain* (1935), Anstey and Elton's *Housing Problems* (1935), Harry Watt's *The Saving of*

Bill Blewitt (1937), Wright and Watt's *Night Mail* (1936), distinguished by W. H. Auden's verse and Britten's music, both used again by Cavalcanti in *Coal Face* (1936). Grierson produced, advised, wrote and travelled, and established British documentary in its particular form of social realism as a world influence.

The Nazis found in **Leni Riefenstahl** (*b* 1902) a woman documentary film-maker with a brilliant editing technique and gave her full facilities to make the powerful *The Triumph of the Will* (1934) and *The Olympic Games* (1938).

In the U.S.A. the Film and Photo League made newsreels and other films about labour conflict and Seymour Stern showed Californian labour exploitation in *Imperial Valley* (1931), but the figure who compares with John Grierson in the development of social documentaries is **Pare Lorentz** (*b* 1905) a graduate, journalist and successful film critic who became films adviser to the Resettlement Agency set up by Roosevelt's New Deal to deal with farming problems. With a crew of experienced photographers (Ralph Steiner, Leo Hurwitz, and Paul Strand) Lorentz made *The Plow That Broke the Plains* (1936) about the Dust Bowl, a key film which brought emotion and meaning to a social problem. Lorentz followed it with *The River* (1937) about the Mississippi, obtained cinema screenings, and secured the formation of the United States Film Service. Through this was made Lorentz's *The Fight for Life* (1939) about childbirth and malnutrition, Ivens's *Power and the Land* (1941), and Flaherty's *The Land* (1941), as well as Lorentz's unfinished film on unemployment. But Congress, disliking Roosevelt, and probably under pressure from Hollywood interests that resented government film sponsorship, refused the Service funds after 1940.

March of Time

The *March of Time* series, later to be much copied in style, was launched in American cinemas in 1935, and, produced by Louis de Rochemont and Roy Larsen for *Time* magazine, used a punchy commentator, newsreel material, interviews and acted scenes to study political subjects in depth. 1935 also saw the establishment of a 16mm film library at the New York Museum of Modern Art, the circulation of British documentaries, and the growth of sub-standard distribution. At the New York World's Fair in 1939 many short films were shown including **Willard Van Dyke** (*b* 1906) and Ralph Steiner's *The City* (1939), propagating Lewis Mumford's ideas. Willard Van Dyke had worked with Lorentz and later formed his own company to make the vivid *Valley Town* (1940) about unemployment. He should not be confused with W. S. Van Dyke (1899–1943) who went with Flaherty to the South Seas. *kg*

Most Dutchmen believe instinctively that films, like watches and cars, are best imported from abroad. But while this prejudice, combined

Panic during a bombing raid, in Ivens's SPANISH EARTH

with other problems such as that of language, has impeded the growth of a feature film tradition in the Netherlands, it has not prevented the progress of the documentary. In **Joris Ivens** (*b* 1898) and Bert Haanstra, the Dutch have two of the greatest figures in the short film field. Albert and Willy Mullens were the pioneers in this *genre*. In 1902 they made a short fiction film, and during the next dozen years the Hague and Hollandia studios made innumerable documentaries, newsreels, and melodramas. As early as 1918, the Dutch film importers and cinema owners united under the banner of the Nederlandse Bioscoop Bond, which remains today a vital and influential organisation.

In May 1928, Ivens screened his first short, *The Bridge* (*De Brug*), a study of movement about the bridge over the Koningshaven in Rotterdam. He worked in close harmony with Mannus Franken, now undeservedly forgotten. Together they sidestepped all the familiar bulwarks of the film industry—*décor,* studio, acting—and concentrated instead on the development of a realistic documentary style involving movement within the frame and in the montage. *Rain* (*Regen,* 1928) was a dazzling photographic exercise, catching the contrast between sunny streets and a city enveloped by an unexpected shower, rivulets of water coalescing along the tumbled roofs, pedestrians confused beneath umbrellas. *Breakers* (*Branding,* 1929) showed how well Ivens could depict the moods of the sea, too, and by a happy coincidence he

THE NETHERLANDS: JORIS IVENS

found inspiration in the Dutch land reclamation programme of the early Thirties, and in the building of the great barrier dyke across the Zuyder Zee. *Zuiderzee* (1930–34) was his masterpiece on the subject, closing with an ecstatic burst of montage as the last gap in the dyke was filled. Hanns Eisler's music was wedged humorously against the images, giving a choreographic effect to the shots of men tossing stones and carrying pipes in unison.

Ivens resolved to show in his films how man continually adapts himself to his environment and to the demands of nature. A politically committed man, he concentrated on the struggle between the miners and the Belgian authorities in *Misère au Borinage* (1933); the battle between "the will of the military" and "the will of the people" in *Spanish Earth* (1937), which was filmed at the height of the Civil War in close collaboration with his brilliant cameraman, John Fernhout; and, in *Indonesia Calling!* (1946), the stubborn refusal by Australian dockers to handle Dutch ships that were bent on breaking the economy of the young Indonesian republic after the war. *pdc*

ANIMATION

Animation pre-dates the invention of cinematography by many years and, if the cave drawings discovered at Altamira, Northern Spain, in 1879 are taken into account, by centuries. These polychrome paintings, dating from approximately 9,000 B.C., depict bison, horses, hinds and wild boars. The primitive but skilful artists attempted to convey movement by giving the animals four pairs of legs in different positions. This is the earliest known manifestation of man's desire to suggest movement in art.

In later periods elements of surviving Egyptian and Grecian art show that the wish to capture the excitement and beauty of movement remained. Nearer to our own times, during the Sixteenth and Seventeenth centuries, enterprising publishers marketed books of drawings, frequently pornographic in content, which appeared to move when the pages were riffled. Further development of animation occurred during the Nineteenth century with the evolution of Victorian optical toys (see Chapter Eleven).

In Paris in 1876 **Emile Reynaud** invented the Praxinoscope, an extension of the Daedulum. A shallow cylinder with drawings of figures in motion distributed evenly around its inner surface encircled a second cylinder of mirrors, the reflecting surfaces of which were equidistant between the drawings and the common axis of the two cylinders. The pictures were viewed by looking into the mirrors as the cylinder was rotated. Reynaud then discovered that by using lenses, further mirrors and lamps the pictures could be projected on to a screen. To increase the duration of the action he drew on strips of translucent oiled paper which he named Crystalord. These drawings were then projected in conjunction with a background supplied by a magic lantern. In 1892 he opened his Optical Theatre in the Paris Waxworks, where his "films" included *Poor Pierrot* and *A Clown and His Dogs* and lasted up to fifteen minutes each. Thus animation as a public entertainment existed three years before the opening of Lumière's Cinematograph in 1895, which effectively stifled Reynaud's business.

It was eleven years before the first animated film appeared (although a paper print of an animated film from 1900, and executed by an unknown artist working for the Edison Company, exists in the Library of Congress). *Humorous Phases of Funny Faces* was made by English artist **Stuart Blackton** at the American Vitagraph studio in 1906. It showed a man rolling his eyes and blowing smoke at his sweetheart, a gentleman with a large nose and a dog jumping through a hoop. Blackton is believed to have introduced newspaper cartoonist **Winsor McCay** to the medium in 1911 but prior to McCay's *début* there had been renewed activity in France. **Emile Cohl** (1857–1938) had been a cartoonist and photographer, a happy combination of talents which he blended in 1908 in *Fantasmagorie*. His animation was simple and vigorous and Cohl realised the possibilities of the medium for effecting rapid transformations of matter, a discovery used with great fluency in *Un Drame chez les Fantoches* (1908).

Winsor McCay's first film, *Little Nemo* (1911), featured the character from his popular newspaper strip and was followed by a gruesome piece called *How a Mosquito Operates* (1911) in which a gigantic mosquito is seen feeding on a sleeping man. McCay's most famous film is *Gertie the Trained Dinosaur* (1913) and in 1918 he completed his most ambitious project, *The Sinking of the Lusitania*. Released on August 15, 1918, by Jewel Productions it is the first example of animation being used for a serious account of an actual event. *The Sinking of the Lusitania* is a milestone in the development of animation and, when considered in conjunction with McCay's other work, amply disproves Richard Schickel's view of early American animation as being "crude and hasty . . . . . reflecting no more than a suggestion of the skills that were to come."

Although animation remained something of a curiosity, it was popular and a number of series were in production from 1912 onwards. Emile Cohl crossed the Atlantic and devised *Baby Snookums* with newspaper cartoonist *George McManus,* whose strip "Bringing up Father" inspired a series released by William Randolph Hearst's International Feature Syndicate. Most of the early series were adapted from newspaper cartoon strips, including *The Katzenjammer Kids* and **George Herriman's** distinctive *Krazy Kat* (which should not be confused with **Pat Sullivan's** *Felix the Cat*). **John R. Bray** (*b* 1870) announced *The Artist's Dream,* his first cartoon, on June 12, 1913, which was followed the same year by *Col. Heeza Liar in Africa*. Intended as a lampoon of former President Teddy Roosevelt, it was so popular that a series developed from it. On January 14, 1914, Bray filed a patent, granted the same year as 811615, which described a method of registration by which drawings could be held in the same position on the artist's board and beneath the camera. This patent also embraced a system whereby the background was drawn on a transparent sheet placed over the character drawings, eliminating the need to redraw the background for every frame. The quality of the resulting film, however, was unsatisfactory and the system was wisely abandoned in favour of that patented by **Earl Hurd** (878091, granted on June 15, 1915) whereby the characters were drawn on a transparent celluloid sheet and placed over the background. This simple idea has been used as a basic animation technique ever since and is referred to as the "cell" technique, "cell" being an abbreviation of celluloid.

After this early flurry of activity, the early and middle Twenties were relatively quiet. Pat Sullivan's *Felix the Cat* made its mark but, apart from the advent of *Oswald the Rabbit,* there were no really memorable developments until the end of the decade. On September 19, 1928, the world's first sound cartoon was premiered at the Roxy Theatre in New York. The film, which featured Mickey Mouse, was called *Steamboat Willie* and its producer was **Walt Disney.** Following a period as a commercial artist in Kansas, Disney (1901–1966) had moved to Los Angeles where he made the *Alice in Cartoonland* series and films featuring Oswald the Rabbit. Disney has received an inordinate amount of space in books, magazines and newspapers and while his contribution to animation should not be minimised, the work of his contemporaries in Hollywood has too often been overshadowed. Disney himself was no great artist; his early films were largely the creation of **Ub Iwerks** and Disney always employed a large team of directors and artists to make the films which bore his name. His talents lay in the fields of story editing and accurately estimating public taste. In 1929 he made the first "Silly Symphony," *Skeleton Dance;* added colour to his attractions in 1932 with *Flowers and Trees;* and released the first of a long line of feature cartoons, *Snow White and the Seven Dwarfs,* in 1937. Inspired by Disney's success, the major film companies soon had animation units of their own busily turning out "Color Rhapsodies," "Happy Harmonies," "Rainbow Parades," "Merrie Melodies," "Looney Tunes" and so forth.

There is, incidentally, a popular misconception that Disney made the first colour cartoon. He did make the first cartoon in Technicolor's three-colour process but in 1931 **Ted Eshbaugh** (*b* 1906) previewed *Goofy Goat,* filmed in the Multicolor process. And in 1930 **Walter Lantz** (*b* 1900) made a cartoon sequence in Technicolor's two-colour process as an introduction to *King of Jazz.*

As Hollywood studios stepped up production of light, undemanding fare, artists elsewhere were experimenting with animation. A leading

WALT DISNEY

figure in the prewar *avant-garde* was **Oscar Fischinger,** who arrived in America in 1929 from Germany. His films include *Brahms' Rhapsody* (1931) and *Lichtertanz* (1932). He declared that his aim was "to produce only for the highest ideals—not thinking in terms of money or sensations to please the masses," a dictum oddly at variance with his acceptance of a commission to design a sequence based on J. S. Bach's "Toccata and Fugue in D" for Disney which was not, however, included in the final version of *Fantasia* (1940). In common with many intellectuals and critics of the time Fischinger may have regarded Disney as the Messiah of the new medium and did not feel that he was betraying his ideals by working for a blatantly commercial organisation.

In 1933 **Berthold Bartosch,** working in France, produced *L'Idée,* a black-and-white cut-out film with music by Arthur Honegger which was based on a series of woodcuts by **Franz Masereel** (*b* 1889). *L'Idée* traces the birth and progress of an artistic ideal, symbolised by a naked woman, which is crushed and its originator killed although the ideal lives on in the hearts of his followers. It needs little imagination to connect this sombre, brooding work with the rise of the Nazis in Germany.

The following year a very different film emerged from France— *Joie de Vivre* (1934) by Hector Hoppin and Anthony Gross. Where Bartosch's film was grey and gloomy, *Joie de Vivre,* also in monochrome,

From Berthold Bartosch's L'IDEE

was gay and lively. A few years later Hoppin and Gross started a feature-length version of Jules Verne's *Around the World in Eighty Days.* Unfortunately this project was abandoned at the outbreak of hostilities but the subtlety and delicacy of the design, colour and animation in the completed footage indicates that this would have been a rewarding film had it been finished.

Alexeieff

Also in France **Alexandre Alexeieff** (*b* 1901) and his wife **Claire Parker** had perfected their unique pinboard. A vertical wooden board is perforated with thousands of holes in which headless pins are placed, the apparatus being lit by four lights on either side. A picture is created by depressing the pins so that they cast shadows of varying depth and the changes in position of the pins are recorded frame by frame in the camera. Their first film using the pinboard was *Night on a Bare Mountain* (1933) and more recently they made *The Nose* (1963). Alexeïeff has also experimented with animating objects and made some superb commercials by photographing oscillating pendula to which a light source was attached.

In Germany **Lotte Reiniger** was making her famous silhouette films in which her stationery silhouettes were made from black paper and the movable ones from black card and thin metal sheet. She was assisted by Berthold Bartosch when making *The Adventures of Prince Achmed* (1926) and her activities have included a series adapted from Hugh Lofting's *Dr. Dolittle* stories.

Christchurch, New Zealand, is the birthplace of artist and film-maker extraordinary **Len Lye** (*b* 1901). After early experiments with kinetic art and drawing directly on to film, he arrived in London in 1925. He made *Tusalava* in 1928 and during the Thirties he made a series of shorts, including *Colour Box* (1935), *Rainbow Dance* (1936) and *Trade Tattoo* (1937) which were sponsored by the adventurous GPO Film Unit. In these films he combined his "direct" technique, live-action photography and ingenious processing tricks to produce work which was well ahead of its time. In 1958 came his best known film, *Free Radicals,* which won the Grand Prize at the Brussels World's Fair International Experimental Competition. *dr*

10. Economic Trends

EDISON'S KINETOSCOPE peepshow machine provided the first means of commercially exploiting the new invention of motion picture photography. From the beginning in 1894 Kinetoscope parlours quickly sprang up across the U.S.A. and machines were imported into Europe. Initially Edison resisted pressure from showmen to make a projector, believing that this would soon kill the market. He thought that ten projectors would be sufficient for the United States, perhaps fifty for the whole world.

The Kinetoscope took fifty feet of film and the first films, all made in the "Black Maria" studio at West Orange, New Jersey, usually featured vaudeville acts of the day. Major Latham, an enterprising veteran of the Civil War, asked Edison to film a prize fight. Latham showed it, round-by-round, in banks of six Kinetoscopes adapted to take one round each: the result was so successful that he and his sons decided to make their own camera, capable of taking longer films of complete fights. This meant placing a free loop of film between the spools and the intermittent mechanism to absorb the strain—an important principle in the patent disputes which were to follow. In May 1895 the Lathams gave the first commercial motion picture show on a screen, using a crude projector adapted from the Kinetoscope. It had the same continuous film motion so the picture must have been unsteady and very dim, but the shows were a success.

Meanwhile in London, Robert Paul, a scientific instrument maker, agreed to copy the Kinetoscope to meet local demands after he found that Edison had not patented his invention outside America. Within months Paul devised his own camera and applied the intermittent principle to a projector which he demonstrated late in 1895. The Kinetoscope also inspired the Lumière brothers, French manufacturers of photographic materials. They too made cameras and projectors and, in the summer of 1895, began to send their camera-showmen on tours through Europe and Asia photographing, developing and exhibiting their films as they went.

Edison was soon faced with competition from the import of European equipment. The films of Lumière and Paul also seemed more attractive because their cameras were hand-operated and portable. They could picture outdoor scenes across the world when the Kinetoscope camera was held captive in the "Black Maria" by its electric drive. A further threat was posed by the Mutoscope, a rival peepshow machine with pictures printed on cards around the outside of a revolving drum. It soon ousted the Kinetoscope, and a few Mutoscopes still survive as "What the Butler Saw" machines.

In response Edison lent his name to the Vitascope, a projector with

A 35mm Cine Camera made by Baxter and Wray of Bradford, in 1897, the first movie camera to be imported into Japan. (Now in the Barnes Museum of Cinematography, St. Ives, Cornwall)

an intermittent motion designed by an American inventor, Thomas Armat. The Vitascope was leased to showmen for use only in their own territory, but the system broke down under intensive competition. Edison's most powerful rival was American Biograph, launched in 1896 as an offshoot from Mutoscope. In the early stages the Biograph camera used an ingenious system of irregular image registration on the film to avoid conflict with the Edison patents. Biograph also used a larger film, and their projector produced a brighter, sharper picture than its rivals.

For the next decade the film reached its public in America as a ten-minute turn in the vaudeville theatres. Elsewhere they were seen as occasional novelties, presented by travelling showmen. The only exceptions were the prize fights, filmed at greater and greater length and shown as special engagements in theatres and concert halls. It was an era of intense and often unscrupulous competition. The authentic film of the Corbett-Fitzsimmons fight in 1897 was rivalled by a "pirate" version made by Sigmund Lubin in which the fight was re-enacted from the newspaper reports. In 1899 Vitagraph were even more resourceful. They smuggled a camera into the Jeffries-Sharkey fight that Biograph had arranged to film. An alternative form of piracy was simply to copy and re-sell successful films, for it was easy to make a "dupe" negative from a print and prints were sold outright in those early days.

In December 1897 Edison tried to win back control of the medium and began a patent suit against American Mutoscope and Biograph. It was the beginning of a lengthy series of disputes in the courts which dragged on indecisively until 1907. During those years the industry grew rapidly. When interest in the primitive films declined audiences were won back with the story films that followed the innovations of Edwin S. Porter. To accommodate the longer programmes Nickelodeons began to spread across the country. They were primitive and often crudely constructed halls, usually in poorer neighbourhoods, with a five or ten cent admission charge. Within five years many American cities had over a hundred. Their programmes of five or six films were changed every few days, which created an opportunity for film exchanges that bought prints from the producers and then hired them out to the Nickelodeons.

By 1907 the main producers in America were Edison, Biograph, Kalem, Vitagraph, Lubin, Selig, and Essanay. There was also Star Films selling Méliès films, and Pathé. A crucial court decision of 1907 upholding Edison's camera patents led to all except Biograph becoming licensees of Edison. In 1908 Biograph, armed with the Latham patents and an option on Armat's, also settled with Edison and the nine companies formed the Motion Picture Patents Company, a trust which was intended to establish—somewhat belatedly—a patents monopoly. All production would be in the hands of the Trust, who would issue licenses to projector owners allowing them to show only the films made by the Trust.

The establishment of the Trust coincided with the first attempts by government and local administrations to control the industry. In Britain the Cinematograph Act of 1909 came into force. Since the Paris Charity Bazaar fire of 1897 in which nearly 180 people died, the hazard associated with the inflammable cellulose nitrate film had never been far from the public mind. Cinemas now had to be licensed by the local authority, and stringent conditions were laid down for the handling of film and the safety of the audience. Indirectly, however, the act gave the power of censorship to local authorities who cared to insist on the prior approval of the films to be shown. An attempt to resolve a potentially chaotic situation was made by the Kinematograph Manufacturers Association: in 1912 they set up the British Board of Film Censors to provide a system of self-censorship which eventually won general recognition. In America the Trust was faced with a similar problem. After the New York authorities had tried, unsuccessfully, to close the city's five hundred Nickelodeons in 1908 the Motion Picture Patents Company established a National Board of Censorship in an attempt to disarm their opponents.

The Trust next turned its attention to the exchanges, hoping to create a vertically integrated monopoly. Exchanges, like exhibitors,

Second Phase
1908–1919

Early American cinema: THE LIFE OF MOSES

were to be licensed but this created some resentment. Defying the Trust, Bauman and Kessel began production under the "Bison" trademark and Carl Laemmle formed "Imp" in Chicago to provide films for his exchanges. Independent production was fraught with difficulties because the Trust made vigorous and even violent attempts to enforce its monopoly. Films therefore had to be made behind locked doors, and the situation favoured the general movement of independent production away from Chicago and New York to California. To strengthen its hold on distribution the Trust formed the General Film Company in 1910 and by 1912 the new distribution company had bought fifty-seven of the fifty-eight principal exchanges. However, at this point, only just over half of the 10,000 Nickelodeons in America were licensed by the Trust which meant that the independents had no shortage of outlets. Their production problems were also eased somewhat in 1911 when Eastman (later Eastman Kodak) ended their exclusive arrangements with the Trust, fearing anti-trust legislation, and put their raw films on the open market.

The independents consolidated their position by amalgamations which resulted in the Mutual Film Company, formed in 1912, and the Universal Film Manufacturing Company formed by Laemmle around Imp.

Until this time all American production was geared to the Nickelodeons which required a diet of fast-moving films of about fifteen minutes each but in Europe there was a growing interest in adapting famous literary and theatrical subjects at some length and in 1912 Adolph Zukor secured a license from the Trust to import one into the U.S.A. Zukor, a Hungarian immigrant with a career in penny arcades behind him, presented *Queen Elizabeth* (1912, *dir* Louis Mercanton) with Sarah Bernhardt in a Broadway theatre. Its success led Zukor to form Famous Players to produce similar films in America but though the results were acceptable on Broadway they did not appeal to the Nickelodeons. Both the Trust and many independents therefore opposed the idea of longer films even though, the following year, the eight-reel *Quo Vadis* (1912) produced by Cines in Italy effectively showed that length did not necessarily mean boring theatricality.

The star system, which was later to provide the American film with its most potent medium of publicity, effectively began in 1910. Producers had protected themselves from having to pay large salaries to their performers by keeping them anonymous until, in the course of their battle with the Trust, Imp won Florence Lawrence away from Biograph in a blaze of publicity. In 1914 *Photoplay* magazine was founded to satisfy the growing curiosity of an eager public and within another two years Chaplin and Mary Pickford were rivalling each other to be the first to have a million dollar contract.

Between 1914 and 1919 the American film industry went through a period of rapid development and transformation; the pattern created by the rise of the feature film still survives today, along with many of the companies formed at that time. Paramount Pictures Corporation was formed in 1914 by merging a group of independent exchanges; it had a distribution contract with Famous Players, and entered the theatre business the following year. In 1916 Zukor merged Famous Players with Jesse Lasky's production company and acquired Paramount to create a vertical combine, active in production, distribution and exhibition. William Fox, an exhibitor and exchange owner, formed the Fox Film Company in 1914 to secure his supply of pictures. In 1919 Marcus Loew, another prominent theatre owner, bought the Metro Pictures Corporation, along with the services of its secretary Louis B. Mayer and subsequently merged Metro with a company formed by Samuel Goldfish and Edward Selwyn in 1916, called Goldwyn Pictures to form Metro-Goldwyn-Mayer. Goldfish, who had already left the Goldwyn company before the merger, later changed his own name to Goldwyn and, after some dispute with the name's new owners, went his own way as a producer. Harry Warner and his three brothers ventured into production in 1913 after being active in exhibition and exchanges, though the Warner Brothers company of the modern era was not established until 1923. In 1917 the First National Exhibitors Circuit formed a production unit to combat the system of block-booking imposed by some exchanges: First National was eventually merged into Warner Brothers.

Meanwhile the earlier producers began to fall by the wayside as the Nickelodeon era came to an end and more luxurious theatres took their place. In 1917 a court judgement against the Trust put an end to what remained of its patent monopoly but by that time Edison, Kalem, Lubin and Biograph had already shut down, unable or unwilling to compete with feature films. 1918 saw the end of Mutual, and in 1919 the General Film Company was wound up in debt, although Vitagraph survived until it was acquired by Warner Brothers in 1925.

By 1919 most of the film production in America was in the hands of companies formed by entrepreneurs who had first established themselves in exhibition or distribution. There was, however, acute competition between them for the services of the most popular stars and

The founders of United Artists: Fairbanks, Pickford, Chaplin, and Griffith

successful directors; realising their power Douglas Fairbanks, Mary Pickford, Charles Chaplin and D. W. Griffith formed United Artists to distribute their own films. A cynic was heard to remark "So, the lunatics have taken charge of the asylum."

During the 1914–1918 war, film production in France, Britain and Germany suffered a serious set-back. The Italian industry continued for a while to make historical spectaculars and production flourished in the neutral countries of Scandinavia. Sweden was most active, althoug'h the Danish Nordisk company made headroads into the German market. The American industry was quick to exploit its advantage, and the mythology of the American stars that was imprinted on the minds of audiences in the years of war was enough to ensure a ready market in the years that followed.

The decade following 1919 was one of consolidation in America. *Third Phase* There was a large, secure and relatively stable market both at home *1919–1929* and abroad. Indeed the wealth that came with it was accompanied by signs of moral decadence which threatened to destroy Hollywood from within. Matters came to a head when comedian Fatty Arbuckle was implicated in the death of a young actress during an orgiastic party; a public outcry followed, which accelerated the move to draft Will Hays, postmaster general in President Harding's administration, to head a new organisation for self-regulation in the industry. Hays opened the offices of the Motion Picture Producers and Distributors of America Inc. in March 1922, creating the organ of film censorship known as "The Hays Office." The M.P.P.D.A. also brought order to the chaotic commercial conditions of the film business. It established standard forms of contract, and acted as a central negotiating body in matters of government policy and overseas trade.

In Britain there was an upsurge of production during the four years following the war, and an attempt to enter the American market. In 1921 the British National Film League tried to bolster the popularity and prestige of British films with special festive weeks throughout England; the result, however, rebounded to their discredit because there were not enough good films. The general mood of optimism persuaded Cecil Hepworth, one of the leading producers of the preceding decade, to begin an ambitious expansion of his Walton-on-Thames studios but he was trapped by the serious recession that followed in 1923, his company was liquidated and his career came to an end. The situation did not improve until the Cinematograph Act of 1927 imposed a quota system on renters and exhibitors. The Quota Act, as it was known, guaranteed a showing and a reasonable financial return for British films, but it also encouraged the production of "quota quickies"—cheaply made films designed merely to fulfil the requirements of the act at the least cost and greatest profit.

Indigenous production was also stimulated by legislation in France

The city as a force for good and evil in Murnau's SUNRISE

and Germany. As the war ended the German government persuaded the Deutsches Bank to finance the Universum Film A.G., known as Ufa. Local producers were supported by the *Kontingent* law under which every American film was offset by a German production. The favourable conditions encouraged some highly original productions and although their blend of expressionism and mystical fantasy may have reflected a morbid aspect of the nation's postwar outlook it also attracted the attention of serious filmgoers in Britain and America and several prominent German actors and film-makers went to work in Hollywood. It was a trend which accelerated with the rise of the Nazis in the Thirties. British technicians like Hitchcock went to work in the Ufa studios to gather experience while German directors were brought in to impart their style to British films. The rise of the German film in the Twenties did much to extinguish the Danish and Swedish film, while Victor Sjöström was one of the first of many prominent European talents to go to America.

The French film industry had been almost completely paralysed by the war, and failed to recapture its former pre-eminence. The rather chaotic conditions, however, favoured some experimental productions which encouraged members of the fashionable intellectual and artistic movement of the day to work in the medium of film. France also absorbed a group of Russian *émigrés* including the director Volkov and the actor Ivan Mosjoukine who had made films in Russia before the Revolution.

The Revolution of course transformed the Soviet film industry, which was nationalised in 1919. Normal commercial factors were no longer important, for Soviet films were made as propaganda to carry the communistic message to the people. Outside Russia the aesthetic constructed around this purpose by Eisenstein, Pudovkin and others attracted the attention of intellectuals, though the revolutionary impact of films like *Battleship Potemkin* often created problems. In Britain it was banned by the B.B.F.C. and was first shown by the Film Society, formed in London in 1925. Because its shows were private the Film Society avoided censorship, and similar bodies were later established in towns throughout the country. It was the beginning of the film society movement which now extends throughout many countries, providing an outlet for films which cannot, for various reasons, be seen in commercial cinemas.

Edison originally intended to synchronise his Kinetoscope with the phonograph to provide talking pictures but it was not until 1926 that the industry began to revive the idea. The first experiments with short films still used synchronised discs but the success of *The Jazz Singer,* the first sound feature released by Warner Bros. in 1927, quickly established a demand for a system of recording sound on film. In the eight years from 1927 to 1934 Western Electric received twenty million dollars from the sale and licensing of their equipment.

The introduction of sound had a major effect on the financial control of many of the major companies for a good deal of the necessary capital came from Wall Street. The financial institutions had been increasing their hold since 1919, and several companies (Loew, Fox and Pathe) already had stock market quotations: by the late Twenties all the pioneers except Fox and Laemmle had allowed control to pass to banking interests. In 1929, on a wave of prosperity, Fox embarked on three ambitious take-over bids: a prominent theatre circuit, a 49½% voting interest in Gaumont-British and the acquisition of Loews Inc., controlling M-G-M. An alliance between Western Electric and Fox's bankers exploited the vulnerable position in which Fox placed himself through heavy borrowing, Fox was ousted from control, and Western Electric equipment supplanted the Movietone system which Fox had pioneered. Meanwhile an anti-trust action prevented the Fox-Loew merger, and in 1935 the company passed under new management when it was merged with the Twentieth Century company operated by Joseph Schenck and Darryl F. Zanuck.

By 1930 eight companies dominated the industry—"the big five,"

Fox, M-G-M, Warner Brothers, Paramount and RKO, and "the little three," Columbia, Universal and United Artists. Western Electric initially secured contracts with all except RKO, which had been formed by a series of amalgamations to provide an outlet for the RCA sound system. By 1936 it was possible to trace major holdings in all eight companies to the two powerful banking groups of Morgan and Rockefeller.

In Britain the American companies supplied the larger part of the market, as well as making their quota of British productions. Cinemas, however, were mainly in British hands with Gaumont-British and the Associated British Picture Corporation—the two largest groups—each owning some 300 cinemas out of a total of about 4,400 in 1936. Both groups were vertical combines on the American pattern. Gaumont-British developed from the original Gaumont agency under its founder Lt.-Col. A. C. Bromhead, and the subsequent merging of various interests in production, distribution and exhibition; the Ostrer brothers, powerful merchant bankers, controlled the group until Twentieth Century-Fox took a substantial holding. The Associated British Picture Corporation was formed in 1933 by John Maxwell, formerly a solicitor in Scotland, who entered the industry in 1912. It embodied British International Pictures, a major production unit operating Elstree Studios, the Associated British Cinemas circuit and two distribution companies, one of which—Pathe Pictures—had evolved from the original French pioneer's agency in Britain.

For a time it seemed a third group might form around Alexander Korda, an itinerant Hungarian director who founded London Films to make *The Private Life of Henry VIII* in 1933. Produced for little over £50,000, the film was an unparalleled international success, returning almost tenfold on its investment. On the strength of it Korda, financed by the Prudential Assurance Company, built a new studio at Denham to rival Hollywood and joined the board of United Artists, who were backing a new cinema circuit formed by Oscar Deutsch, a Birmingham scrap merchant.

Another backer for Deutsch's Odeon circuit was a wealthy Yorkshire flour miller and prominent Methodist, J. Arthur Rank, who arrived in London to make religious films. When he encountered difficulty in having his first efforts shown Rank also took an interest in General Film Distributors, a company formed by C. M. Woolf, hitherto general manager of Gaumont-British.

In 1936 Maxwell of A.B.P.C. tried to buy out the Ostrer interests and secure control of Gaumont-British, but Twentieth Century-Fox opposed the move. When Maxwell died in 1940 Gaumont-British was in financial collapse and Rank was able to purchase a majority holding. Then Deutsch died in 1941 and Rank also bought Odeon. And when the optimistic bubble inflated by Korda's early success burst in 1939

Rank was asked to take over Denham studios, which he added to Pinewood and the Gaumont-British studios at Shepherds Bush and Islington. Meanwhile Warner Bros. acquired control of A.B.P.C. by buying Maxwell's holdings.

11. Technical Developments

IT MAY SEEM on the face of it, that this section on technical aspects of the cinema devotes an undue proportion of its space to early cinema history, more for instance than the sections about the films themselves, which while dealing faithfully with the landmarks of the past can in good faith report a plenitude of films of quality and depth in later years. But there is a reason. With the cinema, the initial inventions were all-important in determining the shape the new process would take. As with other inventions (the steam engine, the motor car, television) it was the initial steps that needed genius, and subsequent modifications have been just that—important improvements in the practical or commercial sense, but not of the same order as the invention of something new in principle. Another difference common to other spheres is that early workers have often been individualists, pursuing their researches from a sense of adventure and discovery, backed by relatively modest resources and with financial return at the end an uncertain quality. When the invention is successfully established and has acquired a commercial structure and a place in the economy, further developments tend to be a matter of big companies, large financial resources, committees, teams of technicians and not infrequently that admixture of "gimmickry" which the influence of the sales side imports into combined operations. With whatever degree of exaggeration it is to the early days that the stories belong of genius struggling in a garret towards a marvellous new discovery. A final point is that as soon as films became a big capital industry using expensive equipment and purpose-made buildings, conservatism set in, and change became more expensive and more difficult. Both the history of sound and wide-screen illustrate this. The industry resisted the introduction of sound as long as it could, and the only wide-screen process to be universally adopted was the one that required least modification.

The commercial cinema as we know it depends on showing an audience moving pictures on a screen. The first problem the early pioneers solved was that of creating an illusion of movement. Impressions on the eye last for a fraction of a second, and to persuade the human eye that it is seeing continuous movement, it is sufficient to present a series of still pictures (about sixteen a second) showing successive stages of the movement, and hide from the eye the change from one picture to another.

These features were embodied in a simple form in the Phenakistiscope (or Deceive Look) invented by the Belgian philosopher and scientist, **Joseph Antoine Ferdinand Plateau** (1801–1883), in 1832, and in the Zoëtrope (also known as the Daedelum or wheel of life) invented by **William George Horner** (1786–1837), a Bristol inventor and showman, in 1834. Both used a wheel that could be spun by hand, carrying a series of little pictures, but with interruptions in the view which hid the substitution of one picture for another. Plateau's wheel was a flat disc like a circular fan with pictures on one side and slots through which the spectator looked. When held up to a mirror, the spectator saw the successive pictures through the slots, while the spaces between hid the changing of the pictures. Horner's device took the form of a revolving drum with a strip of paper carrying pictures tucked round the inside and slots above, through which the viewer looked and saw the pictures moving on the far side of the drum. It should be noted that both these early toys used hand-drawn pictures and a further element was necessary for the cinema as we know it— photography. The optical properties of the camera obscura (Latin: a dark room), which was first a dark room then a small box, had been known for centuries, and is referred to by the Arabian scholar Ibn Al-Haitham (965–1038). In April 1816, **Joseph Nicéphore Niepce** (1765–1833) began his experiments, and took *the* first photograph in 1826 or 1827. On December 14, 1829, Niepce went into partnership with **Louis Jacques Mondé Daguerre** (1787–1851), after whom the Daguerrotype, the first popular form of photography in the late 1830s and early 1840s, was named. Modern photography may be said to date from this period when these two Frenchmen succeeded in developing and fixing the pictures made in a camera by light acting on sensitive chemicals.

Hand-drawn moving pictures were developed to the limit by **Emile Reynaud** (1844–1918), who, when he was a science teacher at Put-en-Velay, invented the Praxinoscope in 1877. It was generally similar to the toys of Plateau and Horner but used mirrors placed in the centre of the drum to both reflect and animate the images. By using longer and longer strips of pictures, and making other improvements such as projecting on to a screen, Reynaud established his Théâtre Optique in the Cabinet Fantastique of the Musée Grévin on the Boulevard Montmartre in Paris, which showed films of up to fifteen minutes and between 1892 and 1900 played to half a million spectators. In the last years of the Théâtre Optique some of the films were made up of successive phases of action taken with a still camera and pieced together, a recognition that the future belonged to photography.

By the 1830s with the illusion of movement and the process of photography, the elements of the cinema had been invented. But it took sixty years, until the 1890s, to combine the various elements in a

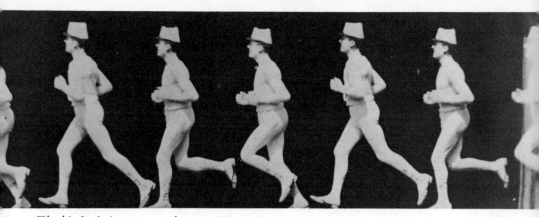

The birth of cinematography: one of E. J. Marey's experiments

sufficiently developed form for them to be used in showing films to an audience. For instance one feature absent from the early devices already mentioned was the projection of the picture on to a screen which not only gave a large, bright image but also enabled a sufficient number of people to view the picture at the same time. Projection was borrowed from the magic lantern performances of the Nineteenth century which used both hand-drawn and photographic transparencies, and the cinema took over the lamp-house and the electric light or lime-light of the magic lantern and added its own film mechanism.

There were many attempts to photograph successive phases of movement. One such attempt was made by the American **Coleman Sellers** (1827–1907) in 1861. In 1852 an Englishman, **Sir Charles Wheatstone** (1802–1875) photographed a series of images and tried to combine them with the principle of the zoëtrope. However, the British photographer, **Eadweard Muybridge** (1830–1904), gained far more attention partly because of his involvement in a sensational trial at which he was accused of killing his wife's lover, as well as his important work as a photographer. The climax to his career came in 1877 when he took successive photographs of a galloping horse, which proved that all four feet of a horse are off the ground at certain moments. He used a series of twenty-four cameras placed side by side along the track, and his work owed a great deal to **E. J. Marey** (1830–1904), a French physiologist, interested in analysing human and animal locomotion.

Marey's first apparatus for photographing movement was the photographic gun or revolver, also used by the French astronomer, Pierre Jules César, when he recorded the passage of Venus across the sun in 1874. Behind the barrel a circular photographic plate was moved intermittently by means of an eccentric wheel giving ten to twelve exposures a second. Marey, impressed by Muybridge's work, devised a chronophotographic camera using both rolls of sensitive paper (1888) and bands of celluloid film (1890). Both LePrince in England (1888) and Albert Londe in Paris made camera-projectors with multiple lenses. Around the same period, other technicians working on cameras and projectors were J. A. R. Rudge (1875), Wordsworth Donisthorpe (1889), F. H. Varley (1890), William Friese-Greene and Mortimer Evans. An assistant of Marey, **Georges Demeney** (1850–1917), attempted to commercialise Marey's work. In 1891 he broke with Marey, and patented his own camera, "the Bioscope." In 1892 and 1893, Demeney attempted, not entirely unsuccessfully, to combine moving pictures and sound.

Demeney's combination with sound followed the work of the famous American inventor, **Thomas Alva Edison** (1847–1937), who in 1877 patented his invention, the phonograph, forerunner of the gramophone. In 1888, as a result of a meeting with Muybridge, Edison assigned one of his collaborators, **W. K. L. Dickson** (1860–1937), to work on a "kineto-phonograph" that would combine sound and images. Edison saw that the two would have to be integrally linked, but he originally tried to link them the wrong way round and to make pictures in a continuous spiral on a cylinder or plate joined to the cylinder of the phonograph. It was not until fifty years later that the linkage was made the other way, by putting a photographic soundtrack on the film alongside the images. Though he failed in synchronising with sound, Dickson succeeded in finding a workable system of moving pictures, and was perhaps the first to use strips of celluloid film manufactured by the Eastman Kodak Company. By 1891 the Edison team had produced a kinetograph (for taking moving pictures) and a kinetoscope (for showing them), and by 1894 kinetoscopes, a sort of peepshow for individual viewing, were being manufactured on a large scale.

THE LUMIÈRES   In Paris the two **Lumière** brothers, **Auguste** (1862–1954) and **Louis** (1864–1948), were to perfect their *cinématographe,* and were to be the first to exploit the invention by distribution and production. The brothers were the owners of a flourishing photographic business at Lyon. In 1895 they patented what was perhaps the final key device in the invention of motion pictures—a claw mechanism with hooks which seized the film (by perforations along the edges), pulled the next frame into place in front of that lamp in a metal "gate" while

194

the lamp was obscured by a moving shutter, held the picture steady while the light shone through it, then pulled down the next frame of the film, and so on. (This device was later supplanted by a maltese cross system which did not tear film so easily.) The Lumière device (which was likened to the shuttle of a sewing machine) was patented in February 1895, and in the same year the Lumière brothers designed a combined camera printer and projector. Various demonstrations to scientific bodies followed and the first public performance to a paying audience took place on Saturday, December 28, 1895 in the basement of the Grand Café in Paris. By the afternoon the queue stretched from the Boulevard des Capucines to the Rue Caumartin.

Edison's kinetoscope inspired others besides the Lumières. In England **R. W. Paul** (1869–1943) and **Birt Acres** (1854–1918) devised their own camera, and produced their first film in February 1895. However, the first public performance in London was by the Cinématographe Lumière in February 1896. In Germany, two showmen, the brothers **Max** (1863–1939) and **Emile Skladanowsky**, specialists in magic lantern shows, invented the bioscope, a projector with two lenses showing two related reels of film simultaneously, superimposed on the same screen, and using metal eyelets for the perforations. Their machine was used at a performance on November 1, 1895, which antedates the Lumière performance. However, it must be remembered that this

LA SORTIE DES USINES LUMIERE

projector could only show a continuous loop of film strip, and the apparatus was out of date by 1896.

As may be seen from the foregoing paragraphs, no one person can claim to have invented the cinema. The honours were widely shared.

THE NEW ART

Although few of them realised it, the inventors had created a new art; and in considering subsequent technical change we should remember that as with other arts, so with the cinema, it is meaningless to speak of progress. There may be an increase in variety and quantity, but the art of an Egyptian painter working thousands of years ago is just as beautiful (that is just as true and moving) as that of Turner or Bacon. The early works of the cinema seem imperfect because we see them as we see battered and broken Greek statues. When (very rarely) brand new prints can be made from perfect negatives the results are a revelation and quite as fine as perfectly preserved and reproduced early photographs. Fortunately, as with Greek statues, the wit, humour, humanity and even grandeur of early films is still discernible through their imperfections.

If not progress, at least there has been plenty of development or change in the cinema, more than in most other arts. Compared with painting, music, or theatre, changes (on the surface at least) have been many and, as intended, often startling. Wide-screen, Cinerama, Circlorama, VistaVision, 3-D, colour systems by the dozen, sound and stereophonic systems by the handful. Most stunning has been cinema architecture, growing from the fairground booths and borrowed halls of the early period (nickelodeons, vaudevilles and converted shops); through eras of wild extravagance with Egyptian, Chinese and Indian temples, starry roofs, arabesque screens, writhing columns, plush foyers; down to the plainer, more functional cinemas of today.

Where there *has* been progress is in the convenience, range and flexibility of film-making equipment. Early equipment was portable but limited in its range. During the Twenties and Thirties equipment became more elaborate but at the same time more elephantine. The years since the Second World War (and no doubt the war helped) have seen the development of light, efficient cameras and sound apparatus, enormous progress in 16mm film-making, increased flexibility of lenses (including the introduction of the zoom lens), more sensitive and more versatile film, both black-and-white and colour. With these have come greater reliability in processing, better editing machines, and more facility in obtaining special effects.

Of all technical changes no doubt the most important have been the addition of sound and colour. Dickson's efforts to combine moving pictures with sound were abandoned, and the popularity of the silent screen with piano or orchestral accompaniment postponed the introduction of sound, although there were a number of experiments during the silent era. Many scientific researchers were active, however, and

The first "talkie": Al Jolson in THE JAZZ SINGER

over two dozen names could be listed of those who worked on photo-electric sound (sound on film) transforming sound waves into light waves and back again, or on systems of sound on gramophone discs. The most important name for the cinema is that of **Lee de Forest** (1873–1961), an American technician who invented the audion tube in 1906, the key invention which made it possible to amplify micro-phonic sound to fill the auditorium, and led to public address systems, and helped in the expansion of radio and electronics, as well as the talkies. Forest's invention, the phonofilm, on which he worked between 1919 and 1924, was based on the principle of photographs of sound waves obtained by means of electrode valves. However, the industry was slow to adopt sound and there were years of delay at every stage. The public was apathetic at first. Silent films could be sold to the masses, and the installation of sound systems required a heavy capital investment. It was only in 1926 that Warner Brothers began to take an interest in a sound on disc process, hoping that it would get them out of their financial difficulties; public acclaim only came fifteen

SOUND

197

months later with the success of *The Jazz Singer,* first screened in New York on October 6, 1927; and the complete change to sound took another three years in America and until the early Thirties in some other countries.

Sound equipment has steadily improved, but the only new feature in the exhibition field has been the introduction of stereophonic sound, an over-publicised device whereby different parts of the soundtracks can be played through loudspeakers in different parts of the auditorium. In the technical field, an important development is the perfection of magnetic instead of optical sound, and this is now used for all original recording. Magnetic sound is used for 70mm films, but has not been generally introduced into cinemas largely because of the cost of converting the sound reproducing heads in all cinema projectors, but it has its advocates.

COLOUR
Colour photography dates back to 1861 when James Clerk Maxwell produced the first colour photograph, of a tartan rosette. It was first successfully applied to films in 1906 by G. A. Smith of the Brighton school of film pioneers, and the system he used was called Kinemacolor. Smith used alternate red and green filters rotated in front of the lens, with the film travelling through the projector at thirty-two frames per second. All colour systems depend on splitting up natural colours into their primary colours, recording these on separate emulsion layers or films and then synthesising them again on the screen. Maxwell's and Smith's systems were both additive, that is the picture on the screen was built up by adding different coloured lights. Various methods were used to obtain the primary colour records, the most important of which were (a) shooting adjacent frames through different coloured filters, (b) using a double-lensed camera with different coloured filters to photograph the same scene on two films simultaneously, (c) using strands of dye to cover the film with a microscopic network containing the three primary colours. The most successful additive system was Dufaycolor, perfected for motion picture work as early as 1925 by Louis Dufay, and first used for a feature film in *Radio Parade* (1934). However, all additive systems suffered from a number of defects; in particular, a bright picture required more light than a cinema projector could supply.

Subtractive systems employ dyes of the three subtractive primary colours, which are complementary to the additive primaries of red, green and blue. Colours are produced on the screen by subtracting their complementary colour from the white light of the projector. The first subtractive system, introduced in 1912, used different coloured emulsions on either side of the film.

Technicolor for its early features, the first of which was *The Gulf Between* (1917), employed an additive method, but this was discontinued in the early Twenties. With *The Toll of the Sea* in 1922

198

Technicolor adopted a subtractive process, and this same process was *Technicolor* still in use in 1929 when the first Technicolor sound feature, *On With the Show,* was released. In common with many early additive systems, however, the process was based on a simplified two colour technique, which gave acceptable, though not completely realistic colour rendition.

It was not until the Thirties that Technicolor, after considerable research, evolved a three-colour subtractive process suitable for production on a large scale. It was used first in Walt Disney's *Flowers and Trees* (1932), and in *La Cucaracha* (1934), and with it colour came gradually into general commercial use. Even so, colour was expensive and the results uncertain, and it was only slowly as time went on that any substantial number of films was made in colour. However, the popularity of colour films—*Becky Sharp* (1935), *Snow White and the Seven Dwarfs* (1938), *Gone with the Wind* (1939), *The Wizard of Oz* (1939), *The Thief of Bagdad* (1940)—led to greater and greater use of colour until today colour features far outnumber black-and-white. *rs, rc, as*

Filming in silent days. Alf Sjöberg (second from right) with his crew on location for THE STRONGEST (1929)

Select Bibliography

Agee, James. *Agee on Film.* 2 vols. New York: Mcdowell Obolensky, 1958 and 1960. London: Peter Owen, 1963.

Anderson, Joseph L. and Donald Richie. *The Japanese Film.* Rutland (Vermont): Charles E. Tuttle, 1959. New York: Grove Press, 1960.

Anderson, Lindsay. *Making a Film.* London: Allen and Unwin, 1952.

Armes, Roy. *Alain Resnais.* London: A. Zwemmer, 1968. New York: A. S. Barnes, 1968.

———. *French Cinema Since 1946.* London: A. Zwemmer, 1970. New York: A. S. Barnes, 1970.

Arnheim, Rudolf. *Film as Art.* Berkeley: University of California Press, 1957. London: Faber, 1967.

Balazs, Bela. *Theory of the Film.* London: Dennis Dobson, 1952.

Balshofer, Fred J. and Arthur C. Miller. *One Reel a Week.* Berkeley: University of California Press, 1967.

Banaskiewicz, Wladyslaw, *and others. Contemporary Polish Cinematography.* Warsaw: Polonia Publishing House, 1962.

Barnouw, Eric and S. Krishnaswamy. *Indian Film.* New York: Columbia University Press, 1963.

Barr, Charles. *Laurel and Hardy.* London: Studio Vista, 1967.

Barry, Iris and Eileen Bowser. *D. W. Griffith.* New York: Museum of Modern Art, 1965.

Baxter, John. *Hollywood in the Thirties.* London: A. Zwemmer, 1968. New York: A. S. Barnes, 1968.

Bazin, André. *Qu'est-ce que le cinéma?* 4 vols. Paris: Editions du Cerf, 1958–62.

Béranger, Jean. *La Grande Aventure du Cinéma Suedois.* Paris: Le Terrain Vague, 1960.

———. *Le Nouveau Cinéma Scandinave.* Paris: Le Terrain Vague, 1969.

Beylie, Claude. *Max Ophuls.* Paris: Editions Seghers, 1963.

Boček, Jaroslav. *Jiří Trnka.* Prague: Artia, 1965.

Bogdanovich, Peter. *John Ford.* London: Studio Vista, 1967.

Brownlow, Kevin. *The Parade's Gone By.* New York: Alfred Knopf, 1968. London: Secker and Warburg, 1969.

Budgen, Suzanne. *Fellini.* London: British Film Institute, 1966.

Butler, Ivan. *Horror in the Cinema.* London: A. Zwemmer, 1970. New York: A. S. Barnes, 1970.

Calder-Marshall, Arthur. *The Innocent Eye: The Life of Robert J. Flaherty.* London: W. H. Allen, 1963.

Cameron, Ian (ed.). *The Films of Robert Bresson.* London: Studio Vista, 1969.

Cameron, Ian and Robin Wood. *Antonioni.* London: Studio Vista, 1968.

Chardère, Bernard. *Jean Renoir*. Lyon: SERDOC, 1962.

Clair, René. Reflections on the Cinema. (Translation from *Réflexion faite*. Paris: Gallimard, 1951.) London: William Kimber, 1953.

Clarens, Carlos. *Horror Movies*. London: Secker and Warburg, 1968.

Colpi, Henri. *Defense et Illustration de la Musique dans le Film*. Lyon: SERDOC, 1963.

Cowie, Peter. *Antonioni, Bergman, Resnais*. London: Tantivy Press, 1963.

————. *The Cinema of Orson Welles*. London: A. Zwemmer, 1965. New York: A. S. Barnes, 1965.

————. *Sweden: an Illustrated Guide*. 2 vols. London: A. Zwemmer, 1970. New York: A. S. Barnes, 1970.

Donner, Jörn. *The Personal Vision of Ingmar Bergman*. Bloomington: Indiana University Press, 1964.

Eisenstein, Sergei. *Film Form* and *Film Sense*. Edited and translated by Jay Leyda. 1 vol. New York: Meridian Books, 1957.

Eisner, Lotte. *The Haunted Screen*. London: Thames and Hudson, 1969.

Everson, William K. *The Western*. New York: Orion Press, 1969.

Eyles, Allen. *The Marx Brothers*. London: A. Zwemmer, 1969. New York: A. S. Barnes, 1969.

Fielding, Raymond (ed.). *A Technological History of Motion Pictures and Television*. Berkeley: University of California Press, 1967.

Finler, Joel. *Stroheim*. London: Studio Vista, 1967.

Ford, Charles. *Max Linder*. Paris: Editions Seghers, 1966.

Gassner, John and Dudley Nichols (ed.). *Twenty Best Film Plays*. New York: Crown Publishers, 1943.

Graham, Peter (ed.). *The New Wave: Critical Landmarks*. London: Secker and Warburg, 1968.

Gregor, Ulrich and Enno Patalas. *Geschichte des Films*. Gütersloh: Sigbert Mohn, 1962.

Halas, John and Roger Manvell. *The Technique of Film Animation*. London: Focal Press, 1959.

Hardy, Forsyth (ed.). *Grierson on Documentary*. London: Faber and Faber, 1966.

Hayne, Donald (ed.). *The Autobiography of Cecil B. DeMille*. London: W. H. Allen, 1960.

Hendricks, Gordon. *The Edison Motion Picture Myth*. Berkeley: University of California Press, 1961.

Higham, Charles and Joel Greenberg. *Hollywood in the Forties*. London: A. Zwemmer, 1968. New York: A. S. Barnes, 1968.

Houston, Penelope. *The Contemporary Cinema*. Harmondsworth: Penguin Books, 1963.

Huff, Theodore. *Charlie Chaplin*. New York: Henry Schuman, 1951.

Hunnings, Neville March. *Film Censors and the Law*. London: Allen and Unwin, 1967.

Jacobs, Lewis. *The Rise of the American Film.* New York: Teachers College Press, 1969.

———— (ed.). *The Emergence of Film Art.* New York: Hopkinson and Blake, 1969.

Jensen, Paul M. *The Cinema of Fritz Lang.* London: A. Zwemmer, 1969. New York: A. S. Barnes, 1969.

Kitses, Jim. *Horizons West.* London: Thames and Hudson, 1969.

Kracauer, Siegfried. *From Caligari to Hitler.* London: Dennis Dobson, 1947. New York: Princeton University Press, 1966.

————. *Nature of Film.* London: Dennis Dobson, 1961.

Kyrou, Ado. *Le Surréalisme au Cinéma.* Paris: Le Terrain Vague, 1963.

Lacassin, Francis. *Louis Feuillade.* Paris: Editions Seghers, 1964.

Leyda, Jay. *Kino.* London: Allen and Unwin, 1960.

————. *Films Beget Films.* London: Allen and Unwin, 1964.

Leprohon, Pierre. *Histoire du Cinéma.* 2 vols. Paris: Editions du Cerf, 1961 and 1963.

Limbacher, James. *Four Aspects of the Film.* New York: Brussel and Brussel, 1968.

Lizzani, Carlo. *Storia del Cinema Italiano 1895–1961.* Florence: Parenti Editore, 1961.

Low, Rachel and Roger Manvell. *The History of the British Film 1896–1906.* London: Allen and Unwin, 1948.

Low, Rachel. *The History of the British Film 1906–1914.* London: Allen and Unwin, 1949.

————. *The History of the British Film 1914–1918.* London: Allen and Unwin, 1950.

MacCann, Richard. *Film: a Montage of Theories.* New York: E. P. Dutton, 1966.

MacGowan, Kenneth. *Behind the Screen.* New York: Delacorte, 1965.

Malerba, Luigi and Carmine Siniscalo (ed.). *Fifty Years of Italian Cinema.* Rome: Carlo Bestotti, 1954.

Manvell, Roger and John Huntley. *The Technique of Film Music.* London: Focal Press, 1957.

Martin, Marcel. *Le Langage Cinématographique.* Paris: Editions du Cerf, 1955.

McVay, Douglas. *The Musical Film.* London: A. Zwemmer, 1967. New York: A. S. Barnes, 1967.

Milne, Tom. *Rouben Mamoulian.* London: Thames and Hudson, 1969.

————. *The Cinema of Carl Dreyer.* London: A. Zwemmer, 1971. New York: A. S. Barnes, 1971.

Nemeskurty, István. *Word and Image.* Budapest: Corvina Press, 1968.

Niver, Kemp R. *The First Twenty Years.* Los Angeles: Locare Research Group, 1968.

O'Dell, Paul. *Griffith and the Rise of Hollywood.* London: A. Zwemmer, 1971. New York: A. S. Barnes, 1971.

Pudovkin, V. *Film Technique and Film Acting.* Translated and edited by Ivor Montagu. London: Vision-Mayflower, 1958.

Quigley, Martin. *Magic Shadows.* New York: Quigley Publications, 1960.

Ramsaye, Terry. *A Million and One Nights.* New York: Simon and Schuster, 1926. London: Frank Cass, 1964.

Reisz, Karel and Gavin Millar. *The Technique of Film Editing.* London: Focal Press, 1968.

Renan, Sheldon. *The Underground Film.* London: Studio Vista, 1967.

Richie, Donald. *The Films of Akira Kurosawa.* Berkeley: University of California Press, 1966.

Robinson, David. *Hollywood in the Twenties.* London: A. Zwemmer, 1968. New York: A. S. Barnes, 1968.

————. *Buster Keaton.* London: Secker and Warburg, 1969.

Rotha, Paul. *Documentary Film.* London: Faber and Faber, 1952.

Roud, Richard. *Jean-Luc Godard.* London: Secker and Warburg, 1967.

Sadoul, Georges. *Georges Méliès.* Paris: Editions Seghers, 1961.

————. *Le Cinéma Français.* Paris: Flammarion, 1962.

————. *The Cinema of the Arab Countries.* Beirut: International Center of Cinema and Television, 1966.

————. *Histoire Generale du Cinéma.* Paris: Denöel, 1946/1954.

Sarris, Andrew. *Interviews with Film Directors.* New York: Bobbs-Merrill, 1967.

————. *The American Cinema: Directors and Directions, 1929–1968.* New York: E. P. Dutton, 1968.

Savio, Francesco (ed. Cinema Section). *Enciclopedia dello Spettacolo.* Rome: Casa Editrice Le Maschere, 1954.

Seton, Marie. *Sergei M. Eisenstein.* London: Dennis Dobson, 1970.

Sharp, Dennis. *The Picture Palace.* London: Hugh Evelyn, 1969.

Slide, Anthony. *Early American Cinema.* London: A. Zwemmer, 1971. New York: A. S. Barnes, 1971.

Spraos, John. *The Decline of the Cinema: an Economist's Report.* London: Allen and Unwin, 1962.

Stack, Oswald (pseud.). *Pasolini on Pasolini.* London: Thames and Hudson, 1969.

Stephenson, Ralph. *Animation in the Cinema.* London: A. Zwemmer, 1967. New York: A. S. Barnes, 1967.

Sternberg, Josef von. *Fun in a Chinese Laundry.* London: Secker and Warburg, 1966. New York: Macmillan, 1965.

Tabori, Paul. *Alexander Korda.* London: Oldbourne, 1959.

Talbot, Daniel. *Film: an Anthology.* New York: Simon and Schuster, 1959. (Shortened version) Berkeley: University of California Press, 1966.

Taylor, John Russell. *Cinema Eye, Cinema Ear.* London: Methuen, 1964.

Truffaut, François and Helen Scott. *Hitchcock*. London: Secker and Warburg, 1968.

Turconi, Davide. *Mack Sennett, il re delle comiche*. Rome: Edizioni del'Ateneo, 1961.

Tyler, Parker. *Classics of the Foreign Film*. London: Spring Books, 1966.

Vê-Hô. *Mizoguchi*. Paris: Editions Universitaires, 1964.

Weinberg, Herman. *The Lubitsch Touch*. New York: E. P. Dutton, 1968.

Writers' Program of the Work Projects Administration in the city of New York (comp.). *The Film Index—the Film As Art*. New York: The Museum of Modern Art and The H. W. Wilson Company, 1941.

Wood, Robin. *Howard Hawks*. London: Secker and Warburg, 1968.

————. *Hitchcock's Films*. London: A. Zwemmer, 1969. New York: A. S. Barnes, 1969.

Zvonicek, Stanislav (ed.). *Modern Czechoslovak Film 1945–1965*. Prague: Artia, 1965.

Victor McLaglen in John Ford's THE INFORMER

Index to Film Titles

A nous la liberté 95
Abraham Lincoln 15
Acciaio 105
Actor's Revenge, An 162
Adam's Rib 36
Adorable Outcast, The 169
Adventures of Prince
  Achmed, The 180
Adventures of Robin
  Hood, The 50
Aelita 137
Aero-Engine 173
Aerograd 153
Affaire Dreyfus, L' 87
Age d'Or, L' 95, **165**, 166
Ah! Wilderness 50
Air Circus, The 61
Air Mail 57
Akrobat har otur, En 125
Alam Ara 164
Alexander Nevsky 154
Alf's Button 78
Alice Adams 38
Alice in Cartoonland 178
All Quiet on the
  Western Front 50, 82
Alone **148**, 150
Amazing Doctor
  Clitterhouse 73
Ame d'Artiste, L' 80, 91
America 15
American Madness 51
Andere, Der 106
Anémic Cinéma 95
Angèle (1934) 97
Angels with Dirty Faces 72, 73
Anna Boleyn 110
Anna Christie (1923) 41
Anna Christie (1930) 50
Anna Karenina 50, 84
Anna the Adventuress 78
Animal Crackers 67
Anniversary of the Oc-
  tober Revolution, The 172
Anthony Adverse 50
Antoinette Sabrier 91
Apaches of Athens 168
Applause 63
Arabesque 91
Are Parents People? 38
Argent, L' 92
Around the World in
  Eighty Days 180
Arrivée d'un Train
  en Gare 85
Arrivée d'un Train en
  Gare Vincennes, L' 86
Arsenal 145

Artist's Dream, The 177
Asphalt 109
Assassinat du Duc
  de Guise, L' 88
Assedio dell' Alcazor, L' 105
Atalante, L' 98
Atlantide, L' 93
Atonement of Gösta
  Berling 127
Au Secours! 89
Auberge Rouge, L' 92
Awakening 157
Awful Truth, The 71

Baby Snookums 177
Balaoo 89
Ballet Mécanique, Le 95
Baltic Deputy 150
Bandéra, La 102
Bank Detective, The 68
Bank Dick, The 68
Barbe-Bleue 87
Barber Shop, The 25
Baroud 36
Barrabas 90
Bas-Fonds, Les 101
Bat and the Cat and the
  Canary, The 15
Battalion, The 155
Battle of Ancre and
  the Advance of the
  Tanks, The 17
Battle of Falkland and
  Coronel Islands, The 171
Battle of Midway, The 59
Battle of the Sexes, The 15
Battle of the
  Somme, The 171
Battleship Potemkin,
  The 116, 119, 141, **142**,
    164, 172, 189
Be my Wife 89
Bébé 89
Becky Sharp 64, 199
Bed and Sofa 138
Beggars of Life 39
Belle Equipe, La 102
Belle Nivernaise, La 92
Ben-Hur (1926) 38
Bengasi 105
Berge in Flammen 119
Bergführer, Der 169
Bergkatze, Die 110
Berlin Alexanderplatz 117, 118
Berlin, die Symphonie
  einer Grosstadt 116, 172
Bête Humaine, La 102
Better 'ole, The 80

Bezhin Meadow 153
Big House, The 72
Big Parade, The 38
Big Swallow, The 77
Big Store, The 68
Big Trail, The 46
Billie the Kid 46
Birth of a Flower, The 171
Birth of a Nation,
  The 10, **11**, **13**, 19
Birth of the Swiss
  Confederation, The 169
Bitter Tea of General Yen 51
Black Cat, The 76
Black Consul, The 153
Blackmail 81, 82
Black Pirate, The 39
Black Watch 56
Blind Husbands 34
Blockheads 31
Blonde Venus, The 54
Bloody Fortnight, The 135
Blue in the Night 25
Blue Angel, The 53, 54, 118
Blue Eagle 56
Blue Express, The 146
Blue Waters 167
Born Reckless 57
Boris Gudunov 135
Boudu sauvé des
  eaux (1932) 95, 97
Boule de Suif 151
Bout-de-Zan 89
Boys Will Be Boys 179
Brahms's Rhapsody 179
Brat, The 57
Bread of Love, The 128
Breakers 175
Bride of Franken-
  stein, The 75
Bridge, The 175
Bright Lights 66
Bright Paths 150
Bringing up Baby 63, 71
Broken Blossoms 14
Bronco Billy and the Baby 41
Brother Orchid 73
Bulgarian Is Gallant, The 159
Bullets or Ballots 72
Bungtheatre 123
Butcher Boy, The 28
Byrakstugan 125

Cabin in the Cotton 50
Cabinet of Dr. Cali-
  gari, The 73, 108, 109
Cabiria 14, 104
Café Electric 123

Calino 90
Captain Blood 50
Carmen 18
Carnet de Bal, Un 103
Carry on Sergeant 167
Case of Lena Smith, The 53
Cat and the Canary, The 75
Ceiling Zero 62
Cendrillon 87
Cenere 104
César (1936) 97
Cesare Borgia 105
Champagne 81
Chang 173
Chapayev 148
Chapeau de paille
d'Italie, Un 94, 95
Charge of the
Light Brigade 50
Chaser, The 31
Chess Fever 143
Chien Andalou,
Un 95, **165**, 166
Chienne, La (1931) 97
Child Saint 164
Childhood of Gorky, The 152
Chimere 105
Chute de la Maison
Usher, La 92, 165
Cigarette Maker's
Romance, The 78
Cimarron 46
Cinq Minutes de
Cinéma Pur 95
Circus 21, 150
Citadel, The 49
City, The 174
City Lights 21
City Streets 63
Civilization 41
Clansman, The 11
Cloak, The 146
Close Up 82
Clown and his Dogs, A 177
Coal Face 174
Cocoanuts, The 66
Coeur Infidèle 92
Col. Heeza Liar in Africa 177
Colour Box 180
Come and Get It 62
Comet over Broadway 66
Comin' thro' the Rye 78
Conquering Power, The 36
Conquering the Women 38
Conquête du Pole, A la 87
Constant Nymph, The 80
Contact 173
Convict 99 84
Cops 29
Coquille et le Clergy-
man, La 91

Coronation of King Peter
in Belgrade, The 159
Corsican Brothers, The 77
Cossacks of the Don 135
Cottage on Dartmoor 81, 82
Counterplan 148
Couronnement du Roi
Edouard VII, Le 87
Covered Wagon, The 45, 46
Cradle Snatchers, The 60
Crainquebille 93
Crazy World of Laurel
and Hardy, The 33
Crime and Punishment 55
Crime de Monsieur
Lange, Le 101, 102
Crime Does Not Pay 72
Criminal Code, The 62, 72
Cripple Creek Bar Room 41
Croix du Cervin, La 169
Crossing the American
Prairies in the
Early Fifties 41
Crossroads 161
Crowd, The 38
Crowd Roars, The 62
Cucaracha, La 199
Cure for Pokeritis, A 23

Daddy-Long-Legs 39
Dame aux Camélias, La 88
Dames 66
Damned Village, The 164
Dance Pretty Lady 82
Dangerous to Know 73
Danger's of a Fisher-
man's Life, The 133
Darling Alfred 77
Date Industry in
Egypt, The 170
Dawn 119, 156
Dawn of Iran 173
Dawn Patrol, The 62
Day at the Races, The 67
Day of the Great
Adventure, The 157
Day's Pleasure, A 19
De Mayerling à Sarajevo 100
Dead End 72
Dead End Kids 73
Death Ray, The 138
December 7th 59
Defence of Sebastopol 135
Dentist, The 25
Dernier Milliardaire, Le 95
Deserter, The 152
Design for Living 49
Destry Rides Again 48
Deux Timides, Les 94
Devil Doll, The 76
Devil Is a Woman, The 54
Devil's Passkey, The 35

Diary of a
Lost Girl, The 115
Diplomatic Bag, The 145
Dirigible 51
Dirnentragödie 109
Dishonoured 54
Divine 100
Docks of New
York, The 34, 53
Dodge City 48, 50
Don Juan's Last Adventure 122
Dough and Dynamite 18
Down on the Farm 24
Downhill Easy Virtue 81
Dr. Bull 57
Dr. Dolittle 100
Dr. Jekyll and
Mr. Hyde (1908) 73
Dr. Jekyll and
Mr. Hyde (1920) 75
Dr. Jekyll and
Mr. Hyde (1932) 63, 75
Dr. Mabuse
the Gambler 108, **111**
Dracula 75, 113
Dracula's Daughter 75
Drag Net, The 34, 53, 54
Drame chez les
Fantoches, Un 177
Dream House 25
Dream of an
Austrian Reservist 122
Dreams of Toyland 78
Drifters 173
Drôle de Drame 103
Drums of Love 15
Duck Soup 67
Dust Be My Destiny 72

Eagle, The 38, 40
East Is East 79
Easy Street 18
Earth **145**, 163
Earth Thirsts, The 147
Ecstasy 156
1860 105
Elephant Boy 84, 173
Emak Bakia 95
Emperor's Candle-
sticks, The 123
End of St. Peters-
burg, The 143, **144**, 172
Engineer Prite's Project 138
Enrico III 104
Entr'acte 94
Episode 123
Erotikon 126, 155
Eternal Light 164
Eternal Love 39
Etoile de Mer, L' 95
Everything that Lives 162
Explosion du Cuirasse, L' 87

Extraordinary Adventures
of Mr. West, The 143
Extraordinary Adventures
of Mr. West in the Land
of the Bolsheviks, The 138

Face on the Bar-room
Floor, The 18
Facing the Wind 147
Fairy Godmother, The 77
Fall of the House
of Russia, The 74
Fall of the Romanov
Dynasty, The 140
Fall of Troy, The 104
Fantasia 179
Fantasmagorie 177
Fantegutten 134
Fantômas 89
Fantôme du
Moulin Rouge, Le 94
Fanny (1932) 97
Far from the Madding
Crowd (1915) 79
Farmer's Wife, The 81
Farinet 170
Fashions of 1934 66
Fatal Glass of Beer, The 25
Father Frost 137
Father Vojtech 155
Faust 114
Favourite Daughter 150
Fazil 60
Fée Carabosse, La 87
Feet First 28
Felix the Cat 177, 178
Femme du Boulanger,
La (1939) 97
Femme disparaît, Une 101
Femme de nulle part 92
Fête Espagnole 91
Feu Mathias Pascal 93
Fièvre 91, 92
Fig Leaves 60
Fight for Life, The 174
Fighting Blood 42
Fighting Heart, The 56
Finis Terrae 92
Fire 9, 77, 147
Five Scouts 163
Five Star Final 50
Flames of Passion 80
Flesh (1932) 57
Flesh and the Devil 38
Floorwalker, The 18
Flötenkonzert von
Sanssouci, Das 118
Flowers and Trees 178, 199
Folie du Dr. Tube, La 93
Foolish Wives 35, 131
Foot Light Parade 66

For the Term of His
Natural Life 168, 169
Forbidden Fruit 36
Forbidden Paradise 39
Forty-First, The 137
Forty Second Street 66
40,000 Horsemen 169
Four Chimneys 162
Four Horsemen of
the Apocalypse 36, 39
Four Men and a Prayer 59
Four Sons 56
Frankenstein 75
Fraternally Yours 70
Freaks 75
Free Radicals 180
Free Soul, A 50
French without Tears 82
Freshman, The 28
Friends 150
From Morning
to Midnight 108
From Saturday to Sunday 156
From the Manger
to the Cross 9
Front Page, The 51, 71
Fugitive, The 60
Fury 38, 52

G-Man 72
Garden of Allah, The 36
Garden of the Moon 66
Gate of Hell 160, 162
Gay Desperado, The 64
General, The 30
General Died at Dawn 51
General Line, The 142
Gens du Voyage, Les 101
Genuine 108
Gertie the
Trained Dinosaur 177
Ghost Goes West, The 83, 95
Ghost of St. Michaels 84
Ghosts 122
Girl Friends 150
Girl from the
Marsh Croft, The 128
Girl in Number
Twenty Nine, The 56
Girl of the Bush, A 168
Girl in the
Limousine, The 24
Girl Who Stayed
at Home, The 14
Giulio Cesare 104
Glace à trois faces, La 92
Go Getter, The 66
Gold Diggers of 1933 50
Gold Diggers of 1935 66
Gold Rush, The 20, 21, 164
Golden Bed, The 36
Golden Boy 65

Golden Mountain, The 134
Golem, Der 106
Golem, The 73
Golem, wie er in die
Welt Kam, Der 106
Gone with the Wind 48, 199
Goodmorning Boys 84
Goofy Goat 178
Gorky Trilogy 152
Grand Duchess and
the Waiter, The 38
Grand Jeu, Le 100
Grande Appello, Il 105
Grande Illusion, La 101, 102
Grandma's Boy 28
Grandma's Reading Glass 78
Grapes of Wrath, The 59
Grass 173
Great Baptism, The 134
Great Big Follies, The 123
Great Citizen, The 151
Great Dictator, The 22
Great Problem, The 36
Great Redeemer, The 37
Great Road, The 140
Great Train Robbery, The 41
Greatest Question, The 14
Greatest Thing
in Life, The 14
Greed 35
Greek Wonder 168
Greenhide 169
Grosse König, Der 119
Gunnar Hedes Saga 127
Guild of the Kutna
Hora Virgins, The 156
Gulf Between 198
Gulliver's Travels 150

Halbblut 111
Hallelujah 49
Hallelujah, I'm a Bum 31
Hamlet (1913) 78
Hands of Orlac 123
Hans Westmar 119
Hangman's House 56
Harold Lloyd's
Funny Side of Life 28
Harold Lloyd's
World of Comedy 28
Hazards of Helen, The 9
Heart of a Savage, The 42
Heart Trouble 31
Hearts Are Trumps 36
Hearts of Oak 56
Hearts of the World 14
Heir to Ghengis
Khan, The 143, 144
Hello Sister 35
Hell's Hinges 44
Henrietta, The 29
High and Dizzy 28

High Pressure 72
High, Wide
and Handsome 64, 65
Hintertreppe 108, 109
His Girl Friday 71
His Trysting Place 18
Histoire d'Amour, Une 99
Histoire d'un Crime, L' 88
Hitlerjunge Quex 119
Holiday 71
Hollywood Hotel 66
Hollywood Review, The 30
Homecoming 124
Homme du Large, L' 92
Homme sans Visage, L' 90
Honeymoon, The 35
Hoodman Blind 56
House of Horror, The 39
House on
Trubnaya Square, The 146
House of Wax 75
Housing Problems 173
Horse Feathers 67
Hôtel du Nord 103
Hotel Sacher 124
How Green was My Valley 59
How a Mosquito Operates 177
Humorous Phases
of Funny Faces 177
Hurdes, Las 166
Hurricane, The 59
Hyppolit the Butler 158

I Am a Fugitive from
a Chain Gang 50, 62, 72
I Am the Law 72
I Claudius 55
I Live for Love 66
I Surrender Dear 25
Idée, L' 179
Idle Class, The 19
Idol Dancer, The 14
If I had a Million 49
I'm No Angel 68
Immigrant, The 18, 19
Immortal Waltz 124
Imperial Valley 174
In Old Arizona 46
In The Big City 147
In the Claws
of the Yellow Devil 135
In the Wake
of the Bounty 169
Indonesia Calling 176
Industrial Britain 173
Informer, The 58
Ingeborg Holm 128
Inhumaine, L' 92, 93
Inn at Osaka, An 162
Innocence Unprotected 159
Inondation, L' 92
Intermezzo 130

Intolerance 11, **14**, 30, 41, 131
Invisible Stripes 72
Invitation au Voyage, L' 91
Iron Mask, The 38, 39
Iron Horse, The 44, 47
Isn't Life Wonderful 15
It Happened
One Night 52, 70
It's a Gift 68
Ivan 152
Ivan the Terrible 141, 155
Iwonka 157

J'accuse (1918) 93, 96
J'accuse (1938) 96
Jack-Knife Man 38
Jackie 56
Jamaica Inn 82
Jan Hus 155
Janosik **155**, 156
Jan Zizka 155
Jazz Singer, The 48, 189, 198
Jenny 103
Jesse James 51
Jeux des reflets
de la vitesse 95
Jezebel 52
Johan 127
Joie de Vivre 179
Jolly Fellow, The 150
Journey's End 75, 82
Joyless Street, The 114, 128
Juarez 52
Jud Suss 119
Judex 89, 90
Judith of Bethulia 11
Juno and the Paycock 59
Just Nuts 25

Kameradschaft 116
Karadjordje 159
Karma 164
Katusha 160
Katzenjamma Kids, The 177
Kentucky Kernels 69
Kentucky Pride 56
Kermesse Héroïque, La 101
Keys to Happiness 136
Kid Auto Races
at Venice 17
Kid Brother, The 28
Kid from Spain, The 66
Kid, The 19, 28
Kiddies in the Ruins 80
Kiki 66
Kinemacolor 77
King Henry **38**, 51
King Kong 76
King of Gamblers 73
King of Jazz 178
King of Kings 36
King Steps Out, The 55

Kino Pravda 139
Kiss Me Again 39
Kiss Me Maritsa 168
Knight without Armour 101
Knitwits 69
Kohlhiesels Töchter 110
Kolberg 119
Komedie om geld 99
Komische Begegnung 125
Komödianten 116
Komsomolsk 151
Koratovič 155
Krazy Kat 177
Kreutzer Sonata, The 155
Kriemhilds Rache 111
Kuhle Wampe **117**, 118

Ladies Love Brutes 73
Lady for a Day 51
Lady of the Pavement 15
Lady Vanishes, The 82
Lady Windermere's Fan 39
Landammann Stauffacher 170
Land, The 174
Land without Bread 166
Last Days of Pompeii 104
Last Command, The 53
Last Laugh, The 108, 113
Last Night, The 150
Last of the Mohicans 37
Last Will of Dr. Mabuse,
The 111
Laughing Gas 18
Law and Order 46
Leaves from Satan's
Book 131
Legion of the Street 157
Lenin in 1918 151
Lenin in October 151
Leopard's Spots, The 11
Leper, The 157
Letter from a Dead
Woman 122
Letzte Kompanie, Die 119
Lichtertanz 179
Liebelei 99
Light of Asia 164
Life 134
Life Is Beautiful 152
Life Is for Living 164
Life of an American
Cowboy, The 41
Life of an American
Fireman, The 9
Life of Bangoku 163
Life of Charles Peace 78
Life of Matsu the
Untamed, The 163
Life of O-Haru, The 161
Liliom 52
Limehouse Nights 14
Little Caesar 50, 71

Little Miss Smiles 56
Little Mother, The 79
Little Nemo 177
Living Corpse, The 160
Local Boy Makes Good 69
Lodger, The 81
Loi du Nord, La 101
London after Midnight 75
Lone White Sail 151
Long Pants 31
Long Voyage Home, The 59
Lonesome Luke's Lively Life 25
Lonesome Luke's Wild Women 25
Look Out Below 28
Lost Horizon 52
Lost Patrol, The 57
Love and Journalism 126
Love Flower, The 14
Love Me Tonight 63
Love Parade, The 49
Loves of Jeanne Ney, The 115
Loyal 47 Ronin, The 160
Lucky Number 82
Lucky Stars 31

M 113
Ma l'amor mio non muore 104
Mad Miss Manton, The 70
Mad Wednesday 28
Madame Bovary (1934) 97
Madame Dubarry 110
Madame Sans-gêne 88
Madness of Dr. Tube, The 74
Magic of Bohemianism 123
Magician, The 36
Making a Living 16
Maltese Falcon 52
Man from Glengarry, The 167
Man I Killed, The 49
Man of Aran 173
Man on the Flying Trapeze, The 68
Manhandled 38
Manslaughter 36
Man with a Gun 151
Man with a Movie Camera, The 139
Manxman, The 81
March of Time, The 174
Mare Nostrum 36
Marie Walewska 50
Marius (1931) 97
Mark of the Vampire, The 76
Mark of Zorro 38
Marriage Circle, The 39, 49

Married Life 24
Marseillaise, La 102
Martyrs of the Alamo 41
Mary of Scotland 59
Maskerade 123
Massacre, The 41
Masses, The 21
Mater Dolorosa (1917) 96
Mater Dolorosa (1932) 96
Matija Gubec 159
Mauprat 165
Max et le Quinquina 88
Max Professeur de Tango 88
Max Toreador 88
Maxim Trilogy 149
Mechanism of the Brain, The 142
Meet John Doe 52
Member of the Government 150
Men and Jobs 151
Men Are Such Fools 66
Men of War 66
Men without Women 56
Merry-Go-Round 35
Metropolis 112
Merry Widow, The 35
Mickey 22
Midnight Taxi 72
Mikaël 132
Million Dollar Legs 24
Million, Le 95
Millionaire Uncle, The 122
Minin and Pozharsky 152
Miracles for Sale 76
Misadventures of a Piece of Veal, The 86
Misérables, Les 88
Misère au Borinage 176
Miss Faithful 133
Miss Julie 130
Misused Love Letters, The 170
Mix, Tom 44, 48
Moana 171, 173
Modern Times 21
Molly-O 22
Money in the Street 123
Monkey Business (1931) 67
Monte Carlo 49
Moon of Israel, The 122
Morocco 54
Most Dangerous Game, The 75
Moscow Nights 82, 83
Moth of Moonbi 169
Mother 37, 143, 144
Mother Machree 56
Mountain Adventure, A 134
Mountain Eagle 81
Movie Crazy 28

Moving Picture World 16
Mr. Deeds Goes to Town 52, 70
Mr. Smith Goes to Washington 48, 52, 70
Müde Tod, Der 109, 111
Mummy, The 76
Murders in the Rue Morgue 52
Mutter Krausens Fahrt ins Glück 117
My Apprenticeship 152
My Little Chickadee 68
My Little Margie 53
My Man Godfrey 70
My Old Dutch 79
My Universities 152
My Wonderful World of Slapstick 30
Mystery of the Wax Museum, The 50, 75
Mysterious X, The 131

Nana 97, 102
Nanook of the North 167, 170
Napoléon (1927) 93, 96
Napoléon (1934) 96
Napoleono 104
Napoleon's Barber 56
Navigator, The 30
Neighbour's Wife and Mine, The 162
Niver Give a Sucker an Even Break 68
New Babylon, The 146
New Gulliver, A 150
Night at the Opera, The 67
Night Mail 173
Night on a Bare Mountain 180
Night Out, A 24
Ninotchka 48, 49
Nogent Eldorado du Dimanche 103
Nose, The 180
Nosferatu 73, 113, 114
Nothing Else Matters 80
Nothing Sacred 70
Notre Dame de Paris 88
Nouveaux Messieurs, Les 101
Nouvelle Mission de Judex, La 89
Nuit du Carrefour, La (1932) 97

October 142, 146
Of Mice and Men 33, 51
Ohm Kruger 119
Oh, Mr. Porter 84

Old and the New,
  The 142, 153
Old Dark House, The 75
Old-Fashioned Way,
  The 68
Old Wives for New 36
Old Wives' Tale, The 79
Olympiade 120
Olympic Games, The 174
On purge bébé 97
On with the Show 199
Once in a Life Time 70
One A.M. 18
One Exciting Night 15
One Family 173
One Hour with You 49
One Million B.C. 33
One Million Years B.C. 15
One Night 130
Onésime 90
Only Angels Have
  Wings 57, **63**
Our Hospitality 29, 30
Operette 124
Oppenheims, The 151
Opium Dreams 131
Organist of St. Vitus,
  The 155
Orlacs Hände 108
Orphans of the Storm 15
Orphée 96
Osaka Elegy 163
Oswald the Rabbit 178
Outlaw and His Wife,
  The 128
Our Daily Bread 49
Our Gang 32
Over the Fence 25
Overland Telegraph 44

Paddy the Next Best
  Thing 80
Page out of Order, A 161
Paid to Love 60
Palmy Days 66
Pandora's Box 115
Paracelsus 116
Par Excellence 120
Parson's Widow, The 131
Paris qui dort 94
Partie de Campagne,
  Une 101
Partie de Cartes, Une 86
Passing Show of 1917,
  The 28
Passion de Notre Seigneur
  Jésus Christ 88
Passion of Joan of
  Arc, The 131, 132
Patriot, The 39
Pauvre Village, Le 169
Pawnshop, The 18

Pay Day 19
Pebble by the Wayside,
  A 163
Penal Servitude 146
Pension Mimosas 100
People of the Vistula 157
People on Sunday 117, 173
Pépé-le-Moko 102
Perfect Clown, The 24
Perfect Day, The 66
Personal Matter 148
Peter the Great 151
Petite Lise, La 99
Petronella 169
Phantasmes 92
Phantom of the Opera 75
Pharmacist, The 25
Piccola mondo antico 105
Picking Peaches 31
Picture of Dorian Gray,
  A 136
Pilgrim, The 19
Pilgrimage 57
Pinky 60
Plainsman, The 46
Platinum Blonde 51, 70
Pleasure Garden, The 81
Plough and the Stars,
  The 59
Plow that Broke the
  Plains, The 174
Poil de Carotte 102
Polikushka 137
Pony Express, The 46
Poor Pierrot 177
Power and the Glory,
  The 60
Power and the Land 174
Pratermizzi 123
Première Sortie 88
Presi di Roma, La 104
President, The 131
Prince and the Beggar
  Boy, The 122
Prince of Avenue A,
  The 56
Prisoner of Shark
  Island, The 59
Private Life of Henry
  VIII, The 83, 190
Private Lives of Elizabeth
  and Essex, The 50
Professor Mamlock 151
Proie du Vent, La 95
Prometheus Bound 168
Propos de Nice 98
Protéa 89
P'tite Lili, La 95
Pueblo Legend, A 42
Public Enemy, The 72
Puppe, Die 110
Pygmalion 82

Quai des Brumes 103
Quatorze Jullet 95
Que Viva Mexico 153
Queen Christina 64
Queen Elizabeth 185
Queen Kelly 35
Queen of Spades 136
Quick Millions 72
Quo Vadis 14, 104, **185**
Quo Vadis (1902) 86

Race 165
Racket Busters 72
Racket Squad 33
Radio Parade 198
Rain 51, 175
Rainbow Dance 180
Rajah Harishchandra 164
Raskolnikoff 108
Rat, The 80
Rebell, Der 119
Red Imps, The 137
Red Line 7000 62
Redman's View, The 42
Regain (1937) 97
Règle du Jeu, La 102
Reine Elisabeth, La 88
Remorques 99
Rescued by Rover 78
Rescued from an Eagle's
  Nest 11, 41
Resurrection 160
Retour à la Raison, Le 94
Return of Maxim, The 149
Reveille 80
Revisor, The 156
Rich Bride, The 150
Rickshaw Man, The 163
Riding School 123
Rien que les Heures 172
Riley the Cop 56
Ring, The 81
Rise of Catherine the
  Great, The 83
River, The 156, 174
Road to Glory, The 60, 62
Road to Life 148
Road to Yesterday, The 36
Roaring Twenties, The 72
Robbery under Arms 168
Robin Hood 38, 39
Roi du Cirque, Le 89
Roman d'un Tricheur
  (1936) 97
Roman Scandals 66, 69
Romance of Margaret
  Catchpole, The 168
Romanze in Moll 120
Romeo and Juliet in
  the Village 170
Romola 38
Rose France 92

Rosenkavalier, Der 123
Rosita 39
Rotaie 105
Roue, La 93
Ruggles of Red Gap 71
Runaway Princess 81

S.A. Mann Brandt 119
Safety Last 28
Saga of Anatahan, The 55
Saint Tukaram 164
Sally Bishop 80
Sally of the Sawdust 15
Sansho the Bailiff 161
Salt for Svanetia 147
Salute 56
Salvation Hunters, The 52
Samson and Dalila 122
San Francisco 15
Sange d'un Poète, Le 96
Sans Lendemain 100
Santa Fe Trail 48
Saphead, The 29
Saving of Bill Blewitt,
   The 173
Sawdust and Tinsel 130
Scarface 62, 72, 73
Scaramouche 36
Scarlett Empress, The 54
Schatz, Der 114
Scherben 109
Schors 153
Schrammeln 124
Scipio Africanus 105
Seal Hunting in New-
   foundland 170
Seas Beneath 57
Secret Six, The 72
Secrets of a Soul 115
Secrets of Nature 171
Sedge Hat, The 163
Sentimental Bloke, The 168
Seven Bold People 151
Seven Footprints to
   Satan 39, 131
Seven Years Bad Luck 89
Seventh Seal, The 128
Shamrock Handicap, The 56
Shanghai Express 54
Shanghai Gesture, The 55
She Done Him Wrong 68
She Had to Say Yes 66
Sheik, The 40
Sherlock Jr. 30
Shooting Stars 81
Shore Acres 36
Shoulder Arms 19
Shriek of Araby, The 24
Siegfrieds Tod 111
Signora per tutti, La 99
Silence, Le 92

Silence of Dean Mait-
   land, The 169
Sin of Harold Diddleback,
   The 28
Sing as we Go 85
Sing, Bing, Sing 25
Sinking of the Lusitania,
   The 177
Sir Arne's Treasure 127
Sisters of the Gion 163
Skeleton Dance 178
Sky Pilot, The 167
Small Town Idol, A 24
Smart Money 72
Smiling Lieutenant, The 49
Smithy 169
Snow White and the
   Seven Dwarfs 48, 178, 199
So This Is Paris 39
Sodom and Gomorrah 122
Soldat Wipf 170
Soldier Man 31
Sole 105
Soldiers of the Cross 168
Some Like It Hot 69
Song of Ceylon 173
Song of Happiness 151
Song of Songs 64
Son of Frankenstein 75
Son of Kong 76
Sonny 38
Sons of Matthew 169
Sons of the Desert 66
Sorrows of Satan, The 15
Sortie des Usines
   Lumière, La 85
Souls on the Road 160
Souriante Madame
   Beudet, La 91
Sous les toits de Paris 95
Spanish Earth 176
Speedy 28
Sperduti Nel Buio 104
Spinnen, Die 111
Spirits, The 131
Spy in Black, The 84
Stage Coach 46, 47, 48
Stage Struck 66
Stanley and Livingstone 51
Stella Dallas 38
Stationmaster, The 137
State Fair 51
Steamboat Bill, Jr. 30
Steamboat round the
   Bend 57
Steamboat Willie 178
Stenka Razin 135
Step by Step 121
Storm over Asia 143
Story of the Kelly
   Gang 168
Strasse, Die 109

Street Angel 39
Street of Sin, The 53
Strike 141
Strong Boy 56
Strong Man, The 21, 31, 136
Strongest, The 130
Struggle, The 15
Student of Prague,
   The 73, 106
Student Prince, The 39
Study in Scarlet, The 80
Submarine Patrol 59
Sunken World, A 122
Sunrise 39, 114
Sutter's Gold 142
Swedenhielms 130
Sweet Blanche 41
Sylvester 109
Symphony of the
   Donbas 147

Three Cornered Moon 69
Three Must-Get-Theres,
   The 89
Three Musketeers,
   The 38, 39, 89
Three on a Match 72
Three Passions, The 36
Three Songs of Lenin 147
Three Women 39
Threepenny Opera,
   The 115, 116
Three's a Crowd 31
Thomas Graal's First
   Child 126
1000 Eyes of Dr.
   Mabuse, The 111
Thunderbolt 54, 71, 73
Thunder over Mexico 153
Thy Shalt Honour
   Thy Wife 132
Thy Soul Shall Bear
   Witness 128
Tiger Shark 62
Tih Minh 90
Tillie's Punctured
   Romance 18, 22, 23
Tilly and Gus 68
Time in the Sun, A 153
Tobacco Road 59
Today We Live 62
Tol'able David 38
Toll of the Sea, The 198
Tonnère, Le 92
Toni (1934) 97
Tony in Warsaw 156
Tabu 173
Tales of Genji 162
Tales of Hoffmann,
   The 123
Tall Timbers 169
Tansy 78

Tartuffe 114
Taxi 72
Teacher, The 151
Tell England 82
Ten Commandments,
The 34, 36
Ten Days that Shook
the World 142
Tendre Ennemie, La 100
Terje Vigen 128
Testament des Dr.
Mabuse, Das 113
Texas Rangers, The 46
Thank You 56
Theodora Goes Wild 70
Thérèse Raquin 93
They Were Expendable 59
They Won't Forget 50
Thief of Bagdad 39, 199
Thieving Magpie, The 137
Thin Man, The 70
Things to Come 83
Thirsty for Love 135
This Is How China
Lives 170
Three Ages, The 29
Topper 33
Tractor Drivers 150
Trade Tattoo 180
Tramp, Tramp, Tramp 31
Tramp, The 18
Trent's Last Case 61
Triumph of the
Will 119, 120, 174
Trouble in Paradise 49
True Heart Susie 14
Turkeys in a Row 163
Turkish 172
Turn of the Road 38
Tusalava 180
Twentieth Century 62
Twenty Thousand Years
in Sing Sing 50
Twenty Years of
Cinema 152

Ugetsu Monogatari 161
Uncivilized 169
Under the Red Robe 130
Underground 81
Underworld 34, 53, 54,
71, 73
Unfinished Symphony,
The 82, 123
Union Pacific 44, 47
Unter den Brücken 120

Untouchable Girl 164
Up the River 57
Upstream 56

Valley Town, The 174
Vampires, Les 89, 90
Vampyr 133
Vanina 108
Vaudeville 123
Vecchia Guardia 105
Victimes de L'alcoolisme,
Les 88
Victory, The 152
Vie de notre Seigneur
Jésus Christ, Le 89
Vie est à nous, La 101
Vienna Blood 124
Vienna in War 122
Vienna Tales 124
Viking, The 167
Virginia City 48
Virginian, The 46
Virginity 156
Volga-Volga 150
Voice of Britain, The 173
Voyage à travers l'im-
possible, Le 87
Voyage dans la lune, Le 87
Voyage imaginaire, Le 94
Vyborg Side, The 149

Walking down Broadway 35
Waltz's from Vienna 82
War on the Plains 42
War Paint 44
Warning Shadows 74
Wax Works 74, 105
Way down East 14
Way out West 66
We from Kronstadt 150
We Live Again 64
We Sail at Midnight 59
Weather Forecast 173
Wee Willie Winkie 59
Wedding March, The 35
Weib des Pharao, Das 110
Welcome Danger 28
Welsh Singer, The 79
Westfront (1918) 115
Wet Parade, The 72
What a Man 68
What Made Her Do It 162
When a Man's a Prince 24
Where the Pavement
Ends 36
White Rose, The 15

White Shadows of the
South Seas 38
White Sister, The 38
White Zombie 76
Whole Town's Talking,
The 57, 73
Whoopee 65
Why Change Your
Wife 36
Wild Boys of the
Road, The 72
Wild Strawberries 130
Wind, The 39, 129
Windbag the Sailor 84
Wings 39
Winning of Barbara
Worth 38
Winter Camellia 160
Witchcraft through
the Ages 74, 131
With Belief in God 159
Wizard of Oz, The
(1925) 24
Wizard of Oz, The
(1939) 48, 50, 199
Wonder Bar 66
Wonderful Story, The 80
World Moves On, The 57
Woman of Affairs, A 38
Woman of Paris, A 19, 20
Woman of Ryazan 146
Woman of the World,
A 39
Woman to Woman 80

Yakov Sverdlov 151
Yoshiwara 100
You and Me 52
You Can't Take It
with You 52, 70
You Only Live Once 52
You Said a Mouthful 69
Young and Innocent 82
Young Forest, The 157
Young Medardus 122
Youth of Maxim 149

Zeebrugge 171
Zenobia 31
Zéro de conduite 95, 98
Zigomar 89
Zigoto 90
Zuiderzee 176
Zürcher Sechseläuten 169
Zvenigora 145